The Right not to Be Subjected to Enforced Disappearance

Ioanna Pervou

The Right not to Be Subjected to Enforced Disappearance

Concept, Content and Scope

Springer

Ioanna Pervou
Law Faculty
Democritus University of Thrace
Komotini, Greece

ISBN 978-3-031-36730-4 ISBN 978-3-031-36731-1 (eBook)
https://doi.org/10.1007/978-3-031-36731-1

This Springer imprint is published by the registered company Springer Nature Switzerland AG
The registered company address is: Gewerbestrasse 11, 6330 Cham, Switzerland

Dedication: to my parents, Yannis and Areti

Preface

The international community was introduced to the concept of enforced disappearances in the second half of the twentieth century, though the phenomenon is a persisting issue. The many numerous occurrences of enforced disappearances throughout the last years, all over the world, have alarmed the international community, which has taken considerable legal steps to tackle the phenomenon. The establishment of the United Nations Convention for the Protection of All Persons from Enforced Disappearance is undoubtedly an important step in the struggle against the phenomenon.

Enforced disappearances have been thoroughly examined by many researchers over the last years, at the United Nations Convention. Almost all aspects of the phenomenon have been analyzed in detail in a scholarly attempt to familiarize readers with the notion of disappearance. This research aims to shed light on a particular manifestation of the phenomenon which theory has tended to pass by: the right not to be subjected to enforced disappearance, stipulated in Article 1(1) of the instrument of the United Nations Convention. The right's provision and legal norm have been long awaited and are anticipated to contribute to comprehending the phenomenon. The right not to be subjected to enforced disappearance is expected to be connected to a conventional provision, given that before the conclusion of the Convention there have been long-standing problems regarding the perception of enforced disappearance.

From 2007 onwards, the Convention against Disappearances has played a central role in this field of human rights. This instrument was expected to decelerate the rate of enforced disappearances worldwide. So far, this goal has not been accomplished; on the contrary, there has been a sharp increase in the number of enforced disappearances, predominantly in Asia, as well as in dangerous conflict zones. Besides, states have adopted new patterns of enforced disappearances, posing serious challenges to international human rights lawyers and to human rights judicial organs. So far, it seems that state practice on enforced disappearance is ultra resistant, undergoing several mutations. For this reason, although the Convention is a new *topos* for addressing the phenomenon, it is still essential to analyze the phenomenon based on other sources of international law (i.e., customary international law). Moreover, references to modern state tactics are deemed necessary for increasing the practical results of this research.

The point of concern which triggered me to write this research monograph is that very little attention has been given to the right not to be subjected against enforced disappearances, that is Art. 1(1) of the UN Convention. This provision was correctly considered as a definite prerequisite for a Convention to come into life. As such, the right against disappearances is a necessary condition for the relevant convention to exist. However, the conventional birth of a right always comes alongside a series of questions.

First, there needs to be doctrinal taxonomy of the norm. The right against disappearance, although a first generation right, or else a civil liberty, is not found, or even implied, in any international general human rights document. The Bill of Rights does not make a single hint of disappearances, since the phenomenon has been misinterpreted for a long time. From this perspective, the conventional right seems to be *prima facie* isolated from the international human rights regime. This question is not only a doctrinal discrepancy rather it plays a significant role when it comes to litigation. International and regional jurisdictional bodies do not have a certain reference point when adjudicating disappearance cases. when disappearance incidents come to their attention. Some courts equate disappearances with torture, while others consider enforced disappearance as a denial of access to justice. There is no stable judicial approach, which means in turn that there is not a solid interpretation of the right's content.

The second question which comes as a reasonable sequence is what happens as soon as a disappearance case reaches a judicial body. The right against disappearances cannot be effectively applied in the legal order, unless it is interpreted in the light of the right to truth, and the right to reparation. Although truth is a multifaceted term which has received in-depth multidisciplinary analysis, the right to know the truth is not well founded in international law. The book offers some key considerations on truth, with the view to better explain how truth and disappearances correlate. From this viewpoint, there is not an exhaustive research on truth, but a more targeted analysis based on the need to understand how the two norms interact. Truth is explained as an ontological, normative, and judicial term. Further, during the study on disappearances it came into attention that the right to reparation has also been a neglected domain in literature. This is mainly due to the fact that as soon as victims reach the courts and speak their truth, reparation follows as a positive outcome. Yet, the forms of reparation vary and have not been explored to the fullest possible extent. This is due to judicial hesitance to apply all forms of reparation, as well as ambiguity regarding what victims and their next of kin wish to receive from the perpetrating states. Overall, secondary rights related to the right against disappearances are necessary for its comprehensive understanding and its application.

The final major point of this research monograph is whether doctrinal isolation tests the effectiveness of an international convention. Undoubtedly, the UN Convention against disappearances is considered a positive step, in both legal and symbolic terms. Still, the question of its interaction with the Bill of Human Rights and the actual protection of people against the practice of disappearance remains.

The greatest challenge is to evaluate the norm's influence beyond the Convention's orbit. This analysis is twofold. First, it involves the customary prohibition against disappearances, with a second phase involving the judicial treatment of enforced disappearance. By shedding light on the customary value of the prohibition on disappearances, there is an attempt to associate this norm with the International Bill of Human Rights. The connection between a disappearance norm and the general principle of human dignity is only possible through the lens of customary enforced disappearance. The second positive element is that reference to a customary prohibition against disappearances broadens its field of application.

Komotini, Greece Ioanna Pervou

Acknowledgments

Throughout this course, I was lucky enough to have the support and advice of many people. I would first like to thank Alison Kesby for her everlasting patience and wise comments, and emeriti Professor Kostas Hadjiconstantinou and Emmanuel Roucounas for their advice and guidance. Finally, I would not be able to accomplish this project without the unquestioning support of my family and friends. My parents, Yannis and Areti, my family Yannis and Kostis, my friends Sofia, Mairi, and Christina, and to everyone who brought jasmine scent to my everyday routine.

Contents

List of Abbreviations

ACHPR	African Commission on Human Peoples Rights
ACHR	American Convention on Human Rights
AP1	First Additional Protocol to the GC
CED	Committee against Disappearances
CoE	Council of Europe
CPED	Convention for the Protection of All Persons from Enforced Disappearance
ECOSOC	Economic and Financial Council
GC 1949	Geneva Conventions
HRC	ICCPR's Human Rights Committee
IACommHR	Inter-American Commission on Human Rights
IACtHR	Inter-American Court of Human Rights
ICC	International Criminal Court
ICCPR	International Covenant for Civil and Political Rights
ICESCR	International Covenant for Economic, Social and Cultural Rights
ICJ	International Court of Justice
ICTY	International Criminal Tribunal for the former Yugoslavia
ISWG	Inter-sessional Open-Ended Working Group
NGOs	Non-Governmental Organizations
OAS	Organization of American States
PACE	Parliamentary Assembly of the Council of Europe
PCIJ	Permanent Court of International Justice
UDHR	Universal Declaration on Human Rights
UN	United Nations
UNGA	United Nations General Assembly
UNSC	United Nations Security Council
UNWGEID	United Nations Working Group on Enforced or Involuntary Disappearance
US	The United States of America
WWII	World War II

Chapter 1
Introduction: The Concept of Enforced Disappearance

1.1 Enforced Disappearances in Antiquity: Between Myths and Widespread Practice

The term "enforced disappearance" (*desapararirición forzada*) was introduced by Latin American Non-Governmental Organizations (hereinafter NGOs)[1] in order to encapsulate a phenomenon that occurred in South America in the second half of the twentieth century. It is fairly considered "a euphemism",[2] because it describes abstractly a sequence of severe human rights violations which eliminate victims and render them helpless. Thereafter, the term has been heavily connected with Latin American practices; for this reason, part of the theory suggests that enforced disappearances are a recent addition to the human rights agenda.[3] However, the phenomenon predates the term, as references to enforced disappearance are common among the myths of different cultures. The theme of an individual taken by the sovereign (a king or emperor, or even a god in mythology) without any information regarding their fate is repeated in mythology, while almost all stories focus on the sorrow of their families. The motif's recurrence signals the fear of unreasonable abductions by the dominants; a fear which infiltrates deep into the collective unconscious of humanity.

In Greek mythology, there is a typical pattern concerning pure and graceful women abducted by the sovereign, with the most infamous example being that of Europa. According to the myth, Europa was the daughter of Agenor, the Phoenician king of Tyre, with whom the god Zeus fell in love. Zeus metamorphosed into a white bull to get close to the virgin and in an effort to escape the disapproving gaze

[1] ECOSOC. (8 January 2002). Civil and Political Rights, Including Questions of Disappearances and Summary Executions. UN Doc E/CN.4/2002/71, para 8.

[2] Maogoto (2002), p. 182.

[3] UN Doc E/CN.4/2002/71, para 7.

I. Pervou, *The Right not to Be Subjected to Enforced Disappearance*,
https://doi.org/10.1007/978-3-031-36731-1_1

of the other gods. As soon as he approached the girl, he took her to Crete, where he revealed his identity, raped and impregnated her. Ovid, in his poem collection "Metamorphoses", depicts Europa's feelings during her kidnapping by the bull, narrating that "[t]he frighted nymph looks backward on the shore, and hears the tumbling billows round her roar".[4] Though Europa is seduced by the bull, for no female could resist Zeus in Greek mythology, the princess is frightened by her unconventional captivity. Zeus stands for the ultimate authority, a god above all gods and superior to all mortals, who accumulates all powers. On the other hand, Europa is the defenseless individual: she is detained unwillingly and unreasonably, as she has not infringed the law by any means. Moreover, Zeus enacts his illegal conduct far from Phoenicia, in a geographically remote area; that is, the god seeks to evade any legal consequences, and to create a legal vacuum. This is why Europa is never allowed to return to her hometown; it is a kind of a protective measure to avoid bringing shame on her, or stigmatize her by the community.

The myth of Europa is known worldwide and has a universal reach and a relatively positive connotation, even though the theme of the myth is a forced abduction. It was considered as a myth of love and not as one of suffering for the victim. In Hesiod's "Cosmogony", it is reported that young girls were easy prey for abductions, either by sovereigns or by gods. Auge, Cyrene, Coronis and Aethra are only some of the victims who suffered under the absolute command of their captors.[5] Furthermore, it is recorded that women's kidnappings were often acts of retaliation between warring city-states: for instance, Io, Medea and Helen were all seized by belligerents. It is noted that

> for as long as there have been men, Greece has had a history: the abductions of Io, Europa, Medea, or Helen [...] have potentially the same role in historical causation as the Aeginetan abduction of status from Epidaurus".[6]

Seemingly, in Greek mythology gender connotes the power disparity existing between individuals and rulers, while rape is the equivalent of mistreatment. We might expect that the myth of Persephone would fall under this category of abductions, the mythological equivalent of the phenomenon of disappearances. Persephone, the daughter of the gods Zeus and Demeter, was violently taken by the god Hades to his kingdom, the underworld. Yet, although the features of violence and kidnapping employed by a sovereign over an unprotected person exist in this story, Persephone's mother is aware of the place of her captivity, even though she cannot visit her daughter. In this respect, Persephone's myth falls more under the notion of incommunicado detention, taking into account that Persephone cannot establish communication with her family for 6 months. Additionally, the fact that she is kept among the dead reaches by definition the threshold of an arbitrary detention.

---

[4] Ovid. *Metamorphoses, Book II* (Sir Samuel Garth et al, Trans.). Gale ECCO.

[5] Strauss Clay (2003), p. 167.

[6] Osborne (2002), p. 497.

The same kidnapping myth, even more cognate with the notion of enforced disappearance, appears in Roman mythology too. The abduction of the Sabine women is connected to the early history of Rome. The Romans sought wives to build their society, but the Sabines refused to allow girls from their tribe to marry them. In response, the Romans decided to abduct the Sabine women during a festival. The plan was state organized, based on the plan that Romulus, the founder of Rome and leader of the Romans, would give the signal to his subordinates to abduct the girls during the ceremonies while the male Sabines were unaware. Both Plutarch and Livy support the idea that the abducted girls were angry with their captors. Their attitude changed only when Romulus promised them that they would become legitimate wives of the Roman men.[7] The massive abduction triggered an armed conflicted between the two tribes, when the Sabines attacked Rome to reclaim the girls. According to the legend, the abducted women managed to reconcile the tribes, as they did not want to mourn either their forebears or their husbands as the result of a conflict between the two groups.

The myth's critical element with respect to enforced disappearance is liberty deprivation conducted by the official state authorities, which caused pain to the abductees' relatives. Furthermore, the turning point in the women's behavior is Romulus' promise that they will become legitimate wives of the Romans. This shift is crucial, for it signifies the women's return to legality, a status that had been overturned by their abduction. As soon as they re-enter the zone of legality, their abduction ceases to be unethical. This metaphor illustrates the connection between disappearance and lawlessness; to wit, how the phenomenon creates a legal black hole for the victim. Or, conversely, as soon as lawlessness is terminated, the suffering of the disappeared is over. Moreover, there is strong resemblance with disappearances committed nowadays by guerillas, or terrorist groups who target young women and girls in particular, with a view to assist them in everyday life activities. Myths not only demonstrate the sovereign-victim nexus, but they also bring to light how gender-based violence (GBV) is one of disappearances' driving forces. Their similarity to recent state practice, namely in Nigeria, Colombia, and Mexico,[8] were disappeared women suffered sexual harassment, or forced impregnation, additionally to general mistreatment is astonishing. It reaffirms how such tactics survived throughout time.

These myths imply that the fear of enforced disappearance existed long before the term was formulated. Certainly they do not correspond exactly to the current perception of enforced disappearance, taking also into consideration how states and the notion of sovereignty evolved all these years. Yet, they all describe human fear of the unlimited mistreatment that a sovereign may cause when the conditions of liberty deprivation are concealed.

---

[7] Brown (1995), p. 295.

[8] Marshall (2008), p. 161.

1.2 Enforced Disappearances in Modern Times: The "Night and Fog Decree"

Enforced disappearances with their contemporary meaning were recorded in their contemporary archetypical form during World War II (hereinafter WWII), when thousands were disappeared as a result of the "Night and Fog Decree" (*Nacht und Nebel Erlass*). Prior to this degree unacknowledged and remote detention existed. There is evidence of its widespread and systematic practice during the Spanish Civil War (1936–1939), when it is estimated that more than a hundred thousand people disappeared and subsequently died as a result of the atrocities ordered by the Franco regime.[9] Moreover, Stalin's infamous commands for the commission of prisoners' of war mass disappearance, which ended up in the execution of thousands of people are also historically affirmed, with the Katyn Forest Massacre being one of the most prominent examples.[10] In this sense, Stalin's regime also endorsed disappearances and adopted them in numerous cases.[11]

Yet, the Night and Fog Decree is the first official recognition of the practice. Moreover, contrary to other regimes, Hitler endorsed enforced disappearance as a desirable method of state terrorism. The Keitel Order proves that disappearances were not just tolerated by the Third Reich but openly promoted by it.[12] The Decree of December 7, 1941 was ordered by Adolf Hitler and signed by the Supreme Commander of the Armed Forces, Wilhelm Keitel (also known as the "Keitel Order"),[13] which provided for the transfer of people who were deemed dangerous for the security of the Third Reich, and who could not be prosecuted quickly, to concentration camps in Germany. According to it,

> prisoners taken to Germany are subjected to military procedure only if particular military interests require this. In case German or foreign authorities inquire about such prisoners, they are to be told that they were arrested, but that the proceedings do not allow any further information.[14]

Vanishing without leaving a trace or providing information was thought to be an appropriate measure for intimidating the potential enemies of the Reich. The perpetrators aimed at disappearing the victims under the fog of night, a rather poetic attempt to euphemize this practice; or else they intended to create nebulous uncertainty around the conditions of their captivity. As has been pointed out:

> the aim of the secret arrest and detention [...] was twofold. First, an individual was to be removed from the protection of law. Second [...] secret arrest and detention served as a

[9] Guarino (2010), p. 63.

[10] Keller and Heri (2014), pp. 735–750.

[11] Matas (1999), p. 351.

[12] Cf Hall (1999), p. 170.

[13] Hall (1999), p. 151.

[14] Nazi Conspiracy and Aggression. (7 December 1941). Night and Fog Decree. 7 L-90. Retrieved March 22, 2023, from http://avalon.law.yale.edu/imt/l-90.asp.

> form of general deterrence, achieved through the intimidation and anxiety caused by the persistent uncertainty among the missing person's family.[15]

The first objective is common to all such orders: deprivation of the victim's liberty with complete lack of due process guarantees. The Night and Fog decree did not differentiate the victim's position vis-à-vis any other person taken to a concentration camp, given that everyone was subjected to ill-treatment indiscriminately. The order targeted primarily the families of those detained; its novel element was the complete secrecy surrounding the conditions of detention, involving a deathly silence shrouding the Reich's plans regarding the disappeared. Disappearance is leaves an open door for hope compared to executions. In this sense, as long as it lasts it augments the anxiety of the victims' relatives, as they are aware of their next of kin severe suffering, but they still hope to reunite.[16]

The victims were by definition doomed: their fate ranged from forced labor to forced participation in cruel experiments.[17] Therefore, ill-treatment was unavoidable, but made it the least horrible option for the families of the detainees, compared to execution. The families' natural anxiety due to the disappearance of their beloved ones was intensified by the regime's policy that aimed deliberately at obfuscation and intimidation. To achieve this goal, Field Marshal Keitel instructed the commanders of concentration camps with prisoners who were classified "Nacht und Nebel" to "entirely cut [them] off from the world and [to allow them] neither to receive nor to send letters".[18] Additionally, there were detailed instructions on how "to dispose of [their] bodies [...] without revealing the place of death".[19] Effectively, these people disappeared without trace, while the German authorities consistently refused to make any announcement about their fate. Keitel's covering letter to the order, which he wrote just a few days after it was issued, encompasses the essence of "Night and Fog"; he explains that

> [e]fficient and enduring intimidation can only be achieved either by capital punishment or by measures by which the relatives of the criminals and the population do not know the fate of the criminal. This aim is achieved when the criminal is transferred to Germany.[20]

Contrary to modern state practices in confronting criminals and terrorists, namely extraordinary renditions, the home state was, for the believers in the Third Reich, the appropriate place to deploy their policies. It was considered a fortress difficult for anyone to surpass. Therefore, the detainees' transfer to Germany was suitable punishment, since the perpetrators had at their disposal all the resources they needed

---

[15] Finucane (2010), p. 176.

[16] Mallinder (2008), p. 230.

[17] Herbert (1997), p. 63.

[18] Nuremberg Trial Proceedings, Indictment: Count 3. Retrieved, March 22, 2023, from http://avalon.law.yale.edu/imt/count3.asp.

[19] Nuremberg Trial Proceedings (27 July 1946). Retrieved, March 22, 2023, from http://avalon.law.yale.edu/imt/07-27-46.asp.

[20] Ibid.

at the Gestapo headquarters, while the disappearances also affected the families of the alleged offenders.

Overall, targeting the family nexus was the extraordinary aspect of "Night and Fog"; Hitler's regime aimed to go beyond the punishment of a few individuals to cause the public fear, and thus obedience.[21] This method was classified as amongst the most painful of their decrees; "Night and Fog" remained in force for approximately 3 years, and it was eventually replaced by the "Terror and Sabotage Decree", an order that put flesh on the bones of the increasingly merciless policy of the Third Reich.[22]

1.3 The Prevalence of Enforced Disappearances in the Americas During the Cold War

The "Night and Fog" policy was adopted as a model in Latin and Central America soon after the end of WWII. Enforced disappearance became synonymous with state terror.[23] It took the form of systematic and widespread governmental practices which sought to obliterate political opposition and suppress society.[24] Under the pretext of fighting threats to national security, enforced disappearances ravaged Latin America, as they had during WWII in Europe. The analogy drawn between the contagion of state terrorism in the Americas and WWII is not unusual, not only for the enormous number of victims, but also because the military regimes saw themselves as embattled in a war comparable to WWII.[25]

The reasons why the phenomenon bloomed in this region are primarily political. More specifically, during the 1960s and the 1970s, and especially within the political context of the Cold War, military juntas seized power in most Latin and Central American countries. The majority of those military juntas served the establishment and enforced the preservation of a capitalist system based upon foreign investments. To some extent, these regimes were the outcome of their push to become major players in the international arena after the end of WWII. In addition, the rise of military juntas in these regions were indicative of the diverse roots set down in the American continent after independence and decolonization. Unlike the United States of America (hereinafter the US), "the independent republics of Latin America did not draw on the philosophical underpinnings of human rights".[26] That is, America's southern hemisphere did not follow a straightforward course towards

[21] Finucane (2010), pp. 181–183.

[22] Nuremberg Trial Proceedings (Indictment).

[23] Giorgou (2013), p. 1004.

[24] Roniger and Sznajder (1999), pp. 7–28.

[25] Brands (2010), pp. 96–101.

[26] Wright (2000), p. 304; Nagle (2000), p. 348.

democratization,[27] rather it pioneered in the Third Wave of democratization.[28] This makes a comparison between the US and the countries of Central and Latin America by definition unsuitable, bearing in mind the involvement of the former in the latter states' political life in the second half of the twentieth century.

The dictatorships that ruled most of the countries in these regions are usually referred to as "bureaucratic–authoritarian" regimes,[29] and they are deeply rooted in the Americas. Historically, it has been suggested that their occurrence is due to

> the embodiment of a centuries-old system in which a ruling elite maintains control by manipulated interaction among and within the three branches of government in order to preserve the status quo of a ruling class composed of large landowners in control of vast natural resources, and a powerful merchant class capable of manipulating trade and commerce to influence the political landscape".[30]

From a legal perspective, the term "authoritarian regime" equates to the utter encroachment on the principle of separation of powers. The Latin American dictators did not aim to dissolve public institutions, but use them in favor of their regime.[31] Enforced disappearances were the response of ruling elites to the rising middle class in their effort not to lose their power. Anyone that could potentially harm those elites, either through economic growth or by investing in new technologies or educational progress, were characterized as subversive, or, worse, as insurgents.

Consequently, at some level the term "enforced disappearances" became synonymous with the incessant use of military force to obliterate any form of opposition and to ensure public order; "ultimately, the military assume[d] the role of the sole 'legitimate' expression of the national will".[32] Thereby, disappearances were deemed an effective measure for the sustainability of the military juntas. In general, the horrific human rights violations suffered by Latin Americans were an expression of political violence, stemming from long-lasting inadequacies in those states' democratic culture. The military juntas of Latin and Central America followed the same pattern in the commission of enforced disappearance, with slight variations according to each country's political and social idiosyncrasies. Regional state conduct during the Cold War is the epitome of the phenomenon of enforced disappearance, and decisive for the contemporary understanding of enforced disappearance.[33] It was these policies of state terror which brought worldwide attention to the phenomenon, and determined the term's substance. Although the exact conditions under which disappearances occurred during that period are unique and cannot be repeated,

---

[27] However, this geographical generalization is not applicable with regards to disappearance, firstly because Mexico engages in state terrorism, and secondly because the US applies modern methods close to this kind of archetypical enforced disappearance.

[28] McCoy (2008), p. 20.

[29] Malloy (1992), pp. 229–246; Lewis (2006), pp. 31–48.

[30] Nagle (2008), p. 5.

[31] Tushnet (2015), p. 421.

[32] Kleinman (1987), p. 1036.

[33] Dulitzky (2019), p. 428.

by accepting a linear conception of history we can see that they have shaped the phenomenon's collective realization. In this regard, enforced disappearances in the Americas are the classic prototype, envisaged as the traditional, or archetypal form of the phenomenon. This classification helps in mapping the phenomenon in the region. Twelve out of the nineteen states in Central and South America committed systematically enforced disappearances: Argentine, Chile, Uruguay, Paraguay, Brazil, Bolivia, Peru, Colombia, Venezuela, Guatemala, El Salvador and Honduras. Needless to say, incidences of enforced disappearance occurred in the other countries as well.[34] However, it is underlined that the entire region suffered from state terrorism; accordingly, the sole purpose of this taxonomy is to understand the phenomenon's historical context.

The first countries that yielded to state terrorism were Uruguay and Brazil. The regimes that assumed power there are deemed mild in comparison to those of Chile and Argentina, which followed. The harm that took place in Chile and Argentina was unrestricted and soon got out of control. After Chile's and Argentina's "Dirty Wars" against the alleged threat of political dissidents and leftist movements, state terror, and consequently the phenomenon of enforced disappearance, sprawled across Latin and Central America.[35] Enforced disappearances in these countries shared significant similarities, though they were shaped by each dictator's hidden agenda and the specific social stratification of each state. In this context, along with Argentina and Chile, Guatemala and El Salvador also require specific analysis, as the method of enforced disappearance was implemented against indigenous populations and children respectively.

With regards to the remaining countries, Paraguay's historical course is characterized by political stability combined with the curtailment of civil and political rights. From 1955 until 1989 the country was dictated by Alfredo Stroessner. Under his command, arbitrary deprivation of liberty and torture were widespread. Yet there are few reported executions and disappearances, primarily because of the dictator's unquestioned power throughout the country. According to the Paraguayan Commission on Truth and Justice there were 423 cases of disappearances and executions during this period.[36]

Similar to Paraguay, Bolivia has a low record of enforced disappearance complaints. During its fifteen-year struggle towards democratization (1967–1982), enforced disappearances amounted to approximately to 155, most of which were committed at the beginning of the 1980s during the dictatorship of Luis García Meza.[37] The Bolivian paradox, though, lies in the fact that the National Commission

[34] *Heliodoro Portugal v Panama*, Inter-American Court of Human Rights Series C No 186 (12 August 2008); *Tibi v Ecuador*, Inter-American Court of Human Rights Series C No 114 (7 September 2004); *Aloeboetoe et al v Suriname*, Inter-American Court of Human Rights Series C No 15 (10 September 1993).

[35] Wright (2007), pp. 28–31.

[36] Comision de Verdad y Justicia (2008), p. 29.

[37] *Ticona Estrada et al v Bolivia*, Inter-American Court of Human Rights Series C No 191 (27 November 2008) paras 47–48.

of Inquiry into Disappearances was unable to produce a final report. Although the state was the first to permanently abandon the regional crisis of state terrorism, and consequently the first to launch a national truth commission as early as 1982, the commission did not deliver a final report due to inadequate funding and political unwillingness. Consequently, information on Bolivia's dark period remains sparse.[38]

1.3.1 Chile and the Pinochet Regime

The military coup d'état led by General Augusto Pinochet overthrew the socialist government of Salvador Allende on 11 September 1973 and ruled Chile for almost two decades (1973–1990). The Pinochet regime expanded on the concept of state terrorism by promoting a discourse of "pre-emptive state self-defense". That is, the regime cultivated a rhetoric of rivalry between state agents and insurgents; the latter being an undeterminable part of the population that could eventually demonstrate disobedience and harm the regime. This scheme took later on the form of an extensive network where disappearances were committed by state agents with the assistance of civilians against insurgents as well as foreign nationals.[39] Preemptiveness was a central feature in the campaign of state terrorism: insurgents were to be defeated before they could launch their anti-governmental operations. Practically, the regime was able to target anyone deemed suspicious based on their purported beliefs.

The political repression of the Pinochet regime included the imprisonment or exile of countless citizens, as well as widespread torture and extrajudicial executions.[40] The practice of enforced disappearance was progressively developed by the regime as a means to conceal the marks of excessive torture on the victims' bodies. The disappeared

> were kept in clandestine detention, subjected to torture and eventually summarily executed. Their bodies were disposed of in secret. [...] During the first months of military rule these "disappearances" were not centrally coordinated. But with the establishment of DINA [Direccion de Inteligencia Nacional], the regime's secret police, toward the end of 1973, "disappearances" became a carefully organized method designed to exterminate opponents considered dangerous and to avoid accountability for such crimes.[41]

DINA, the regime's Secret Agency, played a cardinal role in the perpetration of enforced disappearance.[42] The agency is notorious for the brutality of its agents, while there is still ambiguity as to who was at the agency's head. According to

---

[38] United States Institute of Peace, Truth Commission Bolivia. Retrieved March 22, 2023, from https://www.usip.org/publications/1982/10/truth-commission-bolivia.

[39] Edwards (2022), pp. 479–522.

[40] Rojas and Shaftoe (2019), pp. 41–42.

[41] *Report of the Chilean National Commission on Truth and Reconciliation, Vol I/II* (1993), p. 8.

[42] Shamsi (2014), p. 372.

information which remains unconfirmed by Chile, Colonel Walter Rauff, a former Nazi who supervised the concentration camp at Auschwitz, was appointed head of DINA. Chilean authorities vehemently deny the employment of Rauff in any capacity, and he is not mentioned in the Report of the Chilean Commission on Truth and Reconciliation. However, his name appeared in the lists of the Chilean exiles in Mexico as one of DINA's principle advisors.[43] Irrespective of the truthfulness of this information, the potential connection of DINA with a former member of the SS gives a hint of the barbaric methods applied by the agency. The great majority of disappearances in Chile were conducted by DINA, and when the agency was dissolved, approximately 4 years after Pinochet came to power, the number of disappeared victims decreased significantly.[44]

Moreover, Rauff personifies the necessary liaison between the Keitel order and disappearances in Latin America. Of course, it is not suggested that he himself possessed knowledge regarding the practice of disappearances in Latin America, but that the military juntas in Latin America were familiar with the methods employed by the Third Reich; in this respect, suggesting parallels between the results of state terror during the Cold War in the Americas and WWII in Europe is not groundless. Although the politics of state terror in Latin and Central America occurred in a completely different context than in WWII, their effects on the respective populations were the same. In legal terms, WWII was governed by the law of armed conflict, and human rights violations were directed against the occupied populations, whereas in the so-called "Dirty Wars" the international law principles of state sovereignty and political integrity were respected, and the military juntas guaranteed a *prima facie* political stability in their countries. The military juntas abided by the UN standards for the preservation of peace and security, and, therefore, taking international actions against human rights abuses perpetrated by them was thought to be an unlawful intervention in their domestic jurisdiction. Besides, during the 1970s the international law of human rights had not evolved and most states claimed human rights to be a *domain reservé*.[45] In this respect, Latin American authoritarian regimes were not an exception to the rule. Further, the Pinochet regime formally cooperated with monitoring human rights bodies. However, although it allowed the Inter-American Commission on Human Rights (hereinafter IACommHR) and members of the UN Ad Hoc Working Group on the situation of Human Rights in Chile to conduct on-site visits, it did not provide information as to the fate of the disappeared, the detained and the executed victims. Despite the Commission's numerous requests for official information, the regime turned the country into a land of violence and rendered international fact-finding bodies ineffective.[46]

---

[43] Memorandum for CI Staff Chief, 'Possible Leads in [ ] Case' (8 July 1977).

[44] *Report of the Chilean National Commission on Truth and Reconciliation* (1993), pp. 8–9.

[45] Forsythe (1993), pp. 395–396.

[46] UNGA. (20 December 1978). Importance of the experience of the ad hoc Working Group on the situation of human rights in Chile. UNGA Res 33/176; IACommHR. (25 October 1974). Report on the Situation of Human Rights in Chile. OEA/Ser.L/V/II.34, doc 21, Chapter IX.

The Chilean dictatorship initially turned against the members of the Revolutionary Left Movement (*Movimiento de Izquierda Revolucionaria* – MIR). According to estimates, five-hundred members of the group were disappeared by agents of the Pinochet regime, apart from those killed during armed confrontations.[47] Then the regime turned to organizations of university students and trade unions, because they were presumed to be MIR's think tanks. Overall, enforced disappearances were a powerful tool in the institutionalization of state terror in the Chilean "Dirty War". However, the method was not preferred over death squads or the direct extermination of political opponents. The regime launched large-scale operations of summary executions to eliminate its enemies: massive squad killings were a common reality for Chileans.[48] In other words, state terrorism targeted political opponents directly and not their families, although the latter's terrorization was an inevitable side-effect. The brutality of summary executions, mass-scale detentions, and torture was enough to guarantee obedience among the citizens, and so the intentional concealment of the victims' traces was not considered necessary in the deployment of the regime's patterns of human rights violations. The IACommHR noted that the Pinochet regime had "employed virtually every known means for physical elimination of the dissidents, among others: disappearances, summary executions of individuals and groups, executions decreed in proceedings without legal guarantees, and torture".[49]

Finally, the Chilean dictatorship was the mastermind of "Operation Condor", a regional operation of intelligence sharing among the authoritarian regimes of Latin and America. Operation Condor was established officially in 1975 under the auspices of the Chilean DINA.[50] Although information regarding Condor is unverified, a letter from DINA chief Manuel Contreras to the Paraguayan authorities proves the existence of regional information sharing, and sheds light on the operation's organization. The Contreras letter invited the Paraguayan secret police to join in a meeting in Santiago with the purpose of enhancing coordination for the preservation of national security. There is evidence that

> [t]he proposal for the meeting included a plan of action and an organizational structure as well as a security system with three elements: an office of coordination and security, including a computerized central data bank of suspect persons, organizations, and activities, "something similar to Interpol but dedicated to Subversion"; an information center with special communication channels, a cryptography capability, telephones with scrambling mechanisms, and message systems, and permanent working meetings. The Chileans offered Santiago as the headquarters of the system, specifying that the "technical personnel" of the system would be equally represented by participating countries. These technical personnel

---

[47] *Norma Yurich v Chile*, Human Rights Committee (hereinafter HRC) UN Doc CCPR/C/66/D/718/1996/Rev.1, para 2.9.

[48] *Report of the Chilean National Commission on Truth and Reconciliation* (1993), p. 180.

[49] IACommHR. (15 October 1996). Report No 34/96 (*Meneses Reyes et al v Chile*). OEA/Ser.L/V/11.95, doc 7 para 46; IACommHR. (15 October 1996). Report No 36/96 (*Garay Hermosilla et al v Chile*). OEA/Ser.L/V/II doc 7, para 46.

[50] Analysis of the legal aspects regarding Operation Condor and the judicial responses to it is included in Chap. 3.

> would have diplomatic immunity, and the Chileans proposed that they be from the intelligence services. The "technical personnel" were undoubtedly the agents who carried out Condor operations, including disappearances and assassinations.[51]

All in all, subversion was the ultimate goal of the Pinochet regime. Alongside its political connotations, the term soon became synonymous with civil obedience, a cardinal feature in the regime's ideology. The Pinochet regime unfolded a clear state practice endorsing disappearances, involving state intelligence agencies, which refined practice to guarantee civilian obedience and potential impunity for the perpetrators.

1.3.2 Argentina and Indiscriminate Disappearances

Argentina took a parallel political path to that of Chile.[52] Although it was under an authoritarian regime for fewer years than Chile, the number of victims in Argentina was beyond imagining. Argentina took after Chile's example and perfected it. As a result, in terms of human rights violations, the dictatorship regime that ruled in Argentina from 1976 to 1983 is characterized as one of the most egregious; "the Argentine experience had the unfortunate distinction of introducing the term *desaparecido* into the international lexicon".[53] It is estimated that more than 30,000 citizens disappeared during that period.[54] The dictatorship that seized authority in 1976, known as the Gentlemen's Coup,[55] headed by General Jorge Rafael Videla, proceeded immediately towards the "reorganization" of the state (*Proceso de Reorganización Nacional*).[56] To a great extent the "reorganization" focused upon the extinction of the political opponents through its own infamous "Dirty War" (*Guerra Sucia*). [57] The junta launched a campaign against those who could potentially harm national security and pursued their extermination. It targeted anyone who might be a "leftist" or a "subversive". Students, trade union leaders and journalists were only some of the groups that were constantly under attack. The junta targeted even the political opponents' children, because they were considered future threats to the regime.[58] The regime's strategy is best summarized in the words of General Ramón Camps, who proclaimed: "first, we will kill the guerillas. Then we

---

[51] McSherry (2002), p. 41; *see* also, Slack (1996), pp. 492–506.

[52] Kelly (2018), pp. 210–212.

[53] Mignone et al. (1984), p. 120.

[54] IACommHR. (11 April 1980). Report on the Situation of Human Rights in Argentina. OEA/Ser.L/V/II.49 doc 19.

[55] Feitlowitz (1998), pp. 3–18.

[56] Clark (2001), pp. 75–76.

[57] Roniger and Sznajder (1999), p. 11.

[58] *Reggiardo Tolosa Case*, Inter-American Court of Human Rights Series E (19 November 1993) paras 8–9.

will kill the guerrillas' families. Then we will kill the friends of their families, and the friends of their friends, so that there will be no one left to remember who the guerrillas were".[59] In this sense, the Videla junta is characterized as a regime which would target anyone indiscriminately, for the fear of opposition.

Overall, the junta sought to terrorize the population in order to establish civil obedience. Therefore, the authorities turned against civilians regardless of their ideology, making disappearances a part of everyday life for the people of Argentina.[60] The state authorities developed a very specific and detailed mode of operation. The victims were usually carried off from their homes in the presence of their families. Then they were transferred to secret detention centers where they were tortured to death. Torture was not an interrogation method but rather a means of dehumanizing the detainees before death, used not to extract information or to obtain confessions from the victims. They viewed torture as part of their mission to politically cleanse Argentina; opponents had to be punished before being executed. Torturers were obsessed with their "sacred mission" to cleanse society from the subversives. Eventually, torture became "a routine, a bureaucratic activity".[61] It is reported that torturers were almost addicted to torturing the victims; "sometimes they would stay in the torture room for a full 24 hours, never taking time off or resting; or else, they would go home, and then return a couple of hours later, as though the atmosphere of cruelty and violence had drawn them back".[62] The explanation for this collective obsession with torture involves the church, which fueled the "Dirty War" with the necessary moral underpinnings. Victims who survived reported that priests were sometimes present during torture, requiring them to cooperate and testify as a condition of saving their souls. It is also suggested that members of the chaplaincy encouraged the torturers to proceed for the sake of the public interest.[63] In this respect, torturers were convinced of the rightness of their actions, believing that they were the true servants of the will of God and the regime, which coincided.[64]

Over the course of time, the practice of enforced disappearance became more intricate. After excessive torturing, the perpetrators dumped the victims, alive or dead, from airplanes into the ocean. In this way, they rendered the localization and identification of the bodies of the disappeared impossible. Most of the cases ended in extrajudicial executions, and very few victims survived and reappeared.[65] At the same time, as far as the victims' families were concerned the pertinent authorities refused to inform them of their fate, and the authorities denied that the victims had been detained. State terror paralyzed the rest of the society, and the absence of information on the alleged insurgents was a tool for suppressing opposition.

---

[59] Wright (2000), p. 311.

[60] Crenzel (2017).

[61] Donnelly (2007), p. 61.

[62] Ibid p. 63.

[63] Osiel (2004), p. 133.

[64] Gustavo Morello (2015), pp. 60–62.

[65] National Commission on the Disappearance of Persons (CONADEP) (1984).

This situation raised concerns with the IACommHR; after making reference to Argentina's "disappeared" in 1978[66] it sent a fact-finding mission in 1979. It is striking that the Argentinean authorities attempted to mislead the IACHR by presenting false evidence. But the die had been cast, and the Commission began to report on disappearances in other countries which had adopted identical methods.

Overall, although Argentina suffered from the greatest number of disappearances in Latin America, those responsible for committing these acts were never brought before the Inter-American Court of Human Rights (hereinafter IACtHR), because of the country's reservations regarding its competence. Only recently have domestic tribunals prosecuted members of the dictatorship. Former judge Victor Brusa has been sentenced for committing crimes against humanity. Argentinean courts have convicted Reynaldo Bignone, the former president of Argentina from 1982 to 1983, for ordering enforced disappearances and baby thefts in 2013 and 2014.[67]

The thirty-year lapse between the end of the military junta and the administration of justice for the crimes committed is due to the domestic legislation enforced after the regime's overthrow, which halted criminal proceedings in an attempt to establish democracy and accomplish state redemption. The Full Stop Law (Ley de Punto Final) and the Law of Due Obedience (Ley de Obediencia Debida) of 1986 and 1987 respectively, shielded officials who committed human rights abuses.[68]

1.3.3 Guatemala and State Terrorism

Modern Guatemalan history counts over thirty-seven thousand (37,000) victims of extrajudicial executions and disappearances,[69] and the state's path to democratization resembles the journey of Odysseus. The country's political strife dates back to 1954 when the military overthrew the democratically elected government. From that time onwards, the military was actively involved in Guatemala's political life. The situation in the country deteriorated after the political developments in Cuba in 1959, and by the end of 1960 the state had entered a long phase of internal turbulence. The characterization of the situation in the country is a daunting challenge. On the one hand, episodes of violence between armed groups were an everyday phenomenon, a feature which leads many theorists to speak of a civil war, or an internal armed conflict. On the other hand, human rights atrocities are mainly attributed to state agents, who exercised effective control over the state. By elevating the situation to a civil war, one minimizes the intensity of the policy of state terror exerted by the sovereign authorities and downgrades the subsequent systematic

[66] IACHR. (1978). Annual Report. OEA.Ser.L/V/II.47 doc 13, Section 2, Chapter III.

[67] Retrieved March 23, 2023, from http://jurist.law.pitt.edu/paperchase/2009/12/argentina-court-sentences-former-judge.php and http://www.bbc.com/news/world-latin-america-29532804.

[68] Pérez-Solla (2003), pp. 693–694.

[69] Ball et al. (2005), p. 8.

human rights violations. To give the bigger picture, from 1960 until 1996 authoritarian regimes succeeded one another, thus prolonging disorder and depriving the state of political stability and social cohesion.

The commission of enforced disappearance as an expression of state terror altered according to each regime's priorities. Namely, state involvement in the perpetration of enforced disappearances can be split into three distinct periods. From 1960 to 1966 the victims were primarily government opponents. The government attacked citizens potentially linked to communism or socialism, ideologies which were outlawed. Thus, there was a model of selective repression.[70] The second phase, from 1966 until 1982, was marked by the expansion of the government's brutal attacks, not only against insurgents[71] but also against university students and professors,[72] as well as workers and peasants.[73] During this sixteen-year period, disappearances became more frequent, with the years 1966 and 1972 being among the most ferocious in the country's history. Evidently, Guatemala did not escape the epidemic of indiscriminate, state-organized enforced disappearances that had become by that time an obsession among Latin American dictators, although it is not clear whether the country served as an example for other authoritarian regimes, or if it increasingly espoused the "Dirty Wars" pattern.

Yet, this period has three distinct characteristics, dictated by the Guatemalan sociopolitical conditions. Firstly, with regards to political governance, Guatemala's uniqueness lies in the fact that formally the state was not under a dictatorship, since governments were democratically elected. Besides, during this period Guatemala was not associated with a single person alone; on the contrary there were periodic changes of state leadership. Guatemala's persistent problem, though, was the growing power of the military, which ultimately took control, enjoying a state of impunity. Secondly, a significant percentage of disappearances and executions were not officially carried out by the army but by covert military operators, who formed small counterinsurgency groups. More specifically, either members of the army or people who had received the appropriate training by the Guatemalan forces, organized paramilitary groups and committed small-scale enforced disappearances, with the army's support. This tactic hampered efforts to gain proof of the human rights violations that occurred, since there was no standardized pattern in the commission of enforced disappearances. Accordingly, attribution of these squads'

---

[70] Tomuschat (2001), p. 249; Reconstitution de la Memoire Historique (REMHI) (2000), p. 28.

[71] *Chitay Nech et al v Guatemala*, Inter-American Court of Human Rights Series C No 212 (25 May 2010); *Maritza Urrutia v Guatemala*, Inter-American Court of Human Rights Series C No 103 (27 November 2003).

[72] *Myrna Mack Chang v Guatemala*, Inter-American Court of Human Rights Series C No (25 November 2005).

[73] *Tiu Tojín v Guatemala*, Inter-American Court of Human Rights Series C No 190 (26 November 2008); Commission for Historical Clarification (CHC). (25 February 1999). Guatemala Memory of Silence, Tz'inil Na'tab'al'. Retrieved 22 March, 2023, from https://hrdag.org/wp-content/uploads/2013/01/CEHreport-english.pdf, para 26.

activities to the Guatemalan state was not straightforward, and the injured parties could not prove their allegations.[74]

Finally, the third and most important aspect of the national strategy of state terrorism, including enforced disappearances, was the deployment of targeted attacks against indigenous populations, with the view to exterminating them. Indigenous populations were not from the beginning in the state's crosshairs.[75] Guatemalan society was divided: on one side were the residents of the country's capital, and on the other were the inland, mainly indigenous populations. The division between the country's urban and rural populations was visible to the naked eye. The capital was the heart of development, the decision-making center. In contrast, indigenous populations, or more generally the peasants, were constantly neglected by the central government, as they were considered insignificant from a political standpoint. This policy of abandonment switched as soon as the peasants manned the country's emerging industrial sector. Eventually, the state's progressive minds brought to the negotiating table the issue of protecting the rights of the indigenous people, and the latter were approached by the former with the purpose of contributing to the overthrow of the ruling elite. The peasants' participation in the country's political life was thus deemed a destabilizing factor in Guatemala's political integrity, and, as a result, executions and disappearances spread across the state's territory. State agents were exhaustive in their cruelty: summary executions, torture and enforced disappearances were aggravated due to unrestrained discrimination against indigenous populations. In the second phase of Guatemala's internal conflict, then, state terrorism was twofold: apart from coercing civil obedience, it aimed at punishing indigenous populations for taking a moderate part in the state's political life. In other words, political exclusion roused discrimination against them.[76]

State terrorism coupled with racial discrimination increased when General Efraín Ríos Montt came to power in 1982, after conducting a coup d'état. At the start of the third phase of the Guatemalan conflict there were two key changes. The sovereigns were no longer democratically elected; instead there were consecutive coups taking place and the enforced disappearances of peasants intensified. From 1982 onwards, disappearances, alongside other methods, served as means of genocide[77] directed against the Maya and Ladino tribes.[78] As far as the peasants were concerned, Guatemala eventually became a land of modern serfdom. The peak of enforced disappearances recorded at the beginning of the 1980s was accompanied by the

---

[74] Ball et al. (2005), pp. 16–17.

[75] Pinzón González (2016), pp. 102–118.

[76] *Río Negro Massacres v Guatemala*, Inter-American Court of Human Rights Series C No 250 (4 September 2012); *'Las Dos Erres' Massacre v Guatemala*, Inter-American Court of Human Rights Series C No 211 (24 November 2009); *Plan de Sánchez Massacre v Guatemala*, Inter-American Court of Human Rights Series C No 105 (29 April 2004).

[77] Sarkin and Baranowska (2018), pp. 11–50.

[78] CHC (1999) paras 1, 27. For the connection between enforced disappearance and genocide *see* Chap. 3.

state's refusal to accept inspection visits by international and regional fact-finding bodies, or to allow media coverage.[79]

Overall, state terrorism in Guatemala revealed (during its second phase) a deep-rooted racism against indigenous populations, which in turn intensified systematic state patterns of widespread enforced disappearances and summary executions.[80] Guatemala is a unique example for two reasons: first, national history follows closely Cold War phases and the intensification of state terrorism, including disappearances, came during one of the most acute and turbulence periods in international history. Second, Guatemalan practice demonstrates how enforced disappearance may serve genocidal policies.[81]

1.3.4 El Salvador and Children's Enforced Disappearances

El Salvador did not break tradition regarding state terrorism. Although the Salvadoran internal conflict was briefer than in the rest of the region (it began in 1979 and officially ended in 1991), the country mourned a significant number of victims (approximately 75,000).[82] El Salvador was also trapped in the political wrangling of the Cold War. As a result, the situation in the country during the 1980s did not differ much from those previously examined. State violence against political opponents, or militants, spread gradually to include civilians. The threat of subversion turned El Salvador into a lawless land. There is evidence that everyone was considered a potential enemy of the country's stability. As a result, the appearance of corpses in plain sight in the center of cities or villages was commonplace.[83] State agents did not hesitate to wreck entire communities, if they suspected those communities had liaisons with insurgents.[84] In the Salvadoran case, land utilization was the eye of the storm, due to population density. Governmental plans for legal reforms regarding land tenure and the rural economy still torment the country to date.

---

[79] IACommHR (3 October 1985). Third report on the situation of human rights in Guatemala. OEA/Ser.L/V/II.66, Chapter II; IACommHR, (5 October 1983). Report on the situation of human rights in Guatemala. OEA/Ser.L/V/II.61, doc 47, rev 1, Chapters II, IX; IACommHR. (13 October 1981). Report on the situation of human rights in Guatemala. OEA/Ser.L/V/II.53, doc 21, rev 2, Chapter II.

[80] There is joint reference to executions and disappearances, as they were the patterns applied most often by the sovereigns. According to the REMHI report, "[a]près les assassinats (individuels ou collectifs) les disparitions forcées furent la mesure la plus fréquente, (un cas sur cinq enregistrés)'. REMHI (2000), p. 138.

[81] Laplant (2014), p. 642.

[82] Hoover Green and Ball (2019), pp. 781–814.

[83] UNSC. (1 April 1993). Report of the Commission on the truth for El Salvador, from madness to hope. UN Doc S/25500, 27–28.

[84] *The Massacres of El Mozote and Nearby Places v El Salvador*, Inter-American Court of Human Rights Series C No 252 (25 October 2012); IACommHR. (24 September 1992). Report No 26/92 *(Masacre Las Hojas v El Salvador)*. OEA/Ser.L/V/II.83, doc 14.

In this respect, the conflict in El Salvador bears two significant characteristics. Apart from the political underpinnings of state terrorism, authoritarianism aimed at gaining control of property and ensuring the enemy's complete elimination.[85] In this sense, authoritarians aimed at preserving the archaic colonial social culture of the country.[86] Authoritarians sought to intimidate their opponents, or else force them into exile. Moreover, unlike Guatemala, the Salvadoran case involved excessive violence from both state agents and guerillas, which is why is more usually characterized as civil war.[87] Patterns of violence included extrajudicial executions, enforced disappearances and torture, with executions ranking first in the methods applied by state agents, and disappearances counting for twenty-five per cent of all complaints.[88] Thomas Buergenthal, one of the three commissioners of the United Nations (hereinafter UN) Commission on the Truth for El Salvador, offers a record of the incidents which attracted worldwide attention. These were

> particularly the assassination of Archbishop Oscar Anulfo Romero, the killings of six Jesuit Priests, the rape and murder of four American church-women, the assassinations of mayors in the so-called conflictive areas of the country, the Zona Rosa raid in which, among others, four off-duty U.S. Embassy guards were killed, the El Mozote massacre, the abductions and assassinations of important national figures, and the disappearance and torture-deaths of large numbers of civilian sympathizers of one or the other of the combatants.[89]

Alongside such kind of incidents,

> one phenomenon that occurred during the armed conflict in El Salvador was the enforced disappearance of children [...] the phenomenon was part of a deliberate strategy within the violence institutionalized by the State during the period of conflict [...] the children were abducted during the execution of military operations after which their families were executed or forced to flee to save their lives. Children were frequently taken away by military chiefs who brought them up as their own children.[90]

The social and political reasons which led the state to conduct a systematic pattern of enforced disappearances of children remain unidentified, also because an objective assessment of this period is not accomplished, and much evidence is still contested. Although disappearances of children were perpetrated by Argentina and Guatemala as well,[91] the case of El Salvador is unique in this respect because of the relatively high number of child victims and the standardized pattern that it followed, taking into account children's physical and psychological vulnerability.[92]

---

[85] Ching (2016), pp. 209–210.

[86] LeMoyne (1989), p. 106.

[87] Karl (1992), pp. 149–150.

[88] UNSC. Report of the Commission on the truth for El Salvador, from madness to hope, 43.

[89] Buergenthal (1994), p. 503.

[90] UN Doc A/HRC/7/2/Add.2 (26 October 2007) para 23.

[91] *Molina-Theissen v Guatemala*, Inter-American Court of Human Rights Series C No 108 (3 July 2004); *See* also Retrieved March 22, 2023, from http://www.abuelas.org.ar/english/history.ht.

[92] Sarkin and Calvet Martinez (2022), pp. 43-46.

From a humanitarian standpoint, the phenomenon of the enforced disappearance constitutes a flagrant violation of their dignity. Even if they are not subjected to *stricto sensu* torture, separation from their family environment causes irreversible damage to their personality and/or dignity.[93] Additionally, from a political perspective, the elimination of opponents via state terrorism should not involve children, as they cannot pose a direct threat to any regime or more generally jeopardize the social *status quo*. In this regard, the disappearance of children can only be explained as an effort to accomplish social reform by halting the enemy's proliferation. Further, it implies the existence of a deep divide in a particular society, and is not just a symptom of political polarization. Accordingly, the forced disappearance of children has received special attention by the international community, as an aggravated form of disappearance.

More specifically, there are three situations in which children can become victims of enforced disappearance: by forcible abduction from their family (a); if they are born to parents who are in captivity (b); or if their next of kin disappear, and they become in effect indirect victims of enforced disappearance (c).[94] In the Salvadoran conflict the first situation occurred more frequently, while in other countries, such as Argentina, both patterns which can render children direct victims of disappearance were applied. At this point, it is apparent that the perpetrators' intent varied according to the victims' age. That is, if the disappeared children were young enough, then the purpose of their disappearance was adoption. In contrast, the disappearance of adolescents resulted most commonly in their summary execution, given that juveniles could not fit easily into a new family environment. Besides, perpetrators feared their probable participation in the conflict.[95]

The IACommHR has accepted that there have been at least 881 reported requests to the pertinent authorities and to NGOs to trace children who disappeared during the armed conflict in El Salvador. Accordingly, the Asociación Pro-Búsqueda de Niños y Niñas Desaparecidos

> has found children in several different situations: integrated into a family in El Salvador or abroad by adoption within the judicial system (formal adoptions) or by de facto adoption or appropriation by civilians and members of the Armed Forces; brought up in orphanages or in military facilities, and it has learned of 12 cases of children who were murdered. It has found children in El Salvador and in 11 other countries of the Americas and Europe.[96]

This information reveals that children were equally targeted during the conflict. The perpetrators applied enforced disappearances to accomplish family disintegration. State terrorism was not confined to the demolition of social or community structures to achieve civil obedience; rather, it infiltrated deep into family units by attacking its

---

[93] UNGA, Convention on the Rights of the Child, UNTS 1577, entered into force 20/11/1989, Art. 9.

[94] United Nations Working Group on Enforced or Involuntary Disappearances (hereinafter UNWGEID). (14 February 2013). General Comment on Children and Enforced Disappearances. UN Doc A/HRC/WGEID/98/1, para 2.

[95] Stevens (2010), p. 382.

[96] *Serrano-Cruz Sisters v El Salvador*, Inter-American Court of Human Rights Series C No 120 (1 March 2005) para 48(6).

most vulnerable members. Although enforced disappearances of children was a well-established pattern in El Salvador, there is little or no reference to it in the reports of the international investigatory bodies such as the UN-backed Truth Commission. Hence, international recognition of the method was slow, owing mostly to NGO initiatives. In its most recent jurisprudence, the IACtHR acknowledged a systematic pattern of enforced disappearance of children. Therefore, it held that

> the phenomenon of the forced disappearance of children was part of a deliberate strategy in the context of the institutionalized State violence that characterized this period of the conflict. Most of the disappearances occurred between 1980 and 1984, with the highest figures corresponding to 1982 [...] the disappearances formed part of the counterinsurgency strategy developed by the State under the concept of destroying population groups associated with the guerrillas. Under that strategy, it was found useful to abduct children in order to separate them from the "enemy population" and "to educate them under the State's ideology at that time".[97]

Overall, although there are no clear reasons justifying the political ideologies that generated these methods (like in the Guatemalan example), state terrorism reached unprecedented levels in El Salvador, since it was directed against population groups which are by definition vulnerable.

The moral inviolability of children created political and legal embarrassment to the international community. Public and open acceptance of such a state practice would inevitably lead to an international outcry and it would require a vivid response. The fragile international political equilibrium, alongside the heinous nature of this crime, had the result that no particular political and doctrinal attention was paid to committing disappearances against children.

1.4 Enforced Disappearances as a Widespread Phenomenon: An Overview

Nevertheless, enforced disappearances soon spread beyond Latin America. By way of example, during the 1970s many individuals' status was also unknown in Cyprus, as a result of the 1974 Turkish military intervention. This was chronologically the first case, alongside Chile, which gained the attention of the UN. However, these victims are not referred to as "disappeared persons" but as "missing" or "persons unaccounted for", to demonstrate the difference between the causes of their disappearance there from those disappeared in Latin America.[98] This pattern suggests that enforced disappearances were mainly "attributable to political reasons".[99] The Philippines is another example where disappearances served as a tool against

---

[97] *Contreras et al v El Salvador*, Inter-American Court of Human Rights Series C No 232 (31 August 2011) para 53.

[98] UN Doc E/CN.4/2002/71, para 12.

[99] Ibid para 13.

political opposition. During the Marcos dictatorship (1971–1986) the country suffered from innumerable disappearances which were systematically conducted from 1976 onwards.[100] The example of Philippines is usually referred to, as the practice exerted by the Marcos dictatorship resembles the Latin American prototype of disappearances.

Disappearances have occurred in many states after WWII and have taken many different and covert forms, which allowed states to remain at the side of political correctness and perpetrators to go unpunished. The example of Greece is in this regard unique. At the aftermath of WWII, the Greek state underwent a severe civil war (1946–1949). During that time, Frederica, the state's Queen, launched a national campaign according to which the children of the guerillas' had to be evacuated from dangerous zones. Her initiative was introduced by a royal decree of 1947 and was officially entitled "Charity Drive 'Welfare for the Northern Provinces of Greece' Under the High Authority of Her Majesty, the Queen", and it was publicly know in Greece as "Eranos". This initiative turned out to a covert way to eliminate leftist militias, as it targeted their children and forcefully separated from their next of kin. To the degree's implementation, the Queen created fifty-two orphanages, the so-called "Paidoupoleis" where the "happy orphans of Queen Frederica" resigned.[101] This initiative ended, according to moderate estimations, to more than 3000 adoptions of Greek minors to the US, without their family's consent.[102]

This broad network of adoptions constituted a refined form of disappearances. It did not receive proper international interest for two reasons. First, the initiative was ran by the state's Queen who was internationally well-reputed, ergo the initiative was broadly communicated as an attempt to save children from abandonment and starvation. Second, this disappearance practice went unnoticed as it was not committed by a state's executive. At that time, the Queen in Greece had a reduced role in state organization, limited to ensuring constitutional order. In this sense, large scale children disappearances in Greece were acquiesced and not performed by the state. This fact contributed to limited international attention.

The above prove that enforced disappearances are not a regional phenomenon, or one rooted only in regimes perpetrating atrocities only. It also occurs in countries with long-standing internal conflicts.[103] In other cases, enforced disappearances are used by governments to decimate indigenous populations,[104] or they are associated with gender-based violence supported by the authorities.[105] Consequently, the

[100] Dimaranan (1987), pp. 318–320.

[101] van Steen (2019), pp. 61–64.

[102] Kaisidou (2019), p. 92.

[103] UN Doc E/CN.4/2004/58, paras 322–323.

[104] *Coronel and others v Colombia*, HRC (2002) UN Doc CCPR/C/76/D/778/1997; *Vicente and others v Colombia*, HRC (1997) UN Doc CCPR/C/60/D/612/1995.

[105] *González et al. ("Cotton Field") v Mexico (Merits, Reparations and Costs)*, Inter-American Court of Human Rights, Series C No 205 (16 November 2009); UN Doc CEDAW/C/2005/OP.8/Mexico, paras 61–110.

phenomenon has troubled the international community as it continues to proliferate[106] and because the perpetrators usually remain unpunished.[107] Moreover, contemporary practices of the "War on Terror" have opened up new aspects of the issue.[108] In the name of national security, many states launched anti-terrorist campaigns and moved towards strict legislation. To that end, some states introduced the method of "extraordinary renditions" and further developed a new version of the "not in my backyard" doctrine as its legal correlative (see Chap. 2).[109]

1.5 International Legal Responses to Enforced Disappearances

In the beginning, the international community treated the phenomenon of enforced disappearances *in casu* by appointing *ad hoc* Working Groups to monitor the application of human rights standards in Chile and Cyprus.[110] Soon it became clear that a holistic approach was necessary, and the General Assembly adopted resolution 33/173 on "Disappeared Persons",[111] requesting the Human Rights Commission to 'consider the question of disappeared persons with a view to making appropriate recommendations'.[112] Hereinafter, the ECOSOC (UN Economic and Social Council) "requested both the Commission on Human Rights to consider the question of disappeared persons as a matter of priority" and the Sub-Commission on Prevention of Discrimination and Protection of Minorities "to consider the subject and make recommendations to the Commission on Human Rights".[113] The Sub-Commission recommended the establishment of a group of experts to collect "all the information [...] and to make the necessary contacts with the Governments and the families concerned".[114] The UNWGEID was established with a resolution adopted without a vote by the Commission on Human Rights.[115]

---

[106] UN Docs A/HRC/10/9, A/HRC/4/41.

[107] There are, however, positive exceptions to impunity, like the Pinochet case. *See* Nicholls (2001), pp. 143–144.

[108] Citroni and Scovazzi (2009), pp. 91–92; Parry (2005), pp. 516–533.

[109] Scovazzi and Citroni (2007), pp. 25–58.

[110] UN Docs A/10285, E/CN.4/1188, A/31/253, E/CN.4/1221; GA Res.32/128 (1977), 33/172 (1978), 36/164 (1981).

[111] UNGA Res A/33/173 (1978).

[112] Ibid op clause 2.

[113] UN ECOSOC Res 1979/38 (1979).

[114] UN Doc E/CN.4/1435, Annex III.

[115] UN Doc E/CN.4/Res/1980/20, op clause 1.

1.5.1 *The Creation of the UNWGEID: The Background*

The establishment of the UNWGEID was not an easy task. As soon as disappearances became part of the UN human rights agenda, tensions grew between states over the appropriate way to address the phenomenon. The drafting of a legally binding instrument was out of the question for almost all delegations, because the phenomenon was relatively new on the global arena and there was a lack of knowledge about the issue.[116]

However, the majority of states had realized that there should be an international response to enforced disappearances and so they suggested the establishment of a thematic mechanism, the UNWGEID.[117] States that applied the policy of enforced disappearances (such as Argentina and Uruguay) opposed the creation of the mechanism; instead, they preferred the adoption of resolutions which would only acknowledge the existence of enforced disappearances. At that point it was the dedication of human rights NGOs to achieve a long-term solution that proved instrumental. Having secured the political and diplomatic support of the American delegation,[118] they tried to rouse public concern over enforced disappearances and to pressurize governments into reaching an agreement. To this end they organized campaigns on enforced disappearances and released particular details on applied governmental practices.[119] Their activities, in conjunction with incessant lobbying, paved the way for the establishment of the UN Working Group. Even states that initially opposed to its creation finally conceded to it, as it was the only way to avoid further criticism of their policies. Overall, certain states considered the UNWGEID to be an important step against enforced disappearances, whereas others saw it as the least problematic approach to the topic.[120] Still, even under these circumstances, the creation of the UNWGEID revealed an aware and alarmed international community.

In this context, the UNWGEID's mandate depended greatly on international politics. Indeed, the group had a narrow but clear mandate to deal with disappearances that involved a degree of governmental involvement and liability. At the same time, it decided not to address disappearances associated with armed conflicts.[121] It also "decided to approach its tasks in a humanitarian spirit",[122] meaning that in the context of the Cold War it would not get involved in or criticize the member-states' domestic politics. It would instead seek governmental cooperation in order to function as a third party between the families of the disappeared and the liable

[116] Foot (2000), p. 40.

[117] The Working Group was the first thematic mechanism of the Commission of Human Rights. UN Doc E/CN.4/2002/71 para 15.

[118] Korey (2001), p. 250.

[119] Scovazzi and Citroni (2007), pp. 10, 17.

[120] Gutter (2006), pp. 82–89.

[121] UN Doc E/CN.4/2002/71, para 3.

[122] Ibid para 30.

governments.[123] Thereafter the UNWGEID was heavily criticized for its hesitant approach to the problem both by several human rights NGOs and theorists. However, it was not the chosen approach that caused dissatisfaction, but the low rate of cases that were resolved and the growing number of enforced disappearances worldwide.[124]

Apart from the UNWGEID's attempts to provide answers for the victims' fate, their relatives continued seeking the truth, either individually or through associations they had created. In a number of cases, their quest for justice led them to submit communications to the HRC (Human Rights Committee) under Art. 5 of the Optional Protocol to the International Covenant on Civil and Political Rights (ICCPR).[125]

1.5.2 The HRC's Views: Setting the Foundations for Individuals' Protection

In the first communication it considered, *Bleier v. Uruguay*,[126] the HRC reached its concluding remarks in 1982. In that case, Mr. Eduardo Bleier was arrested and detained by the Uruguayan police forces and then held at a secret place. His arrest was confirmed as his name appeared on a list of prisoners, although it was officially denied. His relatives made unsuccessful efforts to collect information about his fate. However, they provided the HRC with testimonies by detainees, who witnessed the victim's severe torture and suffering. His ill-treatment was directly linked to his alleged communist activities.[127] Uruguay, in its communications submitted to the HRC, denied complicity and further argued that the victim was a subversive, who had probably gone into hiding to avoid his arrest. The HRC underlined the contradiction between these allegations, and eventually found breaches of Articles 6 (right to life), 7 (prohibition of torture) and 10 (rights of persons deprived of their liberty) of the ICCPR and held that "Eduardo Bleier is either still detained incommunicado by the Uruguayan authorities or has died while in custody at the hands of the Uruguayan authorities".[128]

The importance of this conclusion lies in the reversal of the burden of proof that the HRC established in cases of disappeared people.[129] It held that state parties have

[123] Alston (1995), p. 177.

[124] Livermore and Ramcharan (1989–1990), p. 217.

[125] UN Doc. A/6316 (1966), 999 UNTS 302, entered into force 23/03/1976. According to the Protocol's provisions, the HRC can receive written communications from individuals who claim that their rights as set in the ICCPR have been violated. The HRC informs the state to which the complaint refers, and the latter has to respond within a fixed time limit. The HRC then informs the two sides of its views. The views expressed by the HRC are not enforceable.

[126] *Eduardo Bleier v Uruguay*, HRC (1982) UN Doc Supp.No.40 (A/37/40) at 130 (1982).

[127] Ibid paras 2.2–2.3.

[128] Ibid para 13.

[129] *Quinteros v Uruguay*, HRC (1983) Comm.No.107/1981 (21 July 1983) para 11.

by definition more access to the necessary information than individuals, and their insufficient responses turn in favor of the complainants. The HRC also stated that the parties' undertaking to provide the Committee with the requested information ought to follow their positive obligation to conduct full investigations as to the fate of the disappeared.[130]

Unfortunately, the HRC's lack of enforcement capacity has proved to be an obstacle difficult to surmount. The "naming and shaming" strategy[131] that has been developed by the HRC seems to be an inadequate tool to deter enforced disappearances to this day, added to which, this process was still in its infancy at the time of the *Bleier* case. Therefore, it signaled a considerable advance when the Inter-American system for the protection of human rights accepted the challenge to cope with enforced disappearances and bring the perpetrators to justice.

1.5.3 The Inter-American Court of Human Rights (IACHR): A Leading Authority in Disappearances

On 29 July 1988 the IACHR gave a "landmark ruling"[132] concerning the *Velásquez Rodriguez Case.*[133] The case is of paramount importance not only regarding the domain of enforced disappearances but also for the protection of human rights in the Inter-American system in general, since it was the first time that the IACHR applied its compulsory jurisdiction in a contested case.[134] Moreover, the case is pivotal because the Court established special evidential standards regarding the practice of enforced disappearances, and for the first time a state was held responsible for enacting disappearances. For these reasons, the case warrants a thorough analysis.

During the 1980s, the Inter-American Commission on Human Rights[135] was harshly criticized for not bringing cases of enforced disappearances before the Court, despite the large number of complaints it had received from the late 1970s onwards. Finally, in 1987 the Commission referred the case of *Velásquez Rodriguez*

---

130 *Arévalo v Colombia*, HRC (1989) Comm.No.181/1084 (03 November) 1989, para 10; HRC. (30 April 1982). General Comment No.06: The Right to Life (Art.6) para 4.

131 Hafner-Burton (2008), p. 691.

132 Drucker (1988), pp. 289–322.

133 *Velásquez-Rodriguez v Honduras (Merits)*, Inter-American Court of Human Rights, Series C, No4 (29 July 1988).

134 Grossman (1992), pp. 363–390. Until 1988, the Court had issued only Advisory Opinions for interpreting the American Convention on Human Rights (Art. 64).

135 According to the ACHR, Art. 61(1), only "the State Parties and the Commission shall have the right to submit a case to the Court". Individuals are not able to stand before the Court, instead they have to report the alleged human rights violation to the Commission, which investigates the instance and decides whether to introduce it to the Court or not.

to the Court.[136] This delay was mainly due to the fact that the American Convention on Human Rights (hereinafter the ACHR) requires the state parties' prior acceptance of the jurisdiction of the Court to stand before it (Art. 62(1)). This restriction partly explains[137] why Honduras was the first country to be tried for enforced disappearances, although the phenomenon was not as widespread there as in other Latin American states.[138]

This case attracted much attention not only from a pure human rights' perspective (many NGOs submitted *amici curiae*) but also because of the assassinations of three witnesses during the proceedings.[139] The process prior to the trial was a long one. In 1981, shortly after the alleged disappearance, members of Velásquez Rodriguez's family petitioned the Commission. After conducting an investigation, the Commission informed the Honduran government of the complaint and requested an official response. The government gave no further information on the disappearance of Velásquez Rodriguez, and so the Commission proceeded by applying Article 42 of its Regulations:

> The facts reported in the petition whose pertinent parts have been transmitted to the government of the State in reference shall be presumed to be true if, during the maximum period set by the Commission under the provisions of Article 34 paragraph 5, the government has not provided the pertinent information, as long as other evidence does not lead to a different conclusion. [140]

The Honduran government asked the Commission to re-evaluate the facts, and requested additional time to investigate the case and set out information on it. However, the government released only a brief statement, denying involvement in the case. After these postponements due to procedural claims, the case finally was brought before the Court in 1986.

Concerning the merits of the case, Manfredo Velásquez Rodriguez was a Honduran citizen who was kidnapped in 1981 in Tegucigalpa. Since then, there had been no news about his fate. According to the testimonies of the witnesses, Velásquez Rodriguez was kidnapped by Honduran officials, who acted following a specific pattern in such cases (the kidnappers wore civilian clothes and used disguises, and their cars had covered their license plates or had none).[141] The provided information clearly indicated governmental involvement in this conduct. According to Florencio Caballero (a former member of the Honduran armed forces) the abducted victim, he was told, was taken to a secret detention center, where he was tortured and finally

---

[136] *Velásquez-Rodriguez v Honduras (Preliminary Objections)*, Inter-American Court of Human Rights, Series C No 1 (26 June 1987).

[137] Pasqualucci (1994–1995), pp. 307–308.

[138] Drucker (1988), pp. 291–292.

[139] *Velásquez-Rodriguez v Honduras (Merits)* paras 39–41.

[140] Regulations of the Inter-American Commission on Human Rights, reprinted in Basic Documents Pertaining to Human Rights in the Inter-American System, OEA/Ser.L.V/II.82 doc.6 rev.1, 103 (1992).

[141] *Velásquez-Rodriguez v Honduras (Merits)*, para 99.

executed.[142] The Court, faced with lack of substantial evidence, first ruled that disappearances was a practice persistently used by the government.[143] To underpin this ruling, it entertained testimonies of people who had been "disappeared" by the authorities and had managed to escape or been finally released. It then found that "the disappearance of Manfredo Velásquez fell within the systematic practice of disappearances".[144] The Court proceeded by lowering the required threshold of evidence, as it acknowledged that one of the main aims of disappearances is to efface all evidence.[145] Therefore, it held that "circumstantial evidence, indicia, and presumptions may be considered, so long as they lead to conclusions consistent with the facts".[146]

Finally, in a unanimous ruling the Court found Honduras responsible for the disappearance of the victim. In doing so it declared the violation of several articles of the ACHR, as disappearances were not stipulated *per se* in the Convention. It held that the practice adopted by Honduras was a violation of the right to personal liberty (Art.7), the right to the integrity of the person (Art.5) and the right to life (Art.4).[147] Furthermore, the Court held that the violation of these rights was in direct conjunction with the obligation of state parties of the ACHR to organize their legal orders in a way that guarantees the protection of human rights (Art.1(1)). Consequently, it was established that enforced disappearances violated the ACHR's values, *in toto*.[148]

The ruling created a leading precedent for Inter-American legal order and confirmed the awareness of this regional community on enforced disappearances. The Court used exactly the same argumentation in the case of *Saúl Godínez Cruz* and pinpointed that the common feature of these cases was for the purpose of weakening political opponents[149] and intimidating the population.[150] In both cases, it regarded these disappearances as part of a general and systematic practice applied by the government. The Court, though, drew back from this line of argumentation in some of the following cases of enforced disappearances it dealt with, with the view to strengthening the procedural aspects of the trials. In the cases of *Caballero-Delgado* and *Santana v. Colombia* the Court affirmed that disappearances could arise on an

---

142 Ibid para 113.

143 Ibid para 99.

144 Ibid para 147d(i), (g).

145 Ibid para 131; *Fairén-Garbi and Solís-Corrales v Honduras (Merits)*, Inter-American Court of Human Rights, Series C No 6 (15 March 1989) para 127.

146 *Velásquez-Rodriguez v Honduras (Merits)*, paras 130, 188.

147 Ibid paras 155–157.

148 Ibid para 158.

149 *Godínez-Cruz v Honduras (Merits)*, Inter-American Court of Human Rights Series C No 5 (20 January 1989) para 154b(i).

150 *Caracazo v Venezuela (Merits)*, Inter-American Court of Human Rights, Series C No 58 (11 November 1999); *Blanco Romero v Venezuela (Merits)*, Inter-American Court of Human Rights, Series C No 137 (28 November 2005).

occasional basis and not as part of a systematic practice.[151] In these cases, uncontested evidence was presented on behalf of the victims regarding their disappearance and subsequent execution. The existence of strong evidence determined the Court's decision to a great extent. By contrast, in cases where evidence was insufficient to either indicate either a governmental practice on disappearances or the victims' mistreatment and suffering, the Court did not pronounce a violation of the ACHR. This partly explains the unsuccessful outcome of the case of *Fransisco Fairén Garbi and Yolanda Solís Corrales*, as the Court held that "there was insufficient evidence to relate their disappearance with the governmental practice", which was established in the *Velásquez-Rodriguez* and the *Godínez-Cruz* cases.[152]

The plethora of reported cases revealed how widespread the phenomenon was as well as the cruelty it entailed. The attempts of the HRC and the IACHR to deal with enforced disappearances stumbled at the lack of established international standards that would provide for a common understanding and legal basis for the practice. It gradually became evident that the phenomenon of enforced disappearances could not be captured with reference to already existing norms (this point will be further elaborated in Chap. 4). The need for a more thorough and effective approach based on a set of basic legal principles was evident.

1.5.4 The 1992 UN Declaration and the OAS Convention

The international community took prompt action, leading to the adoption of the 1992 UN Declaration on the Protection of all Persons from Enforced Disappearances (hereinafter 1992 Declaration), where the UNWGEID was assigned to report any obstacles during its application and to monitor its implementation in the member-states.[153] Some of the factors which finally led to the adoption of the Declaration included public awareness and the constant pressure from NGOs towards the drafting of Conventions on Enforced Disappearances, the adoption of the Convention Against Torture (CAT 1984)[154] and the recommendations made by the UNWGEID.[155] Soon after the Declaration, the Organization of American States (OAS) adopted the Convention on Forced Disappearance of Persons.[156] This was the first legally binding document which tackled the phenomenon directly and which was tailored to the

---

151 *Caballero-Delgado and Santana v Colombia (Merits)*, Inter-American Court of Human Rights, Series C No 22 (8 December 1995).

152 *Godínez-Cruz v Honduras (Merits)*, paras 157–158.

153 UNGA. Declaration on the Protection of All Persons from Enforced Disappearance. (adopted 18 December 1992). UN Doc A/Res/47/133 (1992 Declaration); UN Doc. E/CN.4/1994/26, para 74.

154 The adoption of CAT had a "spill-over effect" on disappearances; it accelerated UN action and served as a pattern for the 1992 Declaration. UN Doc E/CN.4/2004/58, 92–97.

155 UN Doc E/CN.4/2002/71, para 44.

156 OAS, Inter-American Convention on Forced Disappearance of Persons, 09/06/1994, entered into force 28/03/1996. Retrieved 22, March 2023, from http://www.oas.org/juridico/English/

specific circumstances of the regional environments it was designed for. Overall, this Convention enhanced the Inter-American system for the protection of human rights and promoted democratization in Latin America countries.

Though the OAS Convention was drafted in 1988, its adoption was delayed due to the reluctance of some member-states. Thus, it is argued that the adoption of the 1992 Declaration reinforced the OAS' Convention potential and led to its adoption.[157] The interaction of the multiple human rights regimes outlines that there was a sort of network operating between the UN and the regional legal orders, serving the protection and promotion of human rights.

These developments are well reflected in the ensuing jurisprudence. In the case of *Blake v. Guatemala*, for example,[158] the Inter-American Commission used data and statistics presented in the UNWGEID's report to substantiate its argument.[159] Moreover, it was the first time that the Court directly referred to the provisions of the 1992 Declaration and to the OAS Convention[160] in order to reach a verdict, at the same time proving its openness to current developments. All the same, there were a few occasions where international courts displayed "very limited understanding of the phenomenon"[161] as they applied formalistic criteria. This happened particularly when the European Court of Human Rights (hereinafter ECtHR) first dealt with enforced disappearances in 1998.[162] As discussed below, the ECtHR's jurisprudence proved inconsistent with the approach of the HRC and the IACtHR up to then. It may be said that different circumstances asked for a different approach, yet there were some instances when the Court's judgments were simply deficient.

1.5.5 The ECtHR: The Fluctuation of Its Jurisprudence

The vast majority of the cases tried by the ECtHR were related to Turkey. They were associated with the internal disturbances in the south-eastern region of the country, which is mostly populated by Kurds.[163] In 1994 enforced disappearances were intensified in the area (a state of emergency was in force at that time), causing the UNWGEID profound concern. According to the report submitted, disappearances

treaties/a-60.html. Inter-American Convention on Forced Disappearance of Persons (adopted 9 June 1994, entered into force 28 March 1996) OAS Treaty Series No 68 (IACFDP).

[157] UN Doc E/CN.4/2002/71, para 47.

[158] *Blake v Guatemala (Merits)*, Inter-American Court of Human Rights Series C No 36 (24 January 1998).

[159] Ibid para 48.

[160] Ibid paras 62–73.

[161] Scovazzi and Citroni (2007), p. 191.

[162] *Kurt v Turkey*, App no 24276/94 (ECtHR 25 May 1998).

[163] *Çakici v Turkey*, App no 23657/94 (ECtHR 8 July 1999); *Ismail Ertak v Turkey*, App no 20764/92 (ECtHR 9 May 2000); *Taş v Turkey*, APP no 24396/94 (ECtHR 14 November 2000); *Ciçek v Turkey*, App no 25704/94 (ECtHR 27 February 2001).

occurred in a systematic way, raising issues of state complicity, along with exposure to torture.[164] The Court, though, did not acknowledge that the cases before it fell within this practice, and tried them on an *ad hoc* basis. Its approach diverged from the one already established by the IACHR.[165]

Moreover, in contrast to the approach of the IACHR and the HRC, the ECtHR decided to apply high evidentiary standards. Thus, it did not accept that a reversal in the burden of proof was necessary and did not lower the evidentiary threshold as it demanded proof "beyond reasonable doubt".[166] As a result, the applicants had to present information they could not access, which was in effect "a sort of *probatio diabolica*".[167] On top of that, the ECtHR created a quantitative formula when it came to violations of the right to life.[168] It held that the victims could be presumed dead only when a considerable period of time had passed without any news from the disappeared,[169] which left unanswered questions as to the status of the people who had disappeared not long ago. It was not until recently that the ECtHR adopted a more flexible approach and acknowledged the relation between enforced disappearance and the threat of death. In the case of *Baysayeva v. Russia* it held that disappearances are life-threatening when the victims disappear under violent circumstances.[170]

However, there are some positive aspects to the ECtHR's jurisprudence, especially when it comes to member-states' duties under the European Convention of Human Rights (ECHR). More specifically, the Court held that states have a duty to investigate every case of disappearance effectively. This duty emanates from the general obligation established under Article 2 of the ECHR to "protect the right to life by law". Therefore, member-states have to conduct prompt and thorough investigations into the fate of the disappeared as soon as they take notice of it; failure to do so constitutes a breach of the ECHR. In other words, the Court did not easily pronounce a violation of the right to life resulting from a disappearance, but at the same time it required that states investigate the alleged violation.[171] It could be said that the establishment of a state's duty to investigate compensated for the ECtHR's hesitance to presume the victims' deaths.

---

[164] UN Doc. E/CN.4/1995/36, paras 394–396.

[165] Taqi (2001), pp. 966–967.

[166] UNCHR. (2006). Report of the Intersessional Open-Ended Working Group to Elaborate a Draft Legally Binding Normative Instrument for the Protection of All Persons from Enforced Disappearances. UN Doc E/CN.4/2006/57, paras 99, 107.

[167] Scovazzi and Citroni (2007), p. 190.

[168] Buckley (2001), pp. 55–64.

[169] In the *case of Timurtaş v Turkey*, the ECtHR set a very high threshold of six and a half years to presume the victim's death. *Timurtaş v Turkey*, App no 23531/94 (ECtHR 13 June 2000) paras 82–86.

[170] *Baysayeva v Russia*, App no 74237/01 (ECtHR 5 April 2007) para 119.

[171] *Mahmut Kaya v Turkey*, App no 22535/93, (Report of the European Commission of Human Rights 23 October 1998) paras 342–343.

1.6 Background of the UN Convention's Adoption

Despite serious developments on the international level – such as the adoption of the 1992 Declaration and the progressive evolution of jurisprudence – there were still unresolved issues which hindered a satisfactory response to the phenomenon. Such inconsistencies could not be easily surmounted without a universal instrument that would directly address the main issues of the phenomenon. In 1998 the Sub-Commission on the Promotion and Protection of Human Rights adopted a Draft International Convention on the Protection of all Persons from Forced Disappearance[172] (hereinafter 1998 Draft), which shed light on key aspects of the phenomenon. Although the 1998 Draft followed the way paved by the 1992 Declaration, it stood as a further indication of the lasting concern of the international community about the issue.

Moving forward, and capitalizing upon previous efforts, the Commission on Human Rights adopted, without a vote, Resolution 2001/46; according to the resolution, an independent expert (Prof. Manfred Nowak, a former member of the UNWGEID) had to examine the existing international human rights framework on enforced disappearances and report on the necessity of a "legally binding normative instrument".[173] Reaffirming the strong concern of the international community, the resolution established an Inter-sessional Open-ended Working Group (hereinafter ISWG) to elaborate a draft legally binding instrument "for the protection of all persons from enforced disappearance",[174] having taken into consideration the recommendations of the expert. Nowak concluded that a legally binding instrument was essential for establishing protection against disappearances, since there existed gaps regarding, *inter alia*, the definition of the term (which will be discussed in greater depth in Chap. 2), punishment of the perpetrators, and prevention of the phenomenon. Thus, he proposed three possible forms:

> a separate human rights treaty such as the draft convention, an optional protocol to the International Covenant on Civil and Political Rights, or an optional protocol to the Convention against Torture.[175]

It was then impingent upon the ISWG to decide the form of the document. The Working Group decided that a separate treaty would be the most appropriate form,[176] and in 2005 it submitted a draft to the Commission on Human Rights.[177] Apart from the pros and cons of the proposed options, the debate mainly focused on the monitoring body established as part of the new legal instrument. The procedures and

---

[172] UN Doc E/CN.4/Sub.2/1998/19, Annex.

[173] UN Doc E/CN.4/2001/46, para 12.

[174] Ibid para 12.

[175] UN Doc E/CN.4/2002/71, para 97.

[176] UNCHR. (2004). Report of the Intersessional Open-Ended Working Group to elaborate a draft legally binding normative instrument for the Protection of All Persons from Enforced Disappearances. UN Doc E/CN.4/2004/59.

[177] UN Doc. E/CN.4/2005/66.

powers of the monitoring body would largely determine the parties' obligations, thus constituting an area of divergence of views.[178]

Finally, the CPED was adopted by the newly created (15 March 2006) Human Rights Council[179] and consecutively by the Third Committee[180] and the General Assembly.[181] The fact that the Convention passed by consensus is not just promising, but, as the European Union representative stated during the GA Plenary Session, "it sends a strong political signal from the international community that this shameful and still widespread practice must come to an end".[182]

Indeed, the Convention fills serious gaps in the protection against disappearances. The creation of the right not to be subjected to enforced disappearance alongside the establishment of quasi-universal jurisdiction (*aut dedere aut judicare*) is probably the most important achievement of the Convention (further elaboration on the Convention's contribution follows in Chap. 4). The high number of signatories is indicative of a successful course for the Convention, but safe conclusions cannot be reached before the Convention enters into force. It is fair to say, though, that the Convention is an "acceptable compromise".[183]

Jurisprudence

IACtHR

Aloeboetoe et al v Suriname, Inter-American Court of Human Rights Series C No 15 (10 September 1993).

Blake v Guatemala (Merits), Inter-American Court of Human Rights Series C No 36 (24 January 1998).

Blanco Romero v Venezuela (Merits), Inter-American Court of Human Rights, Series C No 137 (28 November 2005).

Caballero-Delgado and Santana v Colombia (Merits), Inter-American Court of Human Rights, Series C No 22 (8 December 1995).

Caracazo v Venezuela (Merits), Inter-American Court of Human Rights, Series C No 58 (11 November 1999).

[178] UN Doc E/CN.4/2005/WG.22/CRP.6.

[179] UN Doc A/HRC/1/L.2.

[180] UN Doc A/61/448 para 27.

[181] UN Doc A/Res/61/177. The Convention has already 98 signatories and 70 parties. According to Art.39 it needs twenty ratifications to enter into force. Retrieved March 22, 2023, from http://treaties.un.org/Pages/ViewDetails.aspx?src=TREATY&mtdsg_no=IV-16&chapter=4&lang=en. A synopsis to the background of its adoption is available at http://www.icaed.org/the-convention/history-and-background-of-the-convention/.

[182] UN Doc. A/61/PV.82, 3.

[183] Parliamentary Assembly, Council of Europe (PACE) (2005), p. 962.

Chitay Nech et al v Guatemala, Inter-American Court of Human Rights Series C No 212 (25 May 2010).

Contreras et al v El Salvador, Inter-American Court of Human Rights Series C No 232 (31 August 2011).

Fairén-Garbi and Solís-Corrales v Honduras (Merits), Inter-American Court of Human Rights, Series C No 6 (15 March 1989).

Godínez-Cruz v Honduras (Merits), Inter-American Court of Human Rights Series C No 5 (20 January 1989).

González et al. ("Cotton Field") v Mexico (Merits, Reparations and Costs), Inter-American Court of Human Rights, Series C No 205 (16 November 2009).

Heliodoro Portugal v Panama, Inter-American Court of Human Rights Series C No 186 (12 August 2008).

'Las Dos Erres' Massacre v Guatemala, Inter-American Court of Human Rights Series C No 211 (24 November 2009).

Maritza Urrutia v Guatemala, Inter-American Court of Human Rights Series C No 103 (27 November 2003).

Molina-Theissen v Guatemala, Inter-American Court of Human Rights Series C No 108 (3 July 2004).

Myrna Mack Chang v Guatemala, Inter-American Court of Human Rights Series C No (25 November 2005).

Plan de Sánchez Massacre v Guatemala, Inter-American Court of Human Rights Series C No 105 (29 April 2004).

Reggiardo Tolosa Case, Inter-American Court of Human Rights Series E (19 November 1993).

Río Negro Massacres v Guatemala, Inter-American Court of Human Rights Series C No 250 (4 September 2012).

Serrano-Cruz Sisters v El Salvador, Inter-American Court of Human Rights Series C No 120 (1 March 2005).

The Massacres of El Mozote and Nearby Places v El Salvador, Inter-American Court of Human Rights Series C No 252 (25 October 2012).

Tibi v Ecuador, Inter-American Court of Human Rights Series C No 114 (7 September 2004).

Ticona Estrada et al v Bolivia, Inter-American Court of Human Rights Series C No 191 (27 November 2008).

Tiu Tojín v Guatemala, Inter-American Court of Human Rights Series C No 190 (26 November 2008).

Velásquez-Rodriguez v Honduras (Merits), Inter-American Court of Human Rights, Series C, No4 (29 July 1988).

Velásquez-Rodriguez v Honduras (Preliminary Objections), Inter-American Court of Human Rights, Series C No 1 (26 June 1987).

ECtHR

Baysayeva v Russia, App no 74237/01 (ECtHR 5 April 2007).
Çakici v Turkey, App no 23657/94 (ECtHR 8 July 1999).
Ciçek v Turkey, App no 25704/94 (ECtHR 27 February 2001).
Ismail Ertak v Turkey, App no 20764/92 (ECtHR 9 May 2000).
Kurt v Turkey, App no 24276/94 (ECtHR 25 May 1998).
Taş v Turkey, APP no 24396/94 (ECtHR 14 November 2000).
Timurtaş v Turkey, App no 23531/94 (ECtHR 13 June 2000).

UN Documentation

UN Security Council

UNSC. (1 April 1993). Report of the Commission on the truth for El Salvador, from madness to hope. UN Doc S/25500.

UN General Assembly

UN Doc. A/6316 (1966), 999 UNTS 302, entered into force 23/03/1976.
UNGA. Declaration on the Protection of All Persons from Enforced Disappearance. (adopted 18 December 1992). UN Doc A/Res/47/133 (1992 Declaration).
UNGA, Convention on the Rights of the Child, UNTS 1577, entered into force 20/11/1989.
UNGA Res A/36/164 (1981).
UNGA. (20 December 1978). Importance of the experience of the ad hoc Working Group on the situation of human rights in Chile. UNGA Res 33/176,
UNGA Res A/33/173 (1978).
UNGA Res. 33/172 (1978).
UNGA Res A/32/128 (1977),
UN Doc A/61/448.
UN Doc A/Res/61/177.
A/10285.
A/31/253.
UN Doc. A/61/PV.82.

ECOSOC

UNCHR. (2006). Report of the Intersessional Open-Ended Working Group to Elaborate a Draft Legally Binding Normative Instrument for the Protection of All Persons from Enforced Disappearances. UN Doc E/CN.4/2006/57.
UN Doc. E/CN.4/2005/66.
UN Doc E/CN.4/2005/WG.22/CRP.6.
UNCHR. (2004). Report of the Intersessional Open-Ended Working Group to elaborate a draft legally binding normative instrument for the Protection of All Persons from Enforced Disappearances. UN Doc E/CN.4/2004/59.
UN Doc E/CN.4/2004/58.
ECOSOC. (8 January 2002). Civil and Political Rights, Including Questions of Disappearances and Summary Executions. UN Doc E/CN.4/2002/71.
UN Doc E/CN.4/2001/46.
UN Doc E/CN.4/Sub.2/1998/19.
UN Doc. E/CN.4/1995/36.
UN Doc. E/CN.4/1994/26.
UN Doc E/CN.4/Res/1980/20.
UN ECOSOC Res 1979/38 (1979).
UN Doc E/CN.4/1435.
E/CN.4/1188.
E/CN.4/1221.

HRC

United Nations Working Group on Enforced or Involuntary Disappearances. (14 February 2013). General Comment on Children and Enforced Disappearances. UN Doc A/HRC/WGEID/98/1.
UN Doc A/HRC/7/2/Add.2 (26 October 2007).
Coronel and others v Colombia, HRC (2002) UN Doc CCPR/C/76/D/778/1997.
Norma Yurich v Chile, Human Rights Committee UN Doc CCPR/C/66/D/718/1996/Rev.1.
Vicente and others v Colombia, HRC (1997) UN Doc CCPR/C/60/D/612/1995.
Arévalo v Colombia, HRC (1989) Comm.No.181/1084 (03 November) 1989.
Quinteros v Uruguay, HRC (1983) Comm.No.107/1981 (21 July 1983).
Eduardo Bleier v Uruguay, HRC (1982) UN Doc Supp.No.40 (A/37/40) at 130 (1982).
HRC. (30 April 1982). General Comment No.06: The Right to Life (Art.6).
UN Doc A/HRC/1/L.2.
A/HRC/10/9.
A/HRC/4/41.

Miscellaneous

UN Doc CEDAW/C/2005/OP.8/Mexico.

OAS Documentation

OAS, Inter-American Convention on Forced Disappearance of Persons, 09/06/1994, entered into force 28/03/1996. Retrieved 22, March 2023, from http://www.oas.org/juridico/English/treaties/a-60.html. Inter-American Convention on Forced Disappearance of Persons (adopted 9 June 1994, entered into force 28 March 1996) OAS Treaty Series No 68 (IACFDP).

Regulations of the Inter-American Commission on Human Rights, reprinted in Basic Documents Pertaining to Human Rights in the Inter-American System, OEA/Ser.L.V/II.82 doc.6 rev.1, 103 (1992).

IACommHR. (15 October 1996). Report No 36/96 (*Garay Hermosilla et al v Chile*). OEA/Ser.L/V/II doc 7.

IACommHR. (15 October 1996). Report No 34/96 (*Meneses Reyes et al v Chile*). OEA/Ser.L/V/11.95, doc 7.

IACommHR. (24 September 1992). Report No 26/92 *(Masacre Las Hojas v El Salvador)*. OEA/Ser.L/V/II.83, doc 14.

IACommHR (3 October 1985). Third report on the situation of human rights in Guatemala. OEA/Ser.L/V/II.66.

IACommHR, (5 October 1983). Report on the situation of human rights in Guatemala. OEA/Ser.L/V/II.61, doc 47.

IACommHR. (13 October 1981). Report on the situation of human rights in Guatemala. OEA/Ser.L/V/II.53, doc 21.

IACommHR. (11 April 1980). Report on the Situation of Human Rights in Argentina. OEA/Ser.L/V/II.49 doc 19.

IACHR. (1978). Annual Report. OEA.Ser.L/V/II.47 doc 13.

IACommHR. (25 October 1974). Report on the Situation of Human Rights in Chile. OEA/Ser.L/V/II.34, doc 21.

CoE Documentation

Parliamentary Assembly, Council of Europe (PACE). (2005). *Official Report of Debates*. 2005 Ordinary Sess., 4th Part Vol IV. CoE Publishing.

Mahmut Kaya v Turkey, App no 22535/93, (Report of the European Commission of Human Rights 23 October 1998).

Online Material

Commission for Historical Clarification (CHC). (25 February 1999). Guatemala Memory of Silence, Tz'inil Na'tab'al'. Retrieved 22 March, 2023, from https://hrdag.org/wp-content/uploads/2013/01/CEHreport-english.pdf.
Nazi Conspiracy and Aggression. (7 December 1941). Night and Fog Decree. 7 L-90. Retrieved March 22, 2023, from http://avalon.law.yale.edu/imt/l-90.asp.
Nuremberg Trial Proceedings (27 July 1946). Retrieved, March 22, 2023, from http://avalon.law.yale.edu/imt/07-27-46.asp.
Nuremberg Trial Proceedings, Indictment: Count 3. Retrieved, March 22, 2023, from http://avalon.law.yale.edu/imt/count3.asp.
United States Institute of Peace, Truth Commission Bolivia. Retrieved, March 22, 2023, from https://www.usip.org/publications/1982/10/truth-commission-bolivia. http://www.abuelas.org.ar/english/history.ht.
http://jurist.law.pitt.edu/paperchase/2009/12/argentina-court-sentences-former-judge.php.
http://www.bbc.com/news/world-latin-america-29532804.
http://www.icaed.org/the-convention/history-and-background-of-the-convention/.

References

Books

Alston P (1995) The United Nations and human rights, A critical appraisal. Oxford University Press
Ball P et al (2005) Guatemala, 1960–1996: A quantitative reflection. American Association for the Advancement of Science
Brands H (2010) Latin America's Cold War. Harvard University Press
Brown R (1995) Livy's Sabine women and the ideal of Concordia. Transact Am Philol Assoc 125:291–319
Ching E (2016) Stories of civil qar in El Salvador, A battle over memory. The University of North Carolina Press.
Clark AM (2001) Diplomacy of conscience: Amnesty International and changing human rights norms. Princeton University Press
Comision de Verdad y Justicia (2008) Memoria de Gestión, 2004-2008. Vangraf
Crenzel E (2017) The memory of the Argentina disappearances: the political history of Nunca Mas. Routledge
Donnelly J (2007) International human 5ights, 3rd edn. Westview Press
Feitlowitz M (1998) A lexicon of terror: Argentina and the legacies of torture. Oxford University Press
Foot R (2000) Rights beyond borders, The global community and the struggle over human rights in China. Oxford University Press
Gustavo Morello SJ (2015) The Catholic Church and Argentina's Dirty War. Oxford University Press
Gutter J (2006) Thematic procedures of the United Nations Commission on Human Rights and international law: In search of a sense of community. School of Human Rights Research

Herbert U (1997) Hitler's foreign workers, enforced foreign labor in Germany under the Third Reich. Cambridge University Press

Kelly PW (2018) Sovereign emergencies: Latin America and the making of global human rights politics. Cambridge University Press

Korey W (2001) NGOs and the Universal Declaration of Human Rights, "A Curious Grapevine". Palgrave

Lewis PH (2006) Authoritarian Regimes in Latin America, dictators, despots, and tyrants. Rowman and Littlefield Inc.

Mallinder L (2008) Amnesty, human rights and political transition, Bridging the peace and justice divide. Hart Publishing.

National Commission on the Disappearance of Persons (CONADEP). (1984). Nunca Más (Never Again) Report.

Osiel M (2004) The mental state of torturers: Argentina's Dirty War. In: Levinson S (ed) Torture, a collection. Oxford University Press

Ovid. Metamorphoses, Book II (Sir Samuel Garth et al, Trans.). Gale ECCO

Reconstitution de la Memoire Historique (REMHI) (2000) Guatemala: Nunca Más!. Office de Droits De L'Homme De L'Archeveche de Guatemala

Report of the Chilean National Commission on Truth and Reconciliation, Vol I/II (1993) Notre Dame University Press

Rojas H, Shaftoe M (2019) Human rights and transitional justice in Chile. Palgrave Macmillan

Roniger L, Sznajder M (1999) The legacy of human rights violations in the Southern Cone, Argentina, Chile and Uruguay. Oxford University Press.

Scovazzi T, Citroni G (2007) The struggle against enforced disappearance and the 2007 United Nations Convention. Martinus Nijhoff Publisher and VSP

Strauss Clay J (2003) Hesiod's cosmos. Cambridge University Press

van Steen G (2019) Adoption, memory, and cold war Greece: Kid Pro Quo? University of Michigan Press

Wright TC (2007) State terrorism in Latin America, Chile. Argentina, and international human rights. Rowman and Littlefield

Articles

Buckley C (2001) The European Convention on human rights and the right to life in Turkey. Human Rights Law Rev 1(1):35–66

Buergenthal T (1994) The United Nations Truth Commission for El Salvador. Vanderbilt J Transnatl Law 27(3):497–544

Citroni G, Scovazzi T (2009) Recent developments in International law to combat enforced disappearances. Revista Internacional de Direito e Cidadania 3:89–111

Drucker L (1988) Governmental liability for disappearances: a landmark ruling by the Inter-American Court of Human Rights. Stanford J Int Law 25(1):289–322

Dulitzky AE (2019) The Latin-American flavor of enforced disappearances. Chicago J Int Law 19(2):423–489

Edwards P (2022) Political competition and authoritarian repression: evidence from Pinochet's Chile. World Polit 74(4):479–522

Finucane B (2010) Enforced disappearance as a crime under international law: a neglected origin in the laws of war. Yale J Int Law 35(1):171–198

Forsythe DP (1993) Human rights after the Cold War (Part 1). Netherlands Quart Human Rights 11(4):393–412

Giorgou I (2013) State involvement in the perpetration of enforced disappearance and the Rome Statute. J Int Crim Just 11(5):1001–1022

Grossman C (1992) Disappearances in Honduras: The need for direct victim representation in human rights litigation. Hast Int Comp Law Rev 15(3):363–390

Guarino AM (2010) Chasing ghosts: Pursuing retroactive justice for Franco-era crimes against humanity. Bost Coll Int Comp Law Rev 33(1):61–86
Hafner-Burton EM (2008) Sticks and stones: Naming and shaming the human rights enforcement problem. Int Org 62(4):689–716
Hoover Green A, Ball P (2019) Civilian killings and disappearances during civil war in El Salvador (1980-1992). Demogr Res 41:781–814
Karl TL (1992) El Salvador's negotiated revolution. Foreign Aff 71(2):147–164
Keller H, Heri C (2014) Enforced disappearance and the European Court of Human Rights: a wall of silence, fact-finding difficulties and states as subversive objectors. J Int Crim Just 12(4):735–750
Kleinman HM (1987) Disappearances in Latin America: a human rights perspective. New York Univ J Int Law Polit 19(4):1033–1060
Laplant LJ (2014) Memory battles: Guatemala's public debates and the genocide trial of Jose Efrain Rios Montt. Quinnipiac Law Rev 32(3):621–674
LeMoyne J (1989) El Salvador's forgotten war. Foreign Aff 68(3):105–125
Livermore JD, Ramcharan BG (1989–1990) "Enforced or involuntary disappearances": an evaluation of a decade of United Nations action. Can Human Rights Yearb:217–230
Maogoto JN (2002) Now you see, now you don't: The state's duty to punish disappearances and extra-judicial executions. Aust Int Law J 2002:176–219
Marshall J (2008) Positive obligations and gender-based violence: judicial developments. Int Commun Law Rev 10(2):143–170
Matas D (1999) What happened to Raoul Wallenberg. Manitoba Law J 26(3):335–374
McCoy JL (2008) Democratic transformation in Latin America. Whitehead J Dipl Int Relat 9(1):19–30
McSherry JP (2002) Tracking the origins of a state terror network, Operation Condor. Latin Am Persp 29(1):38–60
Mignone EF, Estlund CL, Issacharoff S (1984) Dictatorship on trial: Prosecutions of human rights violations in Argentina. Yale J Int Law 10(1):118–150
Nagle LE (2000) The Cinderella of government: Judicial reform in Latin America. Calif West Int Law J 30(2):345–380
Nagle LE (2008) On armed conflict, human rights, and preserving the rule of law in Latin America. Pennsylvania State Int Law Rev 27(1):1–44
Nicholls C (2001) Reflections on Pinochet. Virginia J Int Law 41(1):140–151
Parry JT (2005) The shape of modern torture: extraordinary rendition and ghost detainees. Melbourne J Int Law 6(2):516–533
Pasqualucci JM (1994–1995) The Inter-American human rights system: establishing precedents and procedure in human rights law. Univ Miami Inter-Am Law Rev 26(2):297–362, 307–308.
Pérez-Solla MF (2003) Enforced disappearances before Argentinean tribunals: new developments in an endless fight for justice. South Afr J Human Rights 19(4):691–716
Sarkin J, Baranowska G (2018) Why enforced disappearances are perpetrated against groups as state policy: overlaps and interconnections between disappearances and genocide. Católica Law Rev 2(3):11–50
Sarkin J, Calvet Martinez E (2022) The global practice of systematic enforced disappearances of children in international law: Strategies for preventing future occurrences and solving past cases. Catholic Univ Law Rev 71(1):33–104
Shamsi N (2014) From Villa Grimaldi to Guantanamo Bay: remedying human rights abuses in Chile and the United States. Cardozo J Int Comp Law 22(2):355–398
Slack KM (1996) Operation Condor and human rights: a report of Paraguay's archive of terror. Human Rights Quart 18(2):492–506
Stevens P (2010) The International Convention for the Protection of All Persons from Enforced Disappearance – A welcoming response to a worldwide phenomenon with limited relief. Tydskrif vir Hedendaagse Romeins-Hollandse Reg 73(3):368–383

Taqi I (2001) Adjudicating disappearance cases in Turkey: an argument for adopting the Inter-American Court of Human Rights' approach. Fordham Int Law J 24(3):940–987

Tomuschat C (2001) Clarification Commission in Guatemala. Human Rights Quart 23(2):233–255

Tushnet M (2015) Authoritarian constitutionalism. Cornell Law Rev 100(2):391–462

Wright TC (2000) Human rights in Latin America: history and projections for the twenty-first century. Calif West Int Law J 30(2):303–322

Book Chapters

Dimaranan MC Sr (1987) Increasing terror. In: Schirmer DB, Rosskamm Shalom S (eds) The Philippines reader, a history of colonialism, neocolonialism, dictatorship and resistance. South End Press

Hall CK (1999) Enforced disappearance of persons. In: Triffterer O (ed) Commentary on the Rome Statute of the International Criminal Court, Observers' notes, Article by Article. Nomos

Kaisidou V (2019) To remember and forgive: The afterlives of Queen Frederica's childtowns in contemporary Greek fiction. In: Willert TS, Katsan G (eds) Retelling the past in contemporary Greek literature, film and popular culture. Rowman & Littlefield, pp 85–101

Malloy J (1992) Contemporary authoritarian regimes. In: Hawkesworth M, Cogan M (eds) Encyclopedia of government and politics, vol 1. Routledge, pp 229–246

Osborne R (2002) Archaic Greek history. In: Bakker EJ et al (eds) Brill's companion to Herodotus. Brill

Pinzón González ME (2016) Psychosocial perspectives on the enforced disappearance of indigenous peoples in Guatemala. In: Congram D (ed) Missing persons; Multidisciplinary perspectives on the disappeared. Canadian Scholars' Press

Chapter 2
The Content of Enforced Disappearance

2.1 Early Attempts at a Definition

The definition of enforced disappearances has proved to be an issue of legal and political controversy.[1] During the last years, disappearances have been labeled according to a diverse range of characterizations, though have been used almost interchangeably.[2] As a result, once disappearances attracted international concern, attempting to define the substance of the term proved to be a difficult task. In this context, human rights NGOs were the first to respond to the need for 'conceptual clarity'.[3]

In the early 1980s, the International League for Human Rights provided a definition in a reply to the UN Secretary-General, according to which

> ['d]isappearances' describe a practice whereby individuals are abducted through the complicity, consent or conspiracy of government forces: unlike in the case of kidnapping, or the taking of hostages, in a 'disappearance' there is no demand for ransom of any sort.[4]

This definition was an early attempt to take an analytical approach to practices that had been developed by governments, though it did not encompass some of the key elements that a disappearance involves. Similarly, many NGOs engaged in a strenuous quest for a definition[5] despite the difficulties they encountered. For instance, the NGO 'Federación Latinoamericana de Asociaciones de Familiares de Detenidos-Desaparecidos' (the Latin American Federation of Associations for

---

[1] UN Doc. E/CN.4/1999/62.

[2] Characterizations varied from forced, enforced or involuntary, to political or even systematic. Kleinman (1987), p. 1033.

[3] Egeland (1982), p. 189.

[4] UN Doc. E/CN.4/1434 (1981) 22–23.

[5] van Boven (1983), p. 37.

I. Pervou, *The Right not to Be Subjected to Enforced Disappearance*,
https://doi.org/10.1007/978-3-031-36731-1_2

Relatives of the Detained-Disappeared, FEDEFAM),[6] drafted a Convention on Enforced Disappearances which defined the term in Art. 2 as:

> Any act or omission which is designed to conceal the whereabouts of a political opponent or dissident, of whose fate his family, friends or supporters are unaware, and is committed with intent to suppress, prevent or impede opposition or dissidence by persons in government office, by government officials at any level or by organized groups of private individuals acting with the support or permission of the foregoing.[7]

This definition was coupled with Art. 3, which further elaborated on the relevant practices of the state authorities and contained a summary of the minimum elements required to constitute a disappearance.[8]

2.1.1 *The UN Definition*

The United Nations reach consensus until the adoption of the 1992 Declaration. This was the precursor to a definition that states parties concluded in the 2006 United Nations' Convention; however, it was not a part of the Declaration itself, but only a preambular clause. The Resolution declared that states were

> *Deeply concerned* that in many countries, often in a persistent manner, enforced disappearances occur, in the sense that persons are arrested, detained or abducted against their will or otherwise deprived of their liberty by officials of different branches or levels of Government, or by organized groups or private individuals acting on behalf of, or with the support, direct or indirect, consent or acquiescence of the Government, followed by a refusal to disclose the fate or whereabouts of the persons concerned or a refusal to acknowledge the deprivation of their liberty, which places such persons outside the protection of the law.[9]

It is also striking that the Human Rights Commission, in adopting resolutions that related to the term,[10] actually used the term itself without any further explanation.

Nevertheless, the 1992 Declaration has proven instrumental, since its drafters proclaimed it as a body of principles for all states'[11] and was the first international document to declare that 'any act of enforced disappearance is an offence to human dignity' and thus violates a series of human rights. Moreover, the act of enforced disappearance also constitutes an offence under criminal law.[12] This conceptualization clearly illustrates the reasons why the 1992 Declaration was a landmark; it established a definition at the international level and stipulated that enforced

[6] FEDEFAM. Fighting against enforced disappearances in Latin America. Retrieved March 22, 2023, from http://www.desaparecidos.org/fedefam/eng.html.

[7] UN Doc. E/CN.4/1985/15, Annex III, 1.

[8] Lippman (1988), p. 142.

[9] UNGA Res 47/133 (1992).

[10] OHCHR, WGEID Resolutions. Retrieved March 22, 2023, from http://www2.ohchr.org/english/issues/disappear/documents.htm#resolutions.

[11] UNGA Res 47/133 (1992) op clause 1.

[12] Idem, Arts.1,4.

disappearance should be treated as an offence under domestic legal systems. The indispensability of the definition was also due to the fact that the offence of enforced disappearance had been acknowledged and so a domestic legal order could prevent and punish such acts. Given this evident correlation between the definition and the offence and their parallel existence it could be argued that, despite its preambular placement, the definition had been functionally incorporated into the main part of the Declaration. Moreover, the 1992 Declaration has remained important even after the adoption of the Convention, since

> [i]t sets forth a set of rules that all the Member States of the United Nations, without the requirement of a ratification are called upon to apply as a minimum to prevent and suppress the practice,[13]

and because it might be also considered of customary value. [14]

The definition given is principally based on the 'working definition' adopted by the UNWGEID in its annual reports.[15] The UNWGEID, in its general comments on the Declaration, stated which elements a definition of enforced disappearance should include. There are

> three minimum cumulative elements which constitute an act of enforced disappearance: a) deprivation of liberty against the will of the person concerned, b) involvement of governmental officials, at least indirectly by acquiescence, c) refusal to disclose the fate and whereabouts of the person concerned.[16]

These elements are interconnected and reveal the historical truth, actuality and complexity of the crime.[17]

Moreover, it was a breakthrough that disappearances were defined as offences of 'extreme seriousness' (Art.4), legally addressing the calls for justice and the end of impunity for the perpetrators. However, the offence of enforced disappearance also presupposed that there exists governmental involvement, or at least awareness of the perpetrators of the crime, obviously rendering the provision useless if there is no political will to punish the crime and suppress the practice.[18]

The significance of the progress made in 1992 is beyond doubt. Apart from establishing 'the autonomous nature of the crime'[19] it gave impetus to a broader debate upon the issue. Therefore, the next step deemed essential was the creation of a right *per se* not to be subjected to enforced disappearance.[20] Art. 1 of the 2007 Convention established this new right, using a negative formulation, and after intensive negotiations the state-parties finally concluded a definition (Art.2).

---

[13] OHCHR, Enforced or Involuntary Disappearances, Fact Sheet No.6/Rev.3, 6. Retrieved March 22, 2023, from https://www.ohchr.org/Documents/Publications/FactSheet6Rev3.pdf.

[14] Citroni and Scovazzi (2009), p. 93.

[15] UN Doc E/CN.4/2002/71(8 January 2002) para 70.

[16] UN Doc E/CN.4/1996/38, para 55.

[17] UN Doc E/CN.4/1984/21, para 178.

[18] UN Doc E/CN.4/1996/38 para 51.

[19] Citroni and Scovazzi (2009), pp. 92–93.

[20] UN Doc E/CN.4/2002/71 para 43.

2.2 The Convention's Definition: A Thorough Analysis of Its Elements

The term 'enforced disappearance' was the focal point during the negotiations as it would naturally entail specific state obligations. As has already been mentioned, the definition given in Art. 2 of the CPED follows the pattern of the 1992 Declaration, but the formulation of the term is substantially different, although phrasal alterations seem slight. Art. 2 reads as follows:

> 'Enforced disappearance' is considered to be the arrest, detention, abduction or any other form of deprivation of liberty by agents of the State or by persons or groups of persons acting with the authorization, support or acquiescence of the State, followed by a refusal to acknowledge the deprivation of liberty or by concealment of the fate or whereabouts of the disappeared person, which will place such a person outside the protection of the law.

2.2.1 *The First Element: Deprivation of Liberty*

It is explicitly stated that the deprivation of liberty is the first element of an enforced disappearance. The final phrasing is the outcome of negotiations, a compromise between the proposals made during the sessions of the ISWG. The initial wording, proposed in the Working Group by the Chairperson-Rapporteur, referred to 'the deprivation of a person's liberty, in whatever form'.[21] The follow up debate brought to light two different trends. Some states endorsed the Chairperson's suggestion, with a view to ensuring full protection, whereas other states considered the phrasing 'imprecise',[22] thus calling for the use of more specific terms. Although the use of specific terms such as arrest, detention and abduction would be 'by way of example,'[23] meaning that the list in the definition was not exhaustive,[24] it seems that the delegations sought clarity in the definition in order to limit ambiguity.[25]

However, these terms not only serve as examples in the context of the Convention, their explicit enumeration signals that they constitute essential components of a 'disappearance'.[26] They form part of the crime, an element of it (*actus reus*).[27]

---

[21] UN Doc E/CN.4/2005/66, para 17.

[22] UN Doc E/CN.4/2004/59, para 20.

[23] UN Doc E/CN.4/2005/66, para 19.

[24] UN Doc E/CN.4/2004/59, para 20.

[25] UN Doc E/CN.4/2003/71, para 36. Terms like 'arrest', 'detention' and 'abduction' were considered as 'simple and clear'.

[26] *Gangaram-Panday v Suriname (Merits, Reparations and Costs)*, Inter-American Court of Human Rights Series C No16 (21 January 1994).

[27] This approach differs from the one the ECtHR follows. For the ECtHR, a disappearance is an 'aggravated form of arbitrary detention'. For that reason, the Court finds it important that the disappeared are last seen in custody by governmental authorities. The Convention focuses on deprivation of liberty as well, but it does not treat it as a prerequisite for a disappearance to occur. *Akdeniz*

Finally, these terms are of considerable conceptual value because they are invoked in the most important international human rights instruments and their content has been enriched by the interpretation of international courts and tribunals over the years.

Another contested issue during the negotiations was that of lawfulness. Some delegations expressed the opinion that only cases of unlawful deprivation of liberty should be included.[28] But the majority of states did not welcome this approach, stating that it would dramatically limit the term's field of application. Besides, jurisprudence,[29] as well as the UNWGEID's experience, had also shown that deprivation of liberty was essentially related to the third element of a disappearance, namely refusal to acknowledge the deprivation, concealment, or fate or whereabouts of the victim, meaning that lawful arrests or detentions could turn into disappearances.[30] (For the sake of coherent argument, in the following sections the third element is discussed before the second one).

2.2.2 The Third Element: Concealment of the Victim's Fate or Whereabouts

The third element of the term refers to the refusal of the proper national authorities to cooperate with the relatives or the counsel of the victim[31] and inform them about his/her fate. It is not surprising that national authorities might refuse to acknowledge the deprivation of liberty itself[32] or give details about it, and as a result they erase all traces of the victim.

This element is not only related to factual circumstances but is also critical in achieving one of the two aims of the Convention, that of prevention.[33] Therefore it should be read together with Arts 18 to 20. Art. 18 refers to the right to information of those people with a legitimate interest and lists the information accessible to them. Art. 20 frames the exceptions, spelling out when the state can refuse the

and others v Turkey, App no 25165/94 (ECtHR 31 May 2001) paras 75–76, 83; *Orhan v Turkey*, App no 25656/94 (ECtHR 18 June 2002) paras 265, 278; *Tekdag v Turkey*, App no 27699/95 (ECtHR 15 January 2004) paras 66, 68. *See* also UN Doc E/CN.4/2002/71, para76.

[28] UN Doc E/CN.4/2004/59, para 21.

[29] *Cantoral-Benavides v Peru (Merits)*, Inter-American Court of Human Rights Series C No 69 (18 August 2000) paras 90–91; *Neira-Alegría et al. v Peru (Merits)*, Inter-American Court of Human Rights Series C No 20 (19 January 1995).

[30] HRC. (10 January 2008). Promotion and protection of all human rights, civil, political, economic, social and cultural Rights, Including the right to development, Report of the Working Group on Enforced or Involuntary Disappearances, para 26.

[31] Meaning 'any person with a legitimate interest', Art.18.

[32] *Castillo-Páez v Peru (Merits)*, Inter-American Court of Human Rights Series C No 34 (3 November 1997) para 58.

[33] *Mojica v Dominican Republic*, HRC (1994) UN Doc CCPR/C/51/D/449/1991, para 5.5.

provision of information about the detained person. This article caused disagreement until the end of negotiations of the ISWG, as it was thought to distort the instrument and render it ineffective.

The drafters of the Convention were aware of the fact that this provision (Art. 20) could serve as a 'Trojan Horse', capable of bringing the Convention's implementation to a standstill; thus they explicitly restricted its scope of application by establishing both affirmative and negative requirements. In any event, though, Art. 2 enjoys normative supremacy over Art. 20, and in case of conflict it prevails. Art. 20(1) reads as follows:

> [...] In no case shall there be restrictions on the right to information referred to in Article 18 that could constitute conduct defined in Article 2 or be in violation of Article 17, paragraph 1.

However, ambiguity does not arise from the priority being accorded to the two provisions, but rather from which 'conduct' is deemed permissible. During the negotiations, some delegations opted for exceptions to the right to information on the grounds of witness protection, threats to national security, and the protection of the detainee's integrity, whereas others proposed postponement of the information provision instead of refusal.[34]

Overall, it seems that Arts. 2, 18 and 20, when properly interpreted, protect the right to information. As a result, a systemic interpretation would ensure maximum protection for the victim and his/her relatives as well.[35] The right to information and the correlative protection of a person's sensitive personal data attains extra attention during the last years, taking into consideration the proliferation of the protective legislation regarding personal data. In this sense, the systemic interpretation of CPED's provisions shall also be in accordance with personal data legislation,[36] an issue which has not yet been thoroughly explained either by UNWGEID or CED. Information over a detainee or captive is far away from concealment of their whereabouts. In this sense, there is not interpretational clash, or provision conflict.

2.2.3 The Second Element: The Identity of the Perpetrators

The last part to examine is the one related to the status of the perpetrators. According to Art. 2, perpetrators should be 'agents of the State or persons or groups of persons acting with the authorization, support or acquiescence of the State'. This element brings to the foreground the issue of the relationship between human rights law and the law of state responsibility.

According to the definition, enforced disappearances can be committed only by state actors, either directly or indirectly. Non-state actors are excluded from the

[34] UN Doc E/CN.4/2006/57, paras 16–29.

[35] Vienna Convention on the Law of the Treaties (VCLT), Vienna 23 May 1969, entered into force 27 January 1980, UNTS 1155, Art. 31(1).

[36] Kamber (2017), p. 96.

definition and Art. 2 cannot be applied to them, not even by analogy, since there is special provision for these in Art. 3. This approach caused dissatisfaction during the negotiations and proved to be a hard case to negotiate.[37] It has been argued that the UNWGEID[38] and the ISWG adopted a 'traditional notion' on this topic, since they left out non-state actors.[39]

However, a careful reading of ILC's Articles on the Responsibility of States for Internationally Wrongful Acts (ARSIWA)[40] reveals what non-state actors stand for in the law of state responsibility and which entities are finally excluded from the Convention's definition. As Special Rapporteur James Crawford points out, human rights supporters have long demanded the abandonment of a 'firm distinction between the State and the private sector' when the international law of state responsibility is applied to human rights instruments.[41] The request, though, for an 'extension of state responsibility in the private sector' is considered to be 'undue'.[42] According to the ARSIWA, in a number of cases, non-state actors' acts are attributed to the state, namely when they serve as agents of the state, when they function under the direction or the control of a state and, lastly, when armed opposition groups are guided by the state.[43] Even if the ARSIWA guarantee in this manner that there will be no impunity for non-state actors, by equating them to indirect state actors, there are still arguments as to why this does not correspond specifically to the practice of disappearances. The most convincing amongst them is that in disappearances it is almost impossible to prove who has committed the crime and, further to this, whether there has been state involvement or not.[44]

---

[37] The members of the ISWG finally agreed about non-state actors only in its last session. UN Doc E/CN.4/2006/57, para 12.

[38] The UNWGEID repeated its firm position in its General Comment on the definition of enforced disappearance: HRC (2008) para 1; OHCHR, Enforced or Involuntary Disappearances, Fact Sheet No.6/Rev.3, p. 11.

[39] UN Doc E/CN.4/2002/71, para 73.

[40] Crawford (2002); Crawford and Olleson (2006), pp. 451–477.

[41] Crawford, J. Human rights and state responsibility. *12th Raymond & Beverly Sackler Distinguished Lecture Series*, Thomas J Dodd Research Centre, University of Connecticut, para 1. Retrieved March 22, 2023, from http://209.85.229.132/search?q=cache:Tq_ZorrV49oJ:doddcenter.uconn.edu/events/sackler/Crawford%2520transcript.doc+state+responsibility+human+rights&cd=20&hl=en&ct=clnk.

[42] Ibid, para 5.

[43] Ibid, para 2. Yet, regarding armed opposition groups, international tribunals have developed a very high threshold to allow their acts to involve state responsibility. The state has to exercise effective control or overall control over the non-state actor. *See*, *Military and Paramilitary Activities in and against Nicaragua* (Nicaragua v USA) [1986] ICJ Rep 1986; *Prosecutor v Tadić*, Decision on the Prosecutor's motion requesting Protective Measures for victims and witnesses (1995) (ICTY Tr.Ch.).

[44] UN Doc E/CN.4/2002/71, para 73.The case is more complicated in countries where both state actors and non-state actors (usually opposition groups) resort to disappearances so as to weaken their opponents.

The issue of non-state actors provoked serious discord during the sessions. The Chairperson managed to reach a compromise with the inclusion of Art. 3.[45] This article was cautiously phrased, as it refers to 'acts defined in article 2' and not to enforced disappearances, implying that the acts are characterized as such only when there is state involvement. It also leaves it to state authorities to punish these acts and to decide which measures to implement ('appropriate measures') in order to bring those responsible to justice. The provision acknowledges states' discretion in this field.[46] In the meantime it reduces the victim's degree of protection as these acts fall outside the *ratione materiae*.[47] The most serious concerns were expressed by the associations of the families of disappeared persons and by NGOs, who argued that the provision's scope could be distorted by governments in an attempt to justify their policies.[48]

Overall, the above debate can be condensed into two conflicting propositions. First, state involvement is a *sine qua non* condition of enforced disappearance. Second, it is very difficult to prove state involvement in disappearances, especially when it is indirect. Thus, what would seem appropriate (to avoid doctrinal aberrations and encompass the particular attributes of the phenomenon) is to adopt a wide interpretation of the ARSIWA and to lower the applicable evidential threshold in cases where there are allegations of indirect state involvement. This view has already been introduced by the IACtHR in the case of *Masacre de Pueblo Bello v. Colombia*, where the Court held Colombia responsible for disappearances carried out by paramilitary groups.[49]

There are other cases though which remain unresolved. The systematic practice of enforced disappearance by private actors such as drug cartels tallied with the knowledge and subsequent acquiescence of state authorities cannot be easily traced.[50] Of course, impunity in such cases is not a conventional matter, rather an issue of state implementation. The same applies in cases of failed or rogue states which do not have effective control over their territory. In these cases, it is still questionable if CPED's Art. 2 or 3 are applicable.

An incident which attracted international attention and begot doctrinal debate is that of Boko Haram's practices in Nigeria. On April 2014, the terrorist group Boko Haram kidnapped around 276 schoolgirls aged 16 to 18 from the Chibok district school. Their massive kidnapping was followed by loss of their traces as they were

---

[45] Compromise proved difficult on this point, since the states' starting points varied significantly, mostly at the second session of the ISWG. UN Doc E/CN.4/2004/59, paras 27–33.

[46] UN Doc E/CN.4/2003/71, para 35.

[47] McCrory (2007), p. 551.

[48] Joint Statement (Associations of families of the disappeared and other supportive NGOs on the occasion of the adoption of the Draft International Convention for the Protection of All Persons from Enforced Disappearances. Retrieved March 22, 2023, from http://www.icaed.org/the-convention/history-and-background-of-the-convention/.

[49] *Masacre de Pueblo Bello v Colombia*, Inter-American Court of Human Rights, Series C No 140 (31 January 2006) paras 111–153.

[50] Teubner (2006), p. 328.

taken in mountainous and hardly accessible areas held captives by the members of the terrorist organization. Boko Haram took the girls for various reasons. It is suggested that the group used girls as negotiating pawns, seeking for the release of some of their members, or that they were used to take care of the necessary household activities.[51] Others refer to the girls' Christian-Orthodox religion as a specific feature which led to their abduction, or to the fact that Boko Haram's members sought to impregnate them in order to create the next generation of their group.[52] All in all, some of the girls were found and returned to their hometown a few months later, whereas more than 100 girls are still missing, whereas there are reports that some may already be dead.

In this scenery, the massive kidnapping of Chibok girls combines the major elements of a disappearance with regards to the forceful deprivation of their liberty, the lost of their whereabouts and the rupture of communications with their next of kin, as well as their placement outside the protection of the law, in the sphere of lawlessness.[53] However, for the above to constitute an enforced disappearance these acts shall be attributable to the state of jurisdiction, which bears respective responsibility. The Boko Haram incident seems at first sight as a case of non-state actors committing disappearances, where the state has no actual involvement. However, there are two features which need further investigation. First, if the Nigerian state authorities were in a position to do something either to avert their kidnapping, or to accomplish their release. State acquiescence, does not avail it from attribution.

The second feature requiring examination relates to Nigeria's ability to exercise effective control over its territory. Numerous reports, alongside literature, imply that the Nigerian government is not capable of exercise effective control over its entire territory, thus it may well be considered a failed, or rogue state.[54] In the first scenario, according to which authorities were unwilling to take action for the sake of the victims, the state may well be held accountable for the perpetration of enforced disappearance; while in the second case, where Nigeria is considered failed there shall be no attribution and Art. 3 of the Convention is applicable. It is interesting to notice that when the incident took place Nigeria was already a CED member-state;[55] thus, the Convention had been incorporated into national law. Yet, both internationally and on a national level there was not connection of the incident to the concept of disappearances, even though there was international awareness as far as the fate of Chibok girls was concerned.[56]

---

[51] Ogueri (2022), p. 152.

[52] Bailey (2018), p. 78.

[53] Ezeani (2017), p. 15.

[54] Niworu (2013), p. 245.

[55] General Allegation 120th Session, Nigeria. (10–14 February 2020). Retrieved 22 March, 2023, from https://www.ohchr.org/sites/default/files/Documents/Issues/Disappearances/Allegations/120_Nigeria.pdf.

[56] Amnesty International. (14 April 2021). Nigeria: Seven years since Chibok, the government fails to protect children. Retrieved March 22, 2023, from https://www.amnesty.org/en/latest/press-release/2021/04/nigeria-seven-years-since-chibok-the-government-fails-to-protect-children/.

On a doctrinal level, the missing part of this debate pertains to whether a failed state which becomes member to the Convention can be held responsible for enforced disappearances taking place within its territory. This query though, is cardinal to the theory of failed states mostly, and it only applies to disappearances in such incidents.

2.2.4 The Third and a Half Element of the Definition

Still, the treatment of non-state actors committing enforced disappearances is not the most complex part of the definition. The last phrase of Art. 2, which places 'such a person outside the protection of the law', constitutes one of the major weaknesses of the whole text. More specifically, states disagreed on whether the placement of the victim outside the protection of the law should be a fourth element of the definition (the subjective part of the crime, meaning that the intention of the perpetrators should be accordingly evidenced), or a mere consequence of any act of enforced disappearance. Argentina, and in general any state that had experienced enforced disappearances, held that placing the victim outside the protection of the law was an 'inherent consequence' of an enforced disappearance.[57] On the other side, a number of states[58] urged for a fourth constitutive element to be added to the definition. They explained that it would be incompatible with their domestic penal systems to introduce a crime which would not ask for the establishment of the perpetrator's intention. Apart from that, they also referred to the definition provided by the Rome Statute of the International Criminal Court (ICC Statute),[59] of which intent is a critical element.[60] The debates left the issue unresolved, and thus the Chairperson of the ISWG stated that states-parties 'were fully entitled to make an interpretive declaration on the matter at the time of ratification'.[61]

However, the interpretation of this phrase is found in documents prior to the Convention, and leaves no doubt about the meaning of the text. According to the UNWGEID the placement of a person outside the protection of the law is the consequence of a disappearance.[62] Nowak and the ISWG, during its early sessions, also sided with the UNWGEID in identifying only three constitutive elements in a disappearance[63] and expressly avoided making reference to it as the fourth. Nowak also underlined that it would be almost impossible to identify intent in the perpetrators' acts, as in most cases they are trained to carry out only certain tasks for which they

[57] UN Doc E/CN.4/2006/57, para 91.

[58] *Idem*, Annex II, 48 onwards, General Statements.

[59] Rome Statute of the International Criminal Court, Arts 7(1), 7(2)(i).

[60] Andreu-Guzmán (2001), pp. 80–81.

[61] UN Doc E/CN.4/2006/57, para 93. *See* also, the statement made by the United Kingdom after the Convention's adoption, UN Doc A/61/PV.82, 2.

[62] UN Doc E/CN.4/2002/79, para 365.

[63] UN Doc E/CN.4/2002/71, para 74; UN Doc E/CN.4/2003/71, para 33.

could be held responsible, not enforced disappearance as a whole.[64] The most explicit and clear statement which supported this view was the one made in a UN experts' Joint Report on secret detention:

> [T]he definition does not require intent to put the person concerned outside the protection of the law as a defining element, but rather refers to it as an objective consequence of the denial, refusal or concealment of the whereabouts and fate of the person.[65]

The fact that states still have not embraced the approach set up by the UNWGEID over the last decades indicates that this issue touched upon the important matter of reserved jurisdiction and domestic policy and that they have sought to protect their agents and all those who exercise any form of state authority from getting involved in criminal proceedings. The issue gains even more importance when it comes to the evidentiary standard set for disappearances. If 'putting the victim outside the protection of the law' is to be considered an element of the definition, then the alleged victims must prove that the perpetrators had *dolus* in doing so, which undoubtedly makes the evidentiary threshold higher.[66]

However, this debate is totally misleading. The purport of this phrase is properly revealed when it is examined in combination with the provisions of the OAS Convention. The relevant phrase in the OAS Convention is: 'thereby impeding his or her recourse to the applicable legal remedies and procedural guarantees'.[67] Under the Inter-American system, 'outside the protection of the law' means that the victim is denied recourse to legal remedies.[68] This is a material element which concerns the victim's case and not the perpetrator's defence, an aspect which was overlooked during the negotiations.

The fact that the Chairperson of the ISWG referred to it as the 'third and half element'[69] of the definition, trying to reconcile all different views, did not remove ambiguity over this point. This is regrettable[70] because it assigned priority to the crime of enforced disappearance and passed over the right not to be subjected to it. In other words, it set guarantees for the protection of the potential perpetrator and minimized the protection of the victim. Moreover, this ambiguity may result in impunity (at least under domestic criminal law) and the further proliferation of policies favoring disappearances, as perpetrators will remain unpunished and judicial remedies will become futile.

---

[64] UN Doc E/CN.4/2002/71, paras 73–74.

[65] UN Doc A/HRC/13/42, para 28.

[66] This approach was adopted by the ECtHR in some cases and it rendered disappearances' victims helpless. *Bazorkina v Russia*, App no 69481/01 (ECtHR 27 June 2006) para 167.

[67] IACFDP (1994) Art. 2.

[68] Andreu-Guzmán (2001), p. 80.

[69] Summary of the 5th session of the ISWG (2004).

[70] Joint Statement (Associations of families of the disappeared and other supportive NGOs on the occasion of the adoption of the Draft International Convention for the Protection of All Persons from Enforced Disappearances). Retrieved March 22, 2023, from http://www.icaed.org/the-convention/history-and-background-of-the-convention/.

Notwithstanding the above controversies, the Convention's definition enjoys wide acceptance both by states and by human rights NGOs. The Convention offers quite a broad definition, which in turn may well correspond to a wide variety of methods that governments apply. The fact that it recognizes that any kind of deprivation of liberty may result in a disappearance is very important, especially with regards to new methods to which governments may resort. The Convention may also be considered a positive development regarding the identity of perpetrators, even if non-state actors are excluded from the definition. As soon as it enters into force, it will insist upon states parties' responsibility for breaches of its provisions. After all, state responsibility is the way to fill in the gaps in human rights protection.[71]

However, it is difficult for any definition, no matter how comprehensive, to denote what an enforced disappearance actually is. Indeed, this definition failed to capture the danger to which the disappeared are exposed; it also did not refer at all to the ill-treatment that victims most often suffer. This is why jurisprudence is still prominent in this area. The HRC, alongside international tribunals, has repeatedly underlined the risk which enforced disappearances entail for the victims' lives. Lastly, the definition did not manage to clear up doubts as to the victim's placement outside the protection of the law. No matter if this phrase was a fourth constitutive element or a mere consequence of the other elements, the definition left space for ambiguity on this point. Hence, there is a state of uncertainty that may be harmful to the integrity of the human rights protection system concerning enforced disappearances.

2.3 Definitional Challenges for Enforced Disappearances

The interpretation of the Convention's definition in Art. 2 is cardinal to CED's success, for a strict grammatical interpretation will limit significantly its scope of application. Although the definition is widely considered successful by all actors interested in enforced disappearances, it still cannot denote particular implications disappearances entail. In this sense, interpretation may lead the Convention to a standstill, pertaining only to the archetypical methods of disappearances, or adversely it may well transform it to a dynamic legal document, applicable in various occasions. From this angle, there are three domains which prompt further attention. First, the application of Art. 2 definition on practices applied against terrorist groups. Second, CED's contribution to mass disappearances which may arise during international, or national conflicts, and third, CED's potential connection with state practices related to refugee and migratory flows. These three topical questions have arisen during the last decade: the relationship between disappearance and antiterrorist policies appeared first, while only during the last couple of years

[71] Anderson (2006), p. 267.

disappearances are connected with policies to decrease refugee and migratory flows, such as pushbacks.

2.3.1 Enforced Disappearances Within the Anti-Terrorist Spectrum

The 'War on Terror' raised new issues for the law of enforced disappearances, concentrating on the application of two key practices: incommunicado detentions and extraordinary renditions. The Convention's adoption and entry into force were close in time with the global awareness against terrorist attacks. For this reason, it early came in discussion, whether particular state practices applied in the name of anti-terrorist policies could fall under the definition of Art. 2. This section summarizes the record of events and the general context in which these methods emerged and then examines each one separately. Finally, it explores the advantages for individuals' protection if these practices are classified as enforced disappearances.

2.3.1.1 Disappearances After 9/11: A Brief Account of Events

The aftermath of the 9/11 terrorist attacks reinforced the public interest concerning disappearances. The US Administration declared the 'Global War on Terrorism' against Al-Qaeda and against the so-called 'Axis of Evil'.[72] On these grounds, some states, including the USA, took austere legislative measures authorizing human rights restrictions[73] as a safeguard protecting national security,[74] whereas other states went further and officially declared a state of emergency.[75] Moreover, certain states took advantage of the political circumstances and used the terrorism rhetoric to combat opposition groups in their territory.[76]

It was not the first time that such a policy had been implemented by states; since the 1960s the language used by Latin American authoritarian regimes had identified military or paramilitary groups as subversives or terrorists.[77] Yet now the situation

[72] US Department of States, Foreign Press Centers. Pre-2017 Archive. Retrieved March 22, 2023, from http://fpc.state.gov/documents/organization/16801.pdf.

[73] Uniting and Strengthening America by Providing Appropriate Tools Required to Intercept and Obstruct Terrorism (USA Patriot Act). (2001). *Public Law*, 107–56; the Canadian Anti-Terrorism Act. (2001). Bill C-36'; the Indian Prevention of Terrorism Act (POTA). (2002). act no 15; and the Australian Criminal Code Amendment (Terrorism) Bill. (2002). act no 40, 2003.

[74] Gearty (2005), pp. 99–157.

[75] *See*, the British Anti-Terrorism, Crime and Security Act. (2001) c.24; Henning (2002), pp. 1277–1278.

[76] Gray (2008), pp. 234–252.

[77] *Bámaca-Velásquez v Guatemala (Merits)*, Inter-American Court of Human Rights, Series C No 70 (25 November 2000) para 121(b), (d); *The 19 Tradesmen v Guatemala (Merits Reparations and*

was different because the policy had been adopted by democratically elected governments, and more generally by countries which were often referred to as liberal democracies.[78] (It might be argued, though, that the policy was first introduced in the mid-20th century by Western 'democracies' in order to avert decolonization.)[79] In addition, the operations carried out after 9/11 against terrorism were unprecedented in terms of their intensity and state cooperation in intelligence sharing.

One of the effects of these draconian laws was the substantial increase in suspects' detentions,[80] which were mainly done in secret or incommunicado. States adopted new techniques as well, which resulted in the lowering of the applicable human rights standards.[81] Thus, enforced disappearances came to the fore once more, as a result of these circumstances.

2.3.1.2 Incommunicado Detentions

It has already been mentioned that deprivation of liberty is just one of the three constitutive elements of an enforced disappearance. It is also clear, according to the definition in the 2007 Convention, that every kind of deprivation of liberty might turn into a disappearance. Indeed, some methods place the detainee at incredibly high risk and result almost always in a disappearance. 'Incommunicado detention' is, in these terms, a means of erasing all traces of the victim. The term describes the detainee's absolute confinement from the outside world. The victim is not allowed to communicate with people other than his/her captors.[82]

The implications of incommunicado detention are several and relate mostly to the victim's protection. The victim is unable to notify their family of this new situation and the reasons for their custody and also cannot consult a lawyer. Their confinement indicates a further refusal by the victim's captors to bring him/her before the judiciary.[83] Because of these restrictions, the form the detainee's treatment takes is at the captors' absolute discretion and may 'invite other forms of coercion'.[84]

Incommunicado detention is not a novel practice and has already been addressed by the international community.[85] The question, though, is whether an incommunicado detention may amount to or result in an enforced disappearance, given the

Costs), Inter-American Court of Human Rights, Series C No 108 (5 July 2004) para 84(a), (h).

[78] Heywood (2000), pp. 169–170.

[79] Law (2009), pp. 199–200.

[80] Sadat (2006), pp. 309–342.

[81] Paust (2005), p. 855.

[82] Association for the Prevention of Torture. (2 March 2006). Incommunicado, unacknowledged and secret detention under International Law. Retrieved March 22, 2023, from http://www.apt.ch/component/option,com_docman/task,doc_view/gid,280/lang,en/.

[83] Rodley (1999), pp. 333–334.

[84] Bator and Vorenberg (1966), pp. 71–72.

[85] UN Docs E/3048(1957), Annex I, Principles 37–38, A/Res/43/173(1988), Annex, Principles 16, 19; Treves (1990), pp. 581–582.

human rights curtailments that states have already introduced and are willing to undertake during their anti-terrorist campaigns.[86] The UNWGEID has stressed the potential relationship between the two since 2003.[87] According to the UNWGEID's Reports and the Convention, incommunicado detention falls under the states' obligation to take preventive measures against disappearances and to refrain from using any methods that endanger a detainee's security. The Convention does not mention incommunicado detention *expressis verbis*, but it can be argued that it implies it in Art. 17(2)(d) (read in conjunction with Art. 17(1), which refers to secret detention):

> [...][e]ach State Party shall, in its legislation: Guarantee that any person deprived of liberty shall be authorized to communicate with and be visited by his or her family, counsel or any other person of his or her choice, subject only to the conditions established by law, or, if he or she is a foreigner, to communicate with his or her consular authorities, in accordance with applicable international law.

The Convention's rationale shows that the drafters understood incommunicado detention to be a particular form that secret detention may become (incommunicado detention is an aspect of secret detention: Art. 17(2) seeks to address the violations a person suffers when secretly detained). Contrary to this view, some commentators place incommunicado just before disappearances on the scale of severity. In other words, an enforced disappearance is considered 'a heinous form of incommunicado detention'.[88] Apparently, this view misconceives the complexity of an enforced disappearance; however, the value of equating these two practices is obvious only rarely when it comes to newly developed anti-terrorist policies.

In the post 9/11 era, incommunicado detentions have become standard tools to confront terrorism and to avert future attacks. The intent of the measures undertaken is not the individual's extermination (as it was in the 1960s) but the weakening of the terrorist organization's structures. Thus, the captors aim to extract the best available information. To that end, a detainee's confinement enables the authorities to apply severe interrogation techniques affecting his/her treatment,[89] but not to conclude in torture that will cause irreparable damage or end in extrajudicial executions. This, of course, does not guarantee humane treatment for detainees. Recent statistics prove that ill-treatment is almost inevitable during incommunicado detention [90] and that detainees are exposed both to physical and mental suffering.[91]

Furthermore, confinement enables the authorities to leave the suspects incommunicado for a prolonged period (this tactic, apart from the detainees' debilitation, also ensures that there is no communication with other suspected terrorists); this

[86] Waldron (2002), pp. 191–192.

[87] UN Doc E/CN.4/2003/70, 3.

[88] Joseph (2014) p. 170.

[89] Marks and Clapham (2005), p. 77.

[90] Crelinstern (2003), p. 203.

[91] Morentin et al. (2008), pp. 88–89.

constitutes cruel inhuman and degrading treatment *per se*[92] and is a *prima facie* violation of the ICCPR[93] and of the IACHR.[94] The data available show that terrorist suspects are usually held incommunicado for months or even years,[95] even though the HRC held as early as 1979 that even 6 weeks of incommunicado detention are a breach of the Covenant.[96] In addition, the ECtHR found fourteen days' incommunicado detention to be exceptionally long, even when there is a state of public emergency because of a terrorist threat.[97] Prisoners that are under prolonged incommunicado detention are usually referred to as 'Ghost Detainees'.[98] This term describes eloquently the detainees' absolute alienation from society and exposes that their very existence depends solely on the information they possess.

It seems that even prolonged confinement and severe interrogation methods applied to alleged terrorists meet the requirements of Art. 2 of the Convention and set up the causal link between incommunicado detentions and enforced disappearances. Obviously, the current conditions of terrorism suspects' detentions leave no doubt that these individuals are eventually disappeared within the accepted parameters of human rights standards for as long as they are in confinement. The key element is that the state in which they are disappeared also refuses to acknowledge their detention or their whereabouts. The fact that at some point the disappeared may be put on trial or get released does not affect their characterization as disappeared, since neither the 2007 Convention nor international jurisprudence ask for information on the victim's death or interminable capture.[99] This also does not reduce their next of kin's anguish over their fate. Their relatives cannot be aware of the patterns that the intelligence services follow, and therefore they fear for the detainees' life.

The extensive use of incommunicado detentions in the 'War on Terror' may also have marked a turn in the jurisprudence on enforced disappearances. Up until now, international human rights courts have in the majority of cases presumed victims' deaths simply because there have been allegations of ill-treatment. However, contemporary enforced disappearances occur under different conditions. As victims are

---

[92] HRC. (10/03/92). General Comment No.20: Prohibition of Torture and Cruel Treatment or Punishment (Art.7): 10/03/92, para 6.

[93] *Lopez Burgos v Uruguay*, HRC (1981) UN Doc Supp. No. 40 (A/36/40) at 176 (1981), paras 11.5–11.6.

[94] *Suárez-Rosero v Ecuador (Merits)*, Inter-American Court of Human Rights, Series C No 35 (12 November 1997) paras 48–52.

[95] International Committee of the Red Cross. (2007). Report on the treatment of 14 'high value detainees' in CIA Custody, 7–8. Retrieved March 22, 2023, from http://www.nybooks.com/media/doc/2010/04/22/icrc-report.pdf.

[96] *Caldas v Uruguay*, HRC (1979) Comm No 43/1979, para 14.

[97] *Aksoy v Turkey*, App no 21987/93 (ECtHR 26 November 1996) para 78.

[98] Human Rights Watch (HRW) (2004). Retrieved March 22, 2023, from http://www.hrw.org/en/reports/2004/10/12/united-states-disappeared-cias-long-term-ghost-detainees.

[99] *Mónaco v Argentina*, HRC (1995) UN Doc CCPR/C/53/D/400/1990, para 2.1, 10.4; *Loayza-Tamayo v Peru (Merits)*, Inter-American Court of Human Rights, Series C No 33 (17 September 1997) para 46(c), (e), (f).

likely to reappear, because states no longer look to exterminate them but only safeguard national security, courts must now be more cautious about presuming that disappeared persons are dead. Yet courts continue to hold this view, through lack information and to put pressure on states, meaning that disappearances can be dissociated from the right to life. Although it could be argued that a shift in international jurisprudence is coming into view,[100] it is rather premature to anticipate a general change since jurisprudence is only now evolving on the issue.

It is necessary to mention that in previous cases courts had been criticized for hesitating to link disappearances to the right to life.[101] Therefore, this development clearly shows that there is a wide range of enforced disappearances methods which require different treatment.

2.3.1.3 Extraordinary Renditions

Anti-terrorism measures have reasonably incited domestic criticism in the states that adopted them. Human rights NGOs and the mass media have stressed the legal contraventions they entailed and have further enumerated their inconsistencies both with domestic laws and international obligations. As a result, public opinion started opposing some of the adopted rules, despite the fact that terrorism remains on top of the agenda regarding national security and is still considered a potential danger. Therefore, governments have faced constant pressure to disclose information about the detention conditions of terrorist suspects, while their refusal to do so has exacerbated domestic reactions. Some states, in an attempt to evade accusations of human rights violations (at least regarding domestic legal standards), have turned to other methods. This was the critical point when extraordinary renditions became a commonly applied tool in the War on Terror, also affecting enforced disappearances.

'Extraordinary rendition' is neither a legal term[102] nor an entirely new one.[103] In regard to enforced disappearances, it has been helpfully suggested that extraordinary renditions have been used by governments since the 1970s. At that time, the intelligence services of several Latin American countries had created a network of information-sharing for alleged 'subversives/terrorists'. This network was also known as Operation Condor (Operación Condor).[104] However, it was a rather primitive form when compared to the methods that states developed after 9/11.

Extraordinary rendition is now used to describe the transfer of alleged terrorists from the country where they are apprehended to states with underdeveloped and

[100] *Jegatheeswara Sarma v Sri Lanka*, HRC (2003) UN Doc CCPR/C/78/D/950/2000, para 9.6.

[101] *See* Chapter 1, case *Kurt v. Turkey* and the ensuing ECtHR jurisprudence.

[102] Feitlowitz (1998), p. 71.

[103] Extraordinary rendition was initially synonymous with the 'Ker-Frisbie Doctrine', a modern version of the *male captus bene detendus* maxim. Michell (1996), pp. 389–390.

[104] *Goiburú and others v Paraguay*, Inter-American Court of Human Rights, Series C No 153 (22 September 2006).

poor human rights protection. In other words, it is a forcible transboundary movement,[105] a complex method which requires the cooperation of at least three countries: the captor, the accomplice and the extractor state.[106] The suspect is usually caught at the border or in an airport of one country (the accomplice state) by secret agents of another country (the captor state). The victim is then taken to a third country, where he is held in custody and interrogated (the extractor state). In most cases, the interrogation takes place in secret detention centers, over which the captor state's secret services exercise a significant degree of control.[107] Extraordinary renditions have not been standardized up until now, as there is no standard pattern to follow.[108] Despite several variations that have been recorded so far, there is, however, one common feature linking all such incidents: the element of extraterritoriality vis-à-vis the captor state. The suspects are apprehended, detained and interrogated abroad, but on behalf of the captor state; moreover, the victims are always foreign nationals.[109]

Captor states try to accomplish two goals through extraordinary renditions. First, and above all, they prefer increased harshness during interrogations to yield the maximum benefit on intelligence gathering grounds. However, constitutional and legal guarantees, in combination with effective enforcement mechanisms, almost prohibit the use of severe techniques in their own territory, as victims may ask for judicial protection. This explains the second goal, which is to fully deprive access to those transferred to their own judicial system where they can challenge their treatment during detention.[110] In other words, the captor state tries by all means to avoid domestic legislation and instead to create a 'legal *lacuna*'.[111]

The detainees' lives are in jeopardy, since extraordinary rendition reduces their legal protection to the bare-minimum, permitting grave human rights violations. Extraordinary renditions should undoubtedly be placed among practices intended to disappear individuals, as they are 'designed to evade public and judicial scrutiny, to hide the identity of the perpetrators and the fate of the victims'.[112] They also constitute 'a degrading and dehumanizing practice for the victims',[113] because victims are aware of their inability to reach both the outside world and also the judiciary. It is

---

[105] Fitzpatrick (2003), p. 461.

[106] Scovazzi and Citroni (2007), p. 43.

[107] Many commentators argue that transfers to and detentions of alleged terrorists at Guantánamo Bay should be characterized as extraordinary renditions. However, the case of Guantánamo is unique and as such it cannot be categorized. UN Doc E/CN.4/2006/120.

[108] UN Doc A/HRC/4/41, para 454; Mariner (2008), p. 6.

[109] Scovazzi and Citroni concisely refer to extraordinary renditions as 'from abroad to abroad'. Scovazzi and Citroni (2007), p. 42.

[110] Silva (2009), p. 317.

[111] Agamben (2005), pp. 3–4.

[112] Joint Hearing Before the Subcommittee on International Organizations, Human Rights, An Oversight and the Subcommittee on Europe of the Committee on Foreign Affairs House of Representatives, 110th Congress, 1st Session (2007), p. 4.

[113] CoE (2008), p. 45.

this inability that equates extraordinary renditions to enforced disappearances and differentiates them from mere international abductions.[114]

The UNWGEID came round to this view in 2004 and further mentioned that the practice constitutes a breach of the 1992 Declaration.[115] It also came across extraordinary renditions when examining the complaint of Maher Arar. This is one of the very few complaints to have gained publicity up to now, mainly due to efforts made by Canadian human rights NGOs and by the victim's wife.[116] The victim, a national of Canada, was detained in an American airport while returning from Tunisia.[117] He was then transferred to Syria to be interrogated on his alleged links with Al-Qaeda, and he was kept there for nearly a year. After his release, Arar brought his claims before the American courts, only to be rejected on jurisdictional grounds.[118] This is indicative of the juridical difficulties the practice faces. So far, national courts have rejected similar claims based either on lack of jurisdiction or on aspects of national security.[119] Apart from some exceptions,[120] domestic jurisprudence has generally arrived at unsatisfactory judgments for the victims.

2.3.1.4 Unacknowledged Administrative Detention

Administrative detention attracts great legal concern, because it tests the validity and adaptability of general concepts and principles of international law, such as the international rule of law, equality before courts, and effective judicial protection. The term does not appear in international legal instruments, but instead has emerged through state conduct as part of operational terminology.

Initially, administrative detention was generally a practice 'designed to encourage an individual to change or even renounce his opinions, using methods resembling coercion'.[121] In most cases, administrative detention concerned a regime of

---

[114] The CoE referred to the CIA Rendition Program as 'a spider web of disappearances'. PACE (2006), p. 607.

[115] UN Doc E/CN.4/2005/65, paras 13, 368.

[116] Honigsberg (2009), pp. 188–190.

[117] Joint Hearing Before the Subcommittee on International Organizations, Human Rights, An Oversight and the Subcommittee on Europe of the Committee on Foreign Affairs House of Representatives (2007) para 357.

[118] US Court of Appeals, *Maher Arar v Ashcroft et al.*, 532 F.3d 157 (2nd Cir.) decided 30 June 2008, paras 192–193.

[119] American Courts have dismissed most of these cases, relying upon the 'state secrets privilege'. US District Court for the Eastern District of Virginia, Alexandria Division, *El-Masri v Tenet et al.*, decided 12 May 2006. *See*, IACommHR, Report No 21/16 Petition 419/08 (Report on Admissibility, *Khaled El-Masri v US*) OEA/Ser.L/V/II.157 Doc 25 (15 April 2016).

[120] In November 2009, an Italian Court convicted *in absentia* 23 CIA agents for the extraordinary rendition of Abu Omar. Retrieved March 22, 2023, from http://www.spiegel.de/international/europe/0,1518,659418,00.html.

[121] UN Doc E/CN.4/1993/24 (12 January 1993) para 16.

supposedly temporary custody for immigrants and asylum seekers,[122] whilst in countries with totalitarian regimes it was a means to cleanse society of people who could threaten the regime's values.[123] Despite these references, administrative detention was completely redesigned after the 9/11 terrorist attacks and adapted to the discourse of terrorism. In this framework, the term comprised all methods and practices fabricated by states to treat terrorist suspects. Although terrorist attacks have declined since then, the rhetoric of terrorism[124] and the state practices it induces have been consolidated. In the post-9/11 security environment, administrative detentions of suspects remain a central element of many states' security policy, and therefore require a thorough legal analysis.

Preliminary remarks regarding the term would be that it is descriptive, self-contradictory and vague. More specifically, administrative detention is evidently descriptive, as it refers to detentions authorized by the executive instead of the judiciary, a feature which in turn foreshadows the administration's arbitrary prevalence over justice. Indeed, a person's detention as well as their conviction penalties fall *ratione materiae* within the judiciary's powers. Thereby, detentions ruled by the executive annul the rule of law and thus 'present serious problems as far as the administration of justice is concerned',[125] because judicial organs are prevented from controlling or delimiting the discretionary powers of the executive.[126] Clearly, the term is self-contradictory and on the verge of illegality, because it portrays the executive (administrative) as running contrary to the judiciary (detention). Apart from state organization breaches, the illegality of administrative detention rests on the fact that well-established civil and criminal procedures are waived, putting in jeopardy people's human rights.[127] The practices applied by a number of states worldwide illustrate the perils that administrative detentions entail with regard to human rights. It has been reported that detainees are held in custody without any

---

[122] UN Doc E/CN.4/1996/40 (15 December 1995) para 70.

[123] For example, in China the communist regime has enacted laws which authorize the police to detain prostitutes and their clients as well as drug addicts. These acts aim at the rehabilitation of the detained, and administrative detention is the means to make them useful to society. This act is still in force, even though China is progressing slowly towards democratization. Biddulph (2022), pp. 217–218.

[124] In several cases, states which suffered from terrorist attacks declared the so-called 'War on Terror'. This rhetoric generated a debate on whether terrorists are combatants and are thus protected under the Geneva Conventions. This article takes the view that terrorism, and the fight against it, does not meet the requirements of war, and consequently humanitarian law should not apply. For this reason, all observations are limited to human rights law. However, even if the opposing view is accepted, the application of humanitarian law alongside human rights law is by now a well-established principle of international law. Additionally, the relevant national jurisprudence contends that terrorism is 'extraordinary' and therefore exceeds classical legal fields. In this respect, national courts use bits and pieces of both humanitarian and human rights law when necessary. *Boumediene v Bush*, 553 US 723 (2008) 70.

[125] HRC. (13 April 1984). General Comment No. 13: Equality before the courts and the right to a fair and public hearing by an independent court established by law (Art. 14), para 4.9.

[126] Nowak (2005), p. 306.

[127] Radack (2005), p. 544.

charges pressed against them; they are deprived of their right to a fair trial; they are not provided with a counsel of their choice; and they are not permitted to contact their next of kin. Usually, administrative detentions include the above cumulatively.[128] In general, there are no standardized methods, and detainees are subject to any form of possible abuse by the state authorities. As a matter of fact, administrative detention covers a wide range of human rights violations, rendering the term's definition vague and obscure.

2.3.1.5 Terrorism and the 'Duty to Prevent'

In an attempt to circumscribe the term, a rudimentary definition of administrative detention could be the absence or insufficient application of minimum procedural standards during detention. This definition is precise because it points at certain provisions of international instruments which are violated when administrative detentions take place, and it also enables the legal identification of the term. Although administrative detention is not stipulated *per se* in any general human rights convention, the combined reading of Arts 9(3), 10(1) and 14(3)(c) of the ICCPR removes all doubt about its prohibition, as it provides that '[a]nyone [...] detained on a criminal charge [...] shall be treated with humanity [...] and entitled to a trial [...] without undue delay'.[129]

According to Art. 9(1) of the ICCPR, it follows that any form of administrative detention is arbitrary, given that procedural guarantees are eliminated and detainees cannot access justice.[130] States performing such practices have time and again admitted that their ultimate goal is to render terrorist suspects helpless, in order to preserve national security.[131] There arises a typical question: is there an acceptable degree of arbitrariness by reason of national security claims? And in particular, is there a legal justification for administrative detention? The first question brings forward the well-known debate regarding the balancing of the conflicting notions of security and liberty. With the rise of international terrorism, it has been widely accepted that national security outweighs civil liberties. According to the predominant view, in a supposed sliding scale of human rights, the majority's enjoyment of

---

[128] UN Doc A/HRC/10/21 (16 February 2009) para 54.

[129] Arts 9(3), 10(1), 14(3)(c) ICCPR. Both the ECHR and the IACHR contain similar provisions which guarantee detainees' protection, although the terminology differs. The relevant articles of the ECHR and the IACHR (Arts 6 and 8 respectively) refer to detainees' right to a fair trial, and they refrain from using the term 'due process', which is associated with common law systems. This terminology is preferable because it illustrates better detainees' inalienable right to access justice.

[130] HRC. (30 June 1982). General Comment No. 08: Right to liberty and security of persons (Art. 9), para 1.

[131] UN Doc E/CN.4/2006/7 (12 December 2005) para 57.

civil liberties justifies the sacrifice of suspects' rights;[132] however, there has been caution regarding the strengthening of governmental powers.[133]

Although the second question is less theoretical, it is far more disputed. In principle, human rights conventions outlaw administrative detentions, and, *prima facie*, there seems to be no legal underpinning for the practice. In this context, states have recourse mainly to two justifications. The most common reasoning involves invoking a state of emergency due to terrorist threats. After 9/11, the relevant international provision (Art. 4 ICCPR) has been blatantly misinterpreted and governments have authorized the 'suspension' of terrorists' human rights.[134] Indeed, state of emergency clauses have always been treated by states as loopholes for the curtailment of human rights, and they constitute the usual policy argument.

States' second line of argumentation has been more sophisticated, since it revolves exclusively around administrative detentions. States which resort to administrative detentions have genuinely supported the idea that this practice has a preventive purpose: it is a necessary precautionary measure taken in order to avert future terrorist attacks. To back up this argument, states have created the 'sleeper cell' theory, according to which members of terrorist organizations supposedly have trained to pretend to live an ordinary life.[135] Assuming this is the case, then terrorist 'sacs' are potentially everywhere, and therefore only administrative detentions can effectively tackle them.

This view distinguishes detaining from convicting, and consequently suspects' capture, interrogation, and detention became lawful as long as a terrorist act was about to be committed. Under the pretext of prevention, severe measures were taken worldwide, and even countries that were not facing an imminent terrorist threat pronounced laws according to which suspects could be detained for a two-year period without charges being pressing against them.[136] Detention was also possible if two or more people were suspected of having set up a group pertaining to terrorist activities.[137] Overall, the need for prevention served as the theoretical foundation of administrative detention, and soon preventive detention became a synonymous with it.

Moreover, this legal argument was heavily based on Art. 5(1)(c) of the ECHR, which permits detentions aimed at preventing someone from committing an offense in exceptional circumstances. Despite the regional application of the ECHR, this Art extended beyond its European scope and became an implicit point of reference for non-European governments, as it offered a proper legal justification for preventive detentions.[138] It is regrettable that the ECtHR has not treated this provision as an

[132] Dworkin (2002), Gross and Ní Aoláin (2006), p. 105.

[133] Waldron (2002), p. 210.

[134] Dickinson (2002), p. 1433.

[135] Cole (2002), pp. 963–964.

[136] Ziliang (2007), p. 30.

[137] Roth (2008), p. 10.

[138] Stahlberg and Lahmann (2011), pp. 1084–1086.

exception to the rule that no one shall be deprived of his liberty, and that its interpretation has not been restrictive. More specifically, it held that a state's 'investigating authorities [don't need to] have obtained sufficient evidence to bring charges at the point of arrest or while in custody' of a terrorist suspect,[139] given that terrorist crimes form a special category which tests authorities' 'utmost urgency'.[140] Due to the fact that the Court perceives terrorist activities as *sui generis* crimes, it sets a low evidentiary threshold for member-states, thus permitting detentions on almost no factual grounds. As a result, reasonable suspicion is sufficient for states in order to enforce administrative detention to prevent a terrorist act.[141] The executive has almost unlimited power to determine which behaviors pose a terrorist threat to national security.[142] This jurisprudence allows the executive to convert preventive detentions into a covert investigation method; in most cases the authorities purport to obtain information about terrorist networks. If the interrogation proves that the detainee cannot offer valuable information, he is released without charge and before coming to trial. If the authorities suspect that the detainee has strong bonds with a terrorist group and knowledge of that group, he is detained indefinitely. This means that the ECtHR does not identify preventive detention as a form of pre-trial detention, and consequently detention is detached from justice. In this respect, the Court's elastic reading of Art 5(1)(c) partly deviates from the regular standards of the ECHR.

Some authors have also supported the idea that the model of preventive detention exists outside the European legal order as well; it is compatible with, or at least tolerated by, the ICCPR provisions. In particular, it is contended that administrative detention is not explicitly precluded under Art. 9(1) of the Covenant,[143] which *a contrario* places the practice within the frame of legality.[144] However, the post-9/11 application of the practice contravenes the Covenant's specific requirements regarding detention and therefore this argument has little backing. The unprecedented elaboration of the term in relation to anti-terrorist policies has reshaped its meaning; current practices do not conform with international guarantees, even if a dynamic interpretation is applied.

To conclude, the reasoning behind prevention is not a solid legal underpinning for administrative detentions. The major flaw of the preventive detention doctrine is that it prioritizes the preventive functions of criminal justice, whereas criminal laws

139 *Fox, Campbell & Hartley v UK*, App Nos 12244/86, 12245/86, 12383/86 (ECtHR 30 August 1980) para 32.

140 *Murray v UK*, App No 14310/88 (ECtHR 28 October 1994) para 52.

141 *Tuncer & Durmuş v Turkey*, App No 30494/96 (ECtHR 2 November 2004) para 50; Ní Aoláin (2007), pp. 69–75.

142 The same rationale is echoed in the decision of *Al-Marri v Wright* of the fourth Circuit, where the Court affirmed the legality of Al-Marri's detention although there was no evidence of his attachment to terrorist activities. Nevertheless, his detention was deemed imperative so as 'to prevent any future acts of international terrorism against the United States'. *Al-Marri v Wright,* 487 F 3rd 160 (4th Cir 2007).

143 UN Doc E/CN.4/Sub.2/1990/29 (Louis Joinet) (24 July 1990).

144 Macken (2005), pp. 15–16.

are principally designed to address acts repressively.[145] In turn, if prevention is the primary goal of detention, the evidence required for a suspect's detention is diminished, taking into account that the suspect has not yet proceeded to commit material criminal acts. As a result, preventive detention punishes people's propensity to crime and not their crimes as such. Finally, preventive detention reduces the detainees' chances of accessing justice, given that in most cases there are no charges against them. Therefore, detainees are held at the absolute discretion of the executive authorities, since they have either remote or no access to justice. In this context, the potential for human rights violations rises sharply, as the detained are kept outside the protection of the law.[146]

2.3.1.6 Unacknowledged Detentions:[147] Male Detentus ad Infinitum

The separation of detention from trial increases the power of administrative authorities vis-à-vis the detainee and threatens the potential violation of human rights provisions. More specifically, United Nations reports indicate that administrative detentions almost always involve some form of secrecy, especially with regards to alleged terrorists.[148] According to the executive, secrecy is imperative with respect to terrorist suspects, as any leakage of information is to the detriment of national security. In this framework, secrecy has a threefold meaning, and it covers the information provided by the administration: (a) to the detainee concerning the reasons, place and duration of his detention; (b) to the detainee's relatives and counsel;[149] and (c) to anyone with a legitimate interest (authorized international agencies, human rights NGOs and other states' authorities, if the detainee is a foreign national) through the official records of the detained.[150] Evidently, each of these forms

---

145 Waxman (2009), p. 13.

146 Cole (2009), pp. 706–707.

147 The terms 'unacknowledged detention' and 'secret detention' are used interchangeably to denote the lack of information regarding detentions as part of governmental counter-terrorist policies. Yet they differ slightly: unacknowledged detentions are detentions officially denied by the authorities, whereas with secret detentions, the administrative might admit complicity but refuse to disclose any information regarding them. Moreover, unacknowledged detentions are mostly carried out by secret intelligence services, while secret detentions tend to be the responsibility of the military or the police.

148 UN Doc A/HRC/13/42 (26 January 2010) para 223.

149 In the first two cases, when neither the detainees nor their relatives receive sufficient information from the authorities and proper communication cannot be established between them, secret detention is by definition incommunicado. UN Doc A/HRC/16/47 (19 January 2011) para 54. Although incommunicado detention is a narrow term compared to secret detention (usually equated to solitary confinement), ranking them together is to the benefit of the detainee, given that international jurisprudence sets a high threshold regarding the former's violation. *Brannigan & McBride v UK*, App Nos 14553/89, 14554/89 (25 May 1993) para 62; *Aksoy v Turkey*, App No 21987/93 (ECtHR 18 December 1996) para 84.

150 Most often there are no official records attesting to the detention of terrorist suspects and, even if they do exist, the executive denies access to them and protects them as a state secret. Secrecy

constitutes by itself a violation of minimum due process guarantees, comprising secret detention.[151]

However, apart from procedural breaches, secrecy has substantial implications too. From a psychological perspective, lack of information in conjunction with lack of access to justice creates a state of anguish and insecurity both for detainees and their next of kin. In legal terms, psychological pressure is translated into vulnerability to interrogation and enforced civil obedience. More precisely, terrorist suspects are expected to reveal crucial information, whereas relatives are coerced to give up any attempt to challenge the detention.[152] Hence, numerous states have characterized secret detentions as legitimate 'enhanced interrogation techniques' practiced by intelligence agencies against suspects who have been trained not to disclose information or to confess to committing terrorist acts.[153] Furthermore, secrecy has a direct effect on detentions' temporal features. By keeping detentions unacknowledged, the executive has the perfect shield to prolong their duration; as a matter of fact, detainees may be in custody indefinitely, especially when there is no indictment. Therefore, secret detention is considered a means to circumvent 'the legal time limits governing police custody and pre-trial detention [and] the requirement to show reasonable suspicion for […] detention'.[154]

Obviously, secrecy exacerbates the dangers posed to detained terrorist suspects, and contributes to the perpetuation of human rights violations. Despite the perils of secrecy, secret detentions have not been directly addressed until recently, even though, according to international legal documents[155] and jurisprudence,[156] they fall within the concept of arbitrary detention, thus violating the right to personal liberty. However, the CPED introduced a clear prohibition of secret detentions in Art. 17(1), according to which '[n]o one shall be held in secret detention'.[157] Within the

over official documentation extends to the detention's judicial review as well, constituting an insurmountable evidentiary obstacle for the detainee. In addition, excessive classification of documents as secret renders detainees' attempts to reach justice futile. The so-called 'state secret privilege' is a rather popular doctrine in numerous national legal orders, partly accepted by international tribunals too. *Kerimova et al v Russia*, App Nos 17170/04, 20792/04, 22448/04, 23360/04, 5681/05 & 5685/05 (ECtHR 15 September 2011) para 202; *Ameziane v Obama*, 620 F 3rd 1 (DC Cir 2010).

151 Rodley (2005), p. 331.

152 Often, when the authorities seek to intimidate the suspect's relatives, they capture him/her in their presence and make use of intense violence, thus creating 'life-threatening situations'. *Imakayeva v Russia*, App No 7615/02 (ECtHR 9 November 2006) para 141.

153 UN Doc A/HRC/10/3 (4 February 2009) para 43.

154 UN Doc E/CN.4/2005/6 (1 December 2004) paras 61, 63.

155 UN Doc A/HRC/16/47 (n 140) paras 54–55; Inter-American Commission on Human Rights (IACommHR), 'Principles and Best Practices on the Protection of Persons Deprived of Liberty in the Americas' Res 1/08 (13 March 2008) Principle III.

156 *Luluyev et al v Russia*, App No 69480/01 (ECtHR 9 November 2006); *Cyprus v Turkey*, App No 25781/94 (ECtHR 10 May 2001) para 147. See also the applicant's allegations in the case *Al-Nashiri v Romania*, where the legality of secret CIA detention facilities in Romania was challenged. *Al-Nashiri v Romania*, App No 33234/12 (31 May 2018).

157 UN Doc A/61/488 (entry into force 23 December 2010).

Convention's regime, the prohibition of secret detention is a sub-right of the prohibition of enforced disappearance (Art. 1). Still, it is a distinct right which receives special legal protection. More specifically, secret detention is perceived as illegitimate deprivation of liberty which is very likely to incur enforced disappearance.[158] In other words, secret detention presents a great danger to the detainee, as it might efface traces of their existence.[159]

The causal relationship between secret detention and enforced disappearance is the reason why the former is stipulated *per se* in the Convention. The absolute prohibition of secret detention is a means to prevent or reduce the spread of enforced disappearance.[160] To ensure compliance with this prohibition, Arts. 17(2) and (3) of the Convention oblige member-states *inter alia* to: (a) ensure that deprivation of liberty does not occur under life-threatening situations; (b) transfer the captured to supervised detention facilities; (c) allow the establishment of communication between detainees and their relatives, counsel or other authorized persons; (d) permit visits; (e) set effective judicial remedies; and (f) provide up-to-date records of the detained, accessible to anyone with a legitimate interest. These requirements comprise a safety net for detainees and, according to the Convention's wording, they should all be met during any detention. Apparently, the Convention formulates a coherent and integrated legal framework for the protection of detainees, which covers all stages of a detention, from arrest to judicial review.

There are three conclusions that can be drawn from this provision. First, detainees' classifications are rejected under the Convention. Terrorist suspects do not form a special category of detainees, determined by the threats they pose to national security.[161] Hence, the theory of 'high value detainees' who deserve to be secretly detained is incompatible with the Convention, which outlaws secret detention completely ('no one shall'). Second, the above set of guarantees gives a very broad meaning to the concept of secret detention. The violation of a single guarantee suffices to establish secret detention. Therefore, even detainees who are in known detention centers are deemed secretly detained if they are prevented from communicating with the outside world. This wide definition of secret detention broadens the relevant field of protection too. For example, Guantánamo detainees can potentially be regarded as secret detainees, as they cannot contact (at least regularly) their next of kin. That is, according to the Convention the term is not restricted to secret detention facilities or unacknowledged detentions.[162] Although this interpretation of secret detention seems over-expansive at first sight, it is consistent with regards to

[158] UN Doc A/HRC/16/47, para 54.

[159] UN Doc E/CN.4/2002/71, para 74.

[160] Ibid, para 83.

[161] UN Doc E/CN.4/2004/3 (15 December 2003) paras 53, 82.

[162] This view has gained little ground so far, especially with regards to Guantánamo detainees. OAS. (22 July 2011). Regarding the situation of the detainees at Guantánamo Bay, United States. Res No 2/11 MC 259-02; UN Doc E/CN.4/2006/98 (28 December 2005) para 23. Only the CoE seems to endorse it by referring to the 'secret detainees of Guantánamo'. CoE. (8 April 2005). Lawfulness of detentions by the United States in Guantánamo Bay. Doc 10497, para 64.

the subject matter of protection, i.e. the detainee. The main purpose of secret detention practices is to efface the traces of detainees, with the view either to exterminating them or isolating them from other criminal suspects. As a matter of fact, this interpretation aims exactly at preventing these effects: the Convention places the detainee at the epicenter of its protection and adopts a human-centric approach instead of a location-based one. Finally, the third conclusion concerns the relationship between secret and administrative detention. Within the Convention's regime, administrative detention is a notion subsumed under secret detention (Art. 17(2)(f)). This view, though, is not fixed amongst the relevant UN bodies and there are significant discrepancies between their reports.[163] Although administrative and secret detention may overlap (if broadly interpreted), they remain distinct concepts, and they can be implemented simultaneously. The UN Joint Report on secret detention in the context of countering terrorism better demonstrates this point and reconciles these concepts, as it mentions that

> [o]n a global scale, secret detention in connection with counter-terrorist policies remains a serious problem, either through the use of secret detention facilities [...] through declaration of a state of emergency, which allow prolonged secreted detention; or through forms of 'administrative detention', which also allow prolonged secret detention.[164]

This excerpt shows how multiple violations of due process guarantees can take place concurrently: terrorist suspects can be detained for a long time, secretly and without access to justice.[165] This triple violation permanently isolates the prisoner from the outside world, effaces the rule of law, and, finally, results in the detainee's victimization.[166] It is also heinous, and the question to be answered is whether it amounts to enforced disappearance.

2.3.1.7 Secret Administrative Detentions

The risks for detainees who remain in custody without access either to judicial remedies or to their next of kin go far beyond the concept of arbitrariness, as the detainee is isolated from any legal order and from the real world. This double jeopardy came to the forefront mostly with regards to terrorist suspects who were held indefinitely under such conditions.[167] Hitherto, all attempts to analyze the impact of these parallel and mounting violations of detainees' human rights focused primarily on decoding the different forms of a detention's illegality and not on the overall impact on the detainees' legal protection. However, the application of the Convention on

[163] For example, the perspectives of the UN Working Group on Arbitrary Detention and that on Enforced or Involuntary Disappearances diverge. However, their different approaches stem from their dissimilar mandates.

[164] UN Doc A/HRC/13/42, para 165.

[165] Cole (2003), pp. 293–294.

[166] Pervou (2012), pp. 165–166.

[167] CoE, (1st Report Marty) (2008) p. 20; Paust (2004), pp. 1340–1349.

Disappearance provides an all-embracing approach which provides that according to Art. 2 a secret and administrative detention constitutes an enforced disappearance.

More specifically, under the Convention an enforced disappearance occurs when a person is deprived of their liberty by state authorities or by persons or groups who somehow are attached to the state, and who subsequently refuse to disclose information about the person's whereabouts. The definition consists of three major material elements: (a) deprivation of liberty, (b) state complicity, and (c) subsequent concealment of one's fate or whereabouts. The combination of these elements ends up placing the disappeared outside the protection of the law. Clearly, a secret and administrative detention meets the definition's requirements since it is (a) a detention, (b) attributable to state authorities, (c) involves some kind of secrecy, as the pertinent authorities will either deny the detention or interfere with and control the flow of information regarding it. Moreover, the state intends to place the detainee outside the protection of the law. In other words, detainees' inability to access justice is an element of policy, formally proclaimed by states, and not merely a result of the disappearance.[168]

By equating the status of disappeared persons to detainees, their protection is enhanced in three different ways. First, an enforced disappearance denotes an excessive form of violation of human rights; more specifically it implies the use of torture, or at least cruel, inhuman or degrading treatment. Thereby, a secret administrative detention is connected to substantial violations of various human rights, and it is not only a breach of due process guarantees. Second, the concept of enforced disappearance extends protection to the relatives of the victim who cannot properly reach them. If we read between the lines of the Convention's definition, the effacement of the traces does not only affect the disappeared but also his/her next of kin, usually generating fear or anguish. For this reason, the relatives of the disappeared are entitled to reparation for the harm they have suffered because of the disappearance (Art. 24). Finally, the characterization of a secret, administrative detention as an enforced disappearance raises the threshold of protection, given that the right not to be subjected to enforced disappearance is non-derogable[169] and is a peremptory norm of international law.[170] Furthermore, this characterization is of particular significance to terrorist suspects, since the prohibition of enforced

---

[168] Superior state authorities and agents deliberately intend to place detainees outside the protection of the law and to wipe out their traces; consequently, both the objective (*actus reus*) and the subjective *(mens rea)* elements of the crime of enforced disappearance are met, and therefore it should constitute an offense according to the domestic criminal law of member-states to the Convention (Art. 4). Even if the crime of enforced disappearance is not stipulated *per se* in domestic penal codes, state authorities should bear criminal liability for prolonged detention, the creation of life-threatening situations and denial of access to justice. Scovazzi and Citroni (2007), pp. 297–298.

[169] UN Doc CCPR/C/21/Rev.1/Add.11 (31 August 2001) para 13(b), p 8.

[170] *Goiburú et al v Paraguay*, Inter-American Court of Human Rights (IACtHR) Series C No 153 (22 September 2006) para 84.

disappearance constitutes customary law.[171] That is, even states which have not ratified the Convention are customarily bound not to practice disappearances. In this respect, it is argued that no state (not even the United States)[172] can detain and effectively disappear terrorist suspects for the sake of national security. As a result, this reading of secret administrative detentions increases the prospect of vindication and relief for detained terrorist suspects in international fora.

> [A]merican agents seized me and the five others. We were tied up like animals and flown to Guantánamo, the American naval base in Cuba. I arrived on Jan. 20, 2002. I still had faith in American justice. I believed my captors would quickly realize their mistake and let me go. But when I would not give the interrogators the answers they wanted – how could I, when I had done nothing wrong? – they became more and more brutal. I was kept awake for many days straight. I was forced to remain in painful positions for hours at a time. These are things I do not want to write about; I want only to forget [...] I was held there without explanation or charge. During that time my daughters grew up without me. They were toddlers when I was imprisoned, and were never allowed to visit or speak to me by phone.[173]

This testimony shows manifestly that this governmental method exceeds the limits of the usual meaning of arbitrariness. That is, the accumulation of flagrant human rights violations comprises a complex offence which could not have fit the settled and well-founded legal norms until recently. Due to its complexity, this method (detainees who are denied access to justice and cannot properly contact their family and counsel) came under the legal terms of administrative detention and secret detention. However, it is legal rules that should conform to facts and not vice versa, since rules are human constructs which must reflect accurately the truthfulness of facts. In other words, law is just a medium between facts and validity claims.[174]

This coupling of material facts and legal norms can only be achieved through the Convention on Enforced Disappearance. Its legal value lies mainly in two features. First, it offers a broad definition which can capture complex human rights offences. Its primary significance, though, is that it establishes an absolute prohibition of enforced disappearance and of similar practices. Therefore, the emergence of this legal framework corresponds to modern state practices. More specifically, taking into account that international law-making is a response to international phenomena,[175] the Convention sensibly takes a counter-terrorist perspective, as it was drafted and negotiated when global terrorism was on the rise. In the absence of a special legal framework on the rights of prisoners (and detained terrorist suspects), the Convention supplements the general human rights instruments and offers an intrinsic view of the practices of administrative and secret detention. It indicates that these are not merely violations of the procedural rules that govern detention, but

---

[171] Paust (2004), pp. 1352–1353.

[172] *Idem.*

[173] Boumediene, L. (7 January 2012). My Guantánamo Nightmare. *The New York Times*. Retrieved March 22, 2023, from http://www.nytimes.com/2012/01/08/opinion/sunday/my-guantanamo-nightmare.html.

[174] Habermas (1997), p. 8.

[175] Boyle and Chinkin (2007), pp. 3–6.

instead form substantial violations which entail high risks for detainees' right to life and the prohibition of torture.

2.3.1.8 The Convention's Application in Incommunicado Detentions and Extraordinary Renditions

I have already alluded to the fact that states tried to limit their human rights obligations by derogating from major international instruments on grounds of public emergency.[176] Such derogations affected mostly the right to liberty and the due process guarantees attached to it. As noted above, they were enforced by laws which permitted prolonged incommunicado detentions and unlawful renditions.[177] At this point, the 2007 Convention may prove to be a useful tool for enhancing victims' protection.

Characterizing the discussed methods as enforced disappearances has at least two obvious advantages. First of all, their complex nature will be acknowledged. It is a more realistic and systematic approach which affirms the danger for the victims, since they cannot inform anyone of their current status and seek help. Second, under the 2007 Convention the right not to be subjected to enforced disappearance is non-derogable. Art. 1(2) of the Convention contains an absolute prohibition on enforced disappearances, precluding derogations under any possible justification. Prolonged incommunicado detentions and extraordinary renditions will therefore be utterly outlawed since the Convention leaves no space for a gray area in this field. Although human rights commentators link these two practices to enforced disappearances in general, they have not examined them under the Convention's framework, although the latter provides a straightforward and sound response to the current international concerns.

2.3.2 Widespread and Systematic Practice of Enforced Disappearances

One of the aspects which have received least attention by the international community relates to the widespread or systematic practice of enforced disappearance which may well constitute a crime against humanity. According to CPED's Art. 5

---

[176] States made use of Arts. 4(1) of the ICCPR, 27(1) of the ACHR and ECHR 15(1).

[177] However, after a careful reading of the applicable international law, the validity of these derogations may be challenged. UN Doc E/CN.4/2005/6, para 76; OEA.Ser.L./V/II.116, Doc.5 rev.1 corr., 2002, para 24; UN Doc CCPR/C/21/Rev.1/Add.11, para 13(a), (b).

> the widespread or systematic practice of enforced disappearance constitutes a crime against humanity as defined in applicable international law and shall attract the consequences provided for under such applicable international law",[178]

while according to Art. 7(1)(i) of the ICC statute enforced disappearances are stipulated as a crime against humanity.

The provision of Art. 5 carries an inherent conundrum; that is, which are the features that transform disappearance from a human rights violation to a crime against humanity. Disappearances require by definition state complicity and the practice's complexity requires the involvement of state agents throughout every phase. As such, disappearances are almost always the result of deliberate state practice, even when they arise as side-effect of another practice.[179] The involvement of multiple state authorities means that disappearance do not take place accidentally, rather they are predesigned. In these terms, the perpetration in its archetypical form was by definition widespread and systematic.[180]

Enforced disappearances in Latin America satisfied both elements a crime against humanity requires. Nevertheless, they were treated as human rights violations. This observation points to the general deficit of the international legal regime regarding the available, or proper, *fora* to adjudicate cases in which a claim for a crime against humanity exists. On the other hand, the most important issue is that the accumulation of innumerous individual appeals allowed the regional court to reach the conclusion that disappearances were performed systematically and widespread by respondent states. Yet again, the positive affirmation of such state conduct did not alter the Inter-American Court's approach which focused on the human rights aspect of the practice and did not speak of crimes against humanity.

The very same observation applies to the European plane as well. The ECtHR has confronted disappearances as a repetitive human rights violation in particular regions. They were performed in southeastern Turkey against Kurds, or in Caucasus as a state policy to eliminate Chechen opposition. It has not been a practice embraced by most member-states of the Council of Europe. To the contrary, it was applied by particular states aiming at the obliteration of certain groups of people. In this respect, these examples of enforced disappearances that came to Strasbourg's attention were also systematic and widespread. Yet again, the ECtHR avoided speaking of crimes against humanity, while it did not identify a particular pattern early enough.

These examples are illuminating and demonstrate that human rights courts are naturally oriented to examine the existence of human rights violations, and with regards to disappearances, that it takes multiple individual complaints for judicial bodies to identify and establish a pattern.[181] In this sense, it is almost unlikely to verify that a state's practice constitutes a crime against humanity, even if the features of a systematic and widespread practice are proven.

---

[178] Article 5, CPED, UNTS vol. 2716, 3, Doc. A/61/448.

[179] Roberts (2017), p. 10.

[180] Olivera (2019), pp. 144–155.

[181] Grossman (2020), p. 229.

2.3.2.1 Redefining the "Widespread" and "Systematic" Elements

This shortcoming is definitely not the fault of regional human rights courts, as it pertains to the definition of crimes against humanity *per se*. Legal scholars have so far expressed multiple opinions on the notions of "systematic" and "widespread" practice.[182] The predominant view among international criminal lawyers is that the two prerequisites do not have a quantitative character.[183] As such, a widespread and systematic practice is not necessarily repetitious, nor it involves a large number of victims. Crimes against humanity may target a small group of people, or even a single person. In this sense, the two features refer only to state strategy and the intentional commitment of acts which constitute international crimes.[184]

If this interpretation is to be adopted, then archetypical disappearances in Latin America during Cold War qualify as crimes against humanity, and the same applies in cases of disappearances against Kurds and Chechens. All in all, this view is subtly disapproved and international attestations of crimes against humanity cannot be fully dissociated from quantitative criteria. Although this does not form a solid line of argumentation, as it contravenes international theory, nonetheless it reflects current legal practice. After all, for an international crime to threaten the existence of international community strong disapproval and condemnation is needed.[185] In most cases the latter are identical with a crime's magnitude and the number of victims.

2.3.2.2 Massive Disappearances and the Concept of Massacre

Regional courts' jurisprudence cannot offer a definitive solution on the point which the widespread and systematic practice of disappearances qualifies for a crime against humanity. However, their contribution is of great value for massive disappearances during hostilities. There are few cases examined before the IACtHR and ECtHR on this subject. For this reason, the dialogue between the two bodies is not that vivid when massive disappearances are at stake.[186]

An in depth elaboration of this topic includes three aspects: (a) which disappearance incidents qualify as massive, (b) whether the conduct of hostilities transforms the conduct of disappearances and (c) how such incidents can effectively be addressed by juridical human rights bodies.

The term "massive disappearances" does not appear in international legal documents and has mostly a descriptive value. In this sense, it depicts single incidents which resulted in the simultaneous disappearance of many victims. As far as hostilities are concerned, the term is broad incorporates any kind of intrastate or interstate

[182] Kuschnik (2010), p. 519.

[183] Luban (2004), p. 97.

[184] Bassiouni (2011), p. 31.

[185] Moir (2006), p. 103.

[186] Claude (2010), pp. 407–462.

conflict which involves two or more parties. As such, hostilities pertain to the entire set of humanitarian law rules. Thereat, massive disappearances during hostilities apply to any kind of conflict.[187]

The final aspect reveals the discord between the IACtHR and the ECtHR on massive disappearances. The IACtHR has put forward the concept of "massacre" to explain massive disappearances which resulted in most cases in extra-judicial executions. Although this term does not carry a legal value, it accurately explains the concept of massive disappearance during hostilities, allowing the IACtHR to adjust the penalties respectively. More specifically, the Inter-American jurisprudence encountered several incidents with dozens and hundreds of victims disappeared at once. Technically these incidents do not form disappearances, and they would be better conceived as massive extrajudicial executions.

Yet, they took place as part of systematic and widespread strategies of enforced disappearances and the conducting states concealed the victims' fate, as they refused to reveal any information regarding their whereabouts and did not take responsibility over their deaths. What is more, massacres formed part of general state practices deployed by authoritarian regimes aiming at annihilating opposition, or diminishing groups of people which they considered inferior.[188] For example, there are cases where massacres targeted rural populations which were considered perilous to their core principles and values for building a superior society.[189]

Recourse to the term "massacre" has proven a brilliant juridical choice as it avails all difficulties to legally encapsulate such incidents. Massive disappearances (or extra-judicial executions) driven by racial, political or other similar motives may well establish genocidal claims,[190] or generally claims for crimes against humanity. However, the time and context of adjudication did not allow the IACtHR to investigate whether the *mens rea* of these crimes was fulfilled.[191] First, the IACtHR is not vested with the power to initiate criminal proceedings and thus delve into the subjective part of international crimes. Second and most important, these incidents were significantly fewer than individual disappearances claims and it was hard for the Court to speak of a pattern. Massacre explains plainly what the claim is about without complex legal reasoning that would have to balance between human rights violations and crimes against humanity, or demarcate enforced disappearances from genocide and extrajudicial executions.

On the contrary, the ECtHR has rejected this rationale when it dealt with massive disappearances in the context of hostilities.[192] The most profound case before the ECtHR is *Cyprus v. Turkey*. This intrastate application is about the Turkish invasion in the northern part of Cyprus. The European Court could not speak of a massacre

---

[187] Alston and Goodman (2013), p. 699.

[188] Grandin (2011).

[189] *Plan de Sánchez Massacre v Guatemala*, para 51.

[190] Molina Mejia (2010), p. 226.

[191] Medawatte (2017), pp. 227–252.

[192] Barrett (2009), pp. 133–144.

as the international community had already referred to the unaccounted victims of the Turkish invasion as "missing persons". More specifically, soon after the invasion took place the UN General Assembly voted in 1974 for a resolution entitled "Assistance and co-operation in accounting for persons who are missing or dead in armed conflicts",[193] which exposed a legal gap in the 1949 Geneva Conventions that did not contain any provision for people who remained unaccounted for after the termination of an armed conflict. The term "missing persons" prevailed for the unaccounted victims of the Turkish invasion. Although there is no substantial difference between missing and disappearance persons, for some years the former was preferred when referring to unaccounted victims in the context of armed conflicts.

At this point, both Courts take the stance that the victims of massive atrocities during hostilities are to be considered disappeared, even if there is strong evidence that the victims were extrajudicially executed, or if their death is presumed.[194] This perspective is advantageous for two reasons: first, it takes into account that during hostilities the archetypical form of disappearances cannot easily take place. The conflicting parties aim at their strategic and military privilege over their opponent and do not benefit from enforced disappearances as they occurred once in Latin America. Second, the practice of disappearances offers better protection to the victims' next of kin, since the crime is continuous and because it is adjudicated that it creates great anxiety and anguish to the families of the disappeared. These elements are neglected if the victims were simply considered "dead people" (after extrajudicial executions).

2.3.2.3 The Intercontinental Dialogue Regarding Massive Disappearances

Intercontinental dialogue over enforced disappearances is vivid in judicial terms. The two regional bodies engage in a fruitful debate over the phenomenon's treatment. However, historical and geographical proximity of the IACtHR to regimes which rendered disappearances their state strategy gives the Court a clear lead in the relative jurisprudence. On the other hand, the ECtHR seems to gradually comprehend the phenomenon, the constitutive elements of the prohibition and the crime's multiple facets.

With regards to incidents of massive disappearances during atrocities, jurisprudence is limited. The Inter-American Court has adopted a rather radical stance by employing the term "massacre". The term's extralegal character allows the Court to sidestep legal barriers regarding the incidents' characterization and ensuing legal implications. This is not the first time the IACtHR builds its jurisprudence on functional definitions. The same path was followed with the definition of enforced disappearances: the Inter-American Court was primarily based on the functional/working definition provided by non-governmental organizations created by the victims'

---

[193] UNGA Res 3220 (XXIX) (6 November 1974).

[194] Ali Haydar (2022), p. 834.

families. The ECtHR tends to refer to missing persons when disappearances occur in the context of atrocities. This term makes no significance compared to “disappeared” as that they both depict people unaccounted for. Both human rights bodies are reluctant to make direct reference to crimes against humanity and legal bewilderment is definite at this point. This puzzle has rendered CPED’s Art. 5 a provision with of no particular use and gives further rise to queries as to the cases that disappearances are not part of a widespread and systematic state practice.

Overall, this dialogue is so far a privilege for both regional legal orders. It is high time the two Courts pay extra attention to disappearance claims arising during hostilities. The parallel application of human rights and humanitarian law norms is not a novelty, although it is not yet been elaborated regarding enforced disappearance.

2.3.3 Enforced Disappearances and the Refugee Crisis

During the last few years, there is an ever growing trend towards the association of state practices related to high migratory flows with the practice of enforced disappearances. More specifically, many international actors point to the established fact that many migrants who chose unsafe roots to pass international borders end up unaccounted for.[195] In this sense, the practice of pushbacks established by many states, accepting large migratory flows[196] are said to constitute a modern, or covert, form of enforced disappearance.

This view is also shared by the Committee on Enforced Disappearances (CED), on the occasion of its country report for Greece. CED highlights the increased risk migrants and asylum seekers take in their attempt to enter the Greek soil, and thus European territory, in its concluding observations on the report submitted by Greece under its obligation as a CPED member-state. The Committee mentions in particular that it

> is concerned about the reportedly high number of migrants who have disappeared in Greek waters of the Mediterranean Sea and the Evros River while attempting to reach Greece, and it regrets not having received official statistical information thereon [and] urges the State party to ensure that the principle of nonrefoulement enshrined in article 16 (1) of the Convention is strictly respected in all cases and recommends that the State party: (a) Refrain from carrying out pushbacks and collectively expelling migrants and ensure that all allegations of such practices are duly.[197]

---

[195] Migration Data Portal (last updated 14 June 2022). Migrant deaths and disappearances. Retrieved March 22, 2023, from https://www.migrationdataportal.org/themes/migrant-deaths-and-disappearances#:~:text=Since%202014%2C%20more%20than%204%2C000,deaths%20have%20been%20recorded%20globally.

[196] Manfredi (2014), pp. 44–52, 45–46.

[197] Committee on Enforced Disappearances (12 April 2022). Concluding observations on the report submitted by Greece under article 29, paragraph 1, of the Convention. UN Doc CED/C/GRC/CO/1, paras 26–29.

CED's reference to Greece's pushbacks makes an association between the practice and the prohibition of disappearances, further suggesting that this state practice is perilous to a series of human rights and does not relate to the international refugee regime alone.

As far as the disappearance of migrants and asylum seekers is concerned, the Committee's report offers a dynamic interpretation of disappearances, given that the detention, abduction, or other similar acts, coupled with the concealment of their whereabouts, eventually leading to losing track of their whereabouts. In the case of pushbacks, state agents force migrants back over their borders, thus rendering them vulnerable to transnational criminal networks. A grammatical interpretation of the prohibition would not allow for pushbacks to be considered a practice leading to the victims' disappearance and most importantly there is no concealment of the victims' whereabouts on behalf of the state.[198] This requirement is fulfilled only if one equates the absence of effective investigation, or databases containing information which would allow migrants' relatives to locate them. Yet again, this approach contains a leap of logic as states embracing the practice of pushbacks cannot possibly hold record of missing migrants and asylum seekers. In this scheme, it could be argued that the Committee moves to a doctrinally inconsistent interpretation of the prohibition. However, even if one concedes that this approach brings up normative and legal queries, then again CED's report underlines that pushbacks increase the number of missing migrants and make their finding a complex puzzle.

Jurisprudence

ICJ

Military and Paramilitary Activities in and against Nicaragua (Nicaragua v USA) [1986] ICJ Rep 1986.

ICTY

Prosecutor v Tadić, Decision on the Prosecutor's motion requesting Protective Measures for victims and witnesses (1995) (ICTY Tr.Ch.).

[198] Azarova et al. (2022), p. 153.

IACtHR

Bámaca-Velásquez v Guatemala (Merits), Inter-American Court of Human Rights, Series C No 70 (25 November 2000).
Cantoral-Benavides v Peru (Merits), Inter-American Court of Human Rights Series C No 69 (18 August 2000).
Castillo-Páez v Peru (Merits), Inter-American Court of Human Rights Series C No 34 (3 November 1997).
Gangaram-Panday v Suriname (Merits, Reparations and Costs), Inter-American Court of Human Rights Series C No16 (21 January 1994).
Goiburú et al v Paraguay, Inter-American Court of Human Rights (IACtHR) Series C No 153 (22 September 2006).
Loayza-Tamayo v Peru (Merits), Inter-American Court of Human Rights, Series C No 33 (17 September 1997).
Masacre de Pueblo Bello v Colombia, Inter-American Court of Human Rights, Series C No 140 (31 January 2006).
Neira-Alegría et al. v Peru (Merits), Inter-American Court of Human Rights Series C No 20 (19 January 1995).
Suárez-Rosero v Ecuador (Merits), Inter-American Court of Human Rights, Series C No 35 (12 November 1997).
The 19 Tradesmen v Guatemala (Merits Reparations and Costs), Inter-American Court of Human Rights, Series C No 108 (5 July 2004).

ECtHR

Akdeniz and others v Turkey, App no 25165/94 (ECtHR 31 May 2001).
Aksoy v Turkey, App No 21987/93 (ECtHR 18 December 1996).
Al-Nashiri v Romania, App No 33234/12 (31 May 2018).
Bazorkina v Russia, App no 69481/01 (ECtHR 27 June 2006).
Brannigan & McBride v UK, App Nos 14553/89, 14554/89 (25 May 1993).
Cyprus v Turkey, App No 25781/94 (ECtHR 10 May 2001).
Fox, Campbell & Hartley v UK, App Nos 12244/86, 12245/86, 12383/86 (ECtHR 30 August 1980).
Imakayeva v Russia, App No 7615/02 (ECtHR 9 November 2006).
Kerimova et al v Russia, App Nos 17170/04, 20792/04, 22448/04, 23360/04, 5681/05 & 5685/05 (ECtHR 15 September 2011).
Luluyev et al v Russia, App No 69480/01 (ECtHR 9 November 2006).
Murray v UK, App No 14310/88 (ECtHR 28 October 1994).
Orhan v Turkey, App no 25656/94 (ECtHR 18 June 2002).
Tekdag v Turkey, App no 27699/95 (ECtHR 15 January 2004).
Tuncer & Durmuş v Turkey, App No 30494/96 (ECtHR 2 November 2004).

American Courts

Al-Marri v Wright, 487 F 3rd 160 (4th Cir 2007).
Ameziane v Obama, 620 F 3rd 1 (DC Cir 2010).
Boumediene v Bush, 553 US 723 (2008) 70.
US Court of Appeals, Maher Arar v Ashcroft et al., 532 F.3d 157 (2nd Cir.) decided 30 June 2008.
US District Court for the Eastern District of Virginia, Alexandria Division, El-Masri v Tenet et al., decided 12 May 2006.

International Treaties

Vienna Convention on the Law of the Treaties (VCLT), Vienna 23 May 1969, entered into force 27 January 1980, UNTS 1155.
CPED, UNTS vol. 2716, 3, Doc. A/61/448.

National Legislation

Australian Criminal Code Amendment (Terrorism) Bill. (2002). act no 40, 2003.
British Anti-Terrorism, Crime and Security Act. (2001) c.24.
Canadian Anti-Terrorism Act. (2001). Bill C-36'.
Indian Prevention of Terrorism Act (POTA). (2002). act no 15.
Uniting and Strengthening America by Providing Appropriate Tools Required to Intercept and Obstruct Terrorism (USA Patriot Act). (2001). Public Law.

UN Documentation

UNGA

UN Doc A/HRC/16/47 (19 January 2011).
UN Doc A/HRC/13/42 (26 January 2010).
UN Doc A/HRC/10/21 (16 February 2009).
UN Doc A/HRC/10/3 (4 February 2009).
UNGA Res 47/133 (1992).
A/Res/43/173(1988).
UNGA Res 3220 (XXIX) (6 November 1974).
UN Doc A/61/PV.82, 2.
UN Doc A/HRC/16/47.

UN Doc A/HRC/13/42.
UN Doc A/HRC/4/41.
UN Doc A/61/488 (entry into force 23 December 2010).

ECOSOC

UN Doc E/CN.4/2006/120.
UN Doc E/CN.4/2006/98 (28 December 2005).
UN Doc E/CN.4/2006/57.
UN Doc E/CN.4/2006/7 (12 December 2005).
UN Doc E/CN.4/2005/66.
UN Doc E/CN.4/2005/65.
UN Doc E/CN.4/2005/6 (1 December 2004).
UN Doc E/CN.4/2004/59.
UN Doc E/CN.4/2004/3 (15 December 2003).
UN Doc E/CN.4/2003/71.
UN Doc E/CN.4/2003/70.
UN Doc E/CN.4/2002/79.
UN Doc E/CN.4/2002/71.
UN Doc. E/CN.4/1999/62.
UN Doc E/CN.4/1996/40 (15 December 1995).
UN Doc E/CN.4/1996/38.
UN Doc E/CN.4/1993/24 (12 January 1993).
UN Doc E/CN.4/Sub.2/1990/29 (Louis Joinet) (24 July 1990).
UN Doc. E/CN.4/1985/15.
UN Doc E/CN.4/1984/21.
UN Doc. E/CN.4/1434 (1981).
UN Docs E/3048(1957).

HRC

HRC. (10 January 2008). Promotion and protection of all human rights, civil, political, economic, social and cultural Rights, Including the right to development, Report of the Working Group on Enforced or Involuntary Disappearances.
Jegatheeswara Sarma v Sri Lanka, HRC (2003) UN Doc CCPR/C/78/D/950/2000.
UN Doc CCPR/C/21/Rev.1/Add.11 (31 August 2001).
HRC. (10/03/92). General Comment No.20: Prohibition of Torture and Cruel Treatment or Punishment (Art.7): 10/03/92.
Mojica v Dominican Republic, HRC (1994) UN Doc CCPR/C/51/D/449/1991.

HRC. (13 April 1984). General Comment No. 13: Equality before the courts and the right to a fair and public hearing by an independent court established by law (Art. 14).
HRC. (30 June 1982). General Comment No. 08: Right to liberty and security of persons (Art. 9).
UN Doc CCPR/C/21/Rev.1/Add.11.
Lopez Burgos v Uruguay, HRC (1981) UN Doc Supp. No. 40 (A/36/40) at 176 (1981).
Caldas v Uruguay, HRC (1979) Comm No 43/1979.

Miscellaneous

Committee on Enforced Disappearances (12 April 2022). Concluding observations on the report submitted by Greece under article 29, paragraph 1, of the Convention. UN Doc CED/C/GRC/CO/1.
General Allegation 120th Session, Nigeria. (10-14 February 2020). Retrieved 22 March, 2023, from https://www.ohchr.org/sites/default/files/Documents/Issues/Disappearances/Allegations/120_Nigeria.pdf.
OHCHR, WGEID Resolutions. Retrieved March 22, 2023, from http://www2.ohchr.org/english/issues/disappear/documents.htm#resolutions.
OHCHR, Enforced or Involuntary Disappearances, Fact Sheet No.6/Rev.3, 6. Retrieved March 22, 2023, from https://www.ohchr.org/Documents/Publications/FactSheet6Rev3.pdf.

CoE Documentation

CoE. (2008). Secret detentions and unlawful inter-state transfers of detainees in Europe (1st report Marty). CoE Publishing.
PACE. (2006). Official Report of Debates, 2006 Ordinary Sess., 3rd Part, Vol. III. CoE Publishing.
CoE. (8 April 2005). Lawfulness of detentions by the United States in Guantánamo Bay. Doc 10497.

OAS Documentation

IACommHR, Report No 21/16 Petition 419/08 (Report on Admissibility, Khaled El-Masri v US) OEA/Ser.L/V/II.157 Doc 25 (15 April 2016).

Inter-American Commission on Human Rights (IACommHR), 'Principles and Best Practices on the Protection of Persons Deprived of Liberty in the Americas' Res 1/08 (13 March 2008).

OAS. (22 July 2011). Regarding the situation of the detainees at Guantánamo Bay, United States. Res No 2/11 MC 259-02. OEA.Ser.L./V/II.116, Doc.5 rev.1 corr., 2002.

Online Material

Amnesty International. (14 April 2021). Nigeria: Seven years since Chibok, the government fails to protect children. Retrieved March 22, 2023, from https://www.amnesty.org/en/latest/press-release/2021/04/nigeria-seven-years-since-chibok-the-government-fails-to-protect-children/.

Association for the Prevention of Torture. (2 March 2006). Incommunicado, unacknowledged and secret detention under International Law. Retrieved March 22, 2023, from http://www.apt.ch/component/option,com_docman/task,doc_view/gid,280/lang,en/.

Boumediene, L. (7 January 2012). My Guantánamo Nightmare. The New York Times. Retrieved March 22, 2023, from http://www.nytimes.com/2012/01/08/opinion/sunday/my-guantanamo-nightmare.html.

Crawford, J. Human rights and state responsibility. 12th Raymond & Beverly Sackler Distinguished Lecture Series, Thomas J Dodd Research Centre, University of Connecticut, para 1. Retrieved March 22, 2023, from http://209.85.229.132/search?q=cache:Tq_ZorrV49oJ:doddcenter.uconn.edu/events/sackler/Crawford%2520transcript.doc+state+responsibility+human+rights&cd=20&hl=en&ct=clnk.

Dworkin, R. (2002). The threat to patriotism. New York Review of Books. Retrieved March 22, 2023, from http://www.nybooks.com/articles/archives/2002/feb/28/the-threat-to-patriotism/?pagination=false.

FEDEFAM. Fighting against enforced disappearances in Latin America. Retrieved March 22, 2023, from http://www.desaparecidos.org/fedefam/eng.html.

International Committee of the Red Cross. (2007). Report on the treatment of 14 'high value detainees' in CIA Custody. Retrieved March 22, 2023, from http://www.nybooks.com/media/doc/2010/04/22/icrc-report.pdf.

Joint Statement (Associations of families of the disappeared and other supportive NGOs on the occasion of the adoption of the Draft International Convention for the Protection of All Persons from Enforced Disappearances. Retrieved March 22, 2023, from http://www.icaed.org/the-convention/history-and-background-of-the-convention/.

Migration Data Portal (last updated 14 June 2022). Migrant deaths and disappearances. Retrieved March 22, 2023, from https://www.migrationdataportal.org/themes/migrant-deaths-and-disappearances#:~:text=Since%202014%2C%20 more%20than%204%2C000,deaths%20have%20been%20recorded%20 globally.

US Department of States, Foreign Press Centers. Pre-2017 Archive. Retrieved March 22, 2023, from http://fpc.state.gov/documents/organization/16801.pdf.

http://www.spiegel.de/international/europe/0,1518,659418,00.html.

References

Books

Agamben G (2005) State of exception. Chicago University Press

Alston P, Goodman R (2013) International human rights. Oxford University Press

Bassiouni CM (2011) Crimes against humanity, historical evolution, and contemporary application. Cambridge University Press

Boyle A, Chinkin C (2007) The making of international law. Oxford University Press

Crawford J (2002) Articles on state responsibility, introduction, text and commentaries. Cambridge University Press

Citroni G, Scovazzi T (2009) Recent developments in international law to combat enforced disappearances. Revista Internacional de Direito e Cidadania 3:89

Council of Europe (CoE) (2008) Secret detentions and unlawful inter-state transfers of detainees in Europe (1st report Marty). CoE Publishing

Dworkin R (2002) The threat to patriotism. New York Review of Books. http://www.nybooks.com/articles/archives/2002/feb/28/the-threat-to-patriotism/?pagination=false

Feitlowitz M (1998) A Lexicon of Terror: Argentina and the Legacies of Torture. OUP, 71

Gearty C (2005) Can human rights survive? Cambridge University Press

Grandin G (2011) The last colonial massacre, Latin America in the Cold War, updated edn. The University of Chicago Press

Gray C (2008) International law and the use of force, 3rd edn. Oxford University Press

Gross O, Ní Aoláin F (2006) Law in times of crisis, emergency powers in theory and practice. Cambridge University Press

Habermas J (1997) Between facts and norms. Polity Press

Heywood A (2000) Key concepts in politics. Palgrave

Honigsberg PJ (2009) Our nation unhinged: the human consequences of the war on terror. University of California Press

Joint Hearing Before the Subcommittee on International Organizations, Human Rights, An Oversight and the Subcommittee on Europe of the Committee on Foreign Affairs House of Representatives, 110th Congress, 1st Session (2007) ExtraordinaryrRendition in U.S. counterterrorism policy: The impact on transatlantic relations, Ser.No.110–28. US Government Printing Office

Joseph S et al (2014) Seeking remedies for torture victims, a handbook on the individual complaints procedures of the UN Treaty Bodies, 2nd edn. World Organization Against Torture

Kamber K (2017) Prosecuting human rights offences: rethinking the sword function of human rights law. Brill

Law RD (2009) Terrorism, a history. Polity Press.

Mariner J (2008) Double jeopardy, CIA renditions to Jordan. Human Rights Watch Publishing

Marks S, Clapham A (2005) International human rights lexicon. Oxford University Press

Nowak M (2005) U.N. Covenant on Civil and Political Rights, CCPR Commentary, 2nd revised edn. NP Engel

Rodley N (1999) Treatment of prisoners under international law, 2nd edn. Oxford University Press
Rodley NS (2005) The treatment of prisoners under international law, 3rd edn. Oxford University Press
Scovazzi T, Citroni G (2007) The struggle against enforced disappearance and the 2007 United Nations Convention. Martinus Nijhoff Publisher and VSP
van Boven T (1983) Political killings by governments. Amnesty International

Articles

Ali Haydar Y (2022) The presumption of death. Dokuz Eylul Universitesi Hukuk Fakultesi Dergisi 24(2):833–886
Anderson K (2006) How effective is the international convention for the protection of all persons from enforced disappearance likely to be in holding individuals criminally responsible for acts of enforced disappearance? Melbourne J Int Law 7(2):245–277
Andreu-Guzmán F (2001) The draft international convention on the protection of all persons from forced disappearance. ICJ Rev Impunity Crimes Against Human Forced Disapp 62–63:73
Azarova V, Danson Brown A, Mann I (2022) The enforced disappearance of migrants. Boston Univ Int Law J 40(1):133–204
Bailey CM (2018) Women in the crosshairs: expanding the responsibility to protect to halt extreme gender-based violence. Air Force Law Rev 78:75–100
Barrett J (2009) Chechnya's last hope - enforced disappearances and the European Court of Human Rights. Harv Human Rights J 22(1):133–144
Bator PM, Vorenberg J (1966) Arrest, detention, interrogation and the rights to counsel: Basic problems and possible legislative solutions. Columb Law Rev 66(1):62–78
Biddulph S (2022) The production of legal norms: a case study of administrative detention in China. UCLA Pac Basin Law J 20(2):217–277
Claude O (2010) A comparative approach to enforced disappearances in the Inter-American Court of Human Rights and the European Court of Human Rights jurisprudence. Intercult Human Rights Law Rev 5:407–462
Cole D (2002) Enemy aliens. Stanf Law Rev 54(5):953–1004
Cole D (2003) Their liberties, our security, democracy and double standards. Int J Legal Inf 31(2):290–311
Cole D (2009) Out of the shadows: preventive detention, suspected terrorists, and war. Calif Law Rev 97(3):693–750
Dickinson LA (2002) Using legal process to fight terrorism: detentions, military commissions, international tribunals, and the rule of law. Southern Calif Law Rev 75(6):1407–1492
Egeland J (1982) Political 'Disappearances' – a challenge for humanitarian law. Nordisk Tidsskrift Int Ret 57(1):189–202
Ezeani EC (2017) Responding to homegrown terrorism: the case of Boko Haram. Ann Surv Int Comp Law 22:1–32
Fitzpatrick J (2003) Rendition and transfer in the war against terrorism: Guantánamo and beyond. Loyola Los Angeles Int Comp Law Rev 25(3):457–492
Grossman C (2020) ILC Report on prevention and punishment of crimes against humanity and enforced disappearance. Afr J Int Crim Just 2020(2):227–238
Henning VH (2002) Anti-Terrorism, crime and security act: has the United Kingdom made a valid derogation from the European Convention on Human Rights? Am Univ Int Law Rev 17(6):1263–1298
Kleinman HM (1986–1987) Disappearances in Latin America: a human rights perspective. NYU J Int'l L & Pol 19:1033

Kuschnik B (2010) Humaneness, humankind, and crimes against humanity. Goettingen J Int Law 2(2):501–530

Lippman M (1988) Disappearances, towards a declaration on the prevention of the crime of enforced or involuntary disappearances. Connecticut J Int Law 4(1):121–144

Luban D (2004) A theory of crimes against humanity. Yale J Int Law 29(1):85–168

Macken C (2005) Preventive detention and the right of personal liberty and security under the International Covenant on Civil and Political Rights, 1966. Adelaide Law Rev 26(1):1–28

Manfredi MF (2014) Non-refoulement, interception and push-back policies. Cogito Multidiscipl Res J 6(1):44–52

McCrory S (2007) The international convention for the protection of all persons from enforced disappearance. Human Rights Law Rev 7(3):545–566

Medawatte DS (2017) The vanishing act: Punishing and deterring perpetrators through the concurrent application of diverse legal regimes to enforced disappearances. Florida J Int Law 29(2):227–252

Michell P (1996) English-speaking justice: Evolving responses to transnational forcible abduction after Alvarez-Machain. Cornell Int Law J 29(2):383–500

Moir L (2006) Crimes against humanity in historical perspective. New Zealand Yearb Int Law 3:101–130

Morentin B, Callado LF, Idoyaga MI (2008) A follow-up study of allegations of ill-treatment/torture in incommunicado detainees in Spain, failure of international preventive mechanisms. Torture 18(2):87–98

Niworu SM (2013) Boko Haram sect: terrorists or a manifestation of the failed Nigerian state. J Polit Law 6(2):245-[xiv]

Ogueri RN (2022) Genderization of Boko Haram insurgency in Nigeria. Int Rev Law Jurisprud 4(2):151–157

Olivera S (2019) Enforced disappearance as crime against humanity in Rome Statute. CRIMEN: Casopis za Krivicne Nauke 2019(2):144–155

Paust JJ (2004) Post-9/11 overreaction and fallacies regarding war and defense, Guantánamo, the Status of persons, treatment, judicial review of detention, and due process in military commissions. Notre Dame Law Rev 79(4):1335–1364

Paust JJ (2005) Executive plans and authorizations to violate international law concerning treatment and interrogation of detainees. Columb J Transnatl Law 43(3):811–864

Pervou P (2012) The convention for the protection of all persons from enforced disappearance: moving human rights protection ahead. Eur J Legal Stud 5(1):145–173

Radack JA (2005) You say defendant, I say combatant: Opportunistic treatment of rerrorism suspects held in the United States and the need for due process. New York Univ Rev Law Soc Change 29(3):525–554

Roberts C (2017) On the definition of crimes against humanity and other widespread or systematic human rights violations. Univ Pennsylvania J Law Soc Change 20(1):1–28

Roth K (2008) After Guantánamo, The case against preventive detention. Foreign Aff 87(3):9–17

Sadat LN (2006) Ghost prisoners and black sites: extraordinary rendition under international law. Case West Reserve J Int Law 37(2):309–342

Silva M (2009) Extraordinary rendition: a challenge to Canadian and United States legal obligations under the Convention against Torture. California West Int Law J 39(2):313–356

Stahlberg T, Lahmann H (2011) A paradigm of prevention: Humpty dumpty, the war on terror and the power of preventive detention in the United States, Israel and Europe. Am J Comp Law 59(4):1051–1088

Teubner G (2006) The anonymous matrix: human rights violations by private transnational actors. Mod Law Rev 69(3):327–346

Treves T (1990) The UN body of principles for the protection of the detained or imprisoned persons. Am J Int Law 84(2):578–586

Waldron J (2002) Security and liberty: the image of balance. J Polit Philos 11(2):191–210

Waxman M (2009) Administrative detention of terrorists: why detain, and detain whom? J Natl Secur Law Policy 3(1):1–38
Ziliang Y (2007) Preventive detention as a counter-terrorism strategy: they have stopped using it and so should we. Singapore Law Rev 25:24–34

Book Chapters

Crawford J, Olleson S (2006) The nature and forms of international responsibility. In: Evans MD (ed) International law. Oxford University Press
Crelinstern RD (2003) Violence in prisons/torture. In: Heitmeyer W, Hagan J (eds) International handbook of violence research. Kluwer
Molina Mejia R (2010) Bringing justice to Guatemala; The need to confront genocide and other crimes against humanity. In: Esparza M, Huttenbach HR, Feierstein D (eds) State violence and genocide in Latin America, the cold war years. Routledge, pp 209–234
Ní Aoláin F (2007) The individual right of access to justice in times of crisis: emergencies, armed conflict, and terrorism. In: Francioni F (ed) Access to justice as human right. Oxford University Press, pp 57–93

Chapter 3
The Scope of the Right Not to Be Subjected to Enforced Disappearance

3.1 The Right Against Enforced Disappearance as a Latecomer

The stipulation of the right not to be subjected to enforced disappearance in Art. 1(1) of the CPED has been considered a fairly noteworthy step towards the completion of the international human rights regime;[1] certainly, it is a necessary condition for the completion of the phenomenon's regulatory framework as such.[2] The right has been well received based mainly on two grounds: first, it is a definite legal response to the relevant state practices, and second, it represents a kind of formal atonement by the international community for the victims of enforced disappearances (the disappeared and their relatives). Yet, the fact that the right is not mentioned in any of the general universal human rights instruments (either the UDHR or the Covenants, which are usually referred to as the "International Bill of Human Rights")[3] raises interpretive issues regarding the cohesion of these instruments, and

---

[1] The term "international human rights regime" refers to the UN-centered regime for the protection of human rights: the UDHR and the Covenants, as well as all legally binding documents adopted under the Organization's auspices, and the organs and procedural and monitoring mechanisms thereof. In this framework, the UN human rights system is recognized as the only universal human rights regime when compared to the relevant regional systems. Donnelly (1986), p. 605.

[2] Even regional instruments which existed prior to the Convention do not provide for a right. The Inter-American Convention on disappearance adheres to a *rationale* which focuses on the offence of disappearance and does not stipulate a prohibition. This slightly divergent approach is of little practical significance, although there is a clear symbolic distinction. The same applies *mutatis mutandis* to the 1992 Declaration, taking into account the aims that each legal instrument serves. IACFDP Arts I, IV; 1992 Declaration Art. 1(1).

[3] The only explicit reference to the term "disappearance" which could possibly serve as an interpretive connection between the right and the general human rights instruments (the ICCPR and the UDHR in turn) is found in General Comment 6 of the HRC. But the HRC again treats the phenomenon as a peril to the right to life and not as a distinct human rights norm, and therefore it does not

I. Pervou, *The Right not to Be Subjected to Enforced Disappearance*,
https://doi.org/10.1007/978-3-031-36731-1_3

undermines the right's potential to be fully integrated into the current regime of human rights. The late inclusion of the prohibition on disappearance in international conventional texts has attracted critics who identify it as a "testimony to the inadequacy" of the existing positivism-centered human rights system.[4]

Conversely, the absence of references to the right, coupled with its systemic proximity to well-established fundamental human rights (such as the right to life and the prohibition on torture) has long sustained the contention that the prohibition on disappearance does not constitute a distinct right, further casting doubts on its normative character. This view is embraced by eminent scholars, including, among others, Theo van Boven, for whom the right not to be subjected to enforced disappearance is an example of "the further elaboration of the normative scope of [core] human rights", and for whom the Convention in turn does not "define [a] new right" but re-defines and re-conceptualizes "existing human rights in order to make them more explicit and more inclusive".[5] Following the same reasoning, those states which applied disappearance practices during the seventies and onwards attempted to link these considerations to the broader debate on the proliferation of human rights, with the view to maintaining a low threshold on the international protection against enforced disappearance.

However, enforced disappearances cannot fall within the proliferation-fragmentation human rights dilemma, a fact that was addressed by the UN General Assembly during the mid-eighties, since this debate related almost exclusively to so-called solidarity rights: that is, rights aspiring to improve people's standards of living, but which usually lacked strong moral underpinnings. From a theoretical perspective, human rights experts in support of a finite human rights list warned that acknowledging a right lacking in solid moral values would become a destabilizing factor for other, well-founded ones. In this respect, it has been asserted that if every demand were called a human right, then "the currency of our moral language [would become] debased".[6]

It therefore follows that the late manifestation of the right against disappearance cannot not be attached to the proliferation dialectic: first, because the international community has readily proclaimed over the last decades the existence of third generation rights whose scope remains contested;[7] and second, because the right is directed at human existence at its core. The idea of an inseparable bond between an enforced disappearance and the essence of a human being is easy to conceive, taking into account that even thoughts of a potential disappearance are enough to instigate feelings of horror in any person who identifies themselves as a potential victim

allow such an interpretation. HRC. (30 April 1982). General Comment No. 06: The Right to Life (Art. 6), para 4.

[4] Boucher (2009), pp. 249–250.

[5] van Boven (2010), p. 184.

[6] Mulgan (1968), p. 20.

[7] Alston (1984), p. 609.

(just like practices of torture or execution).[8] Hence, its late integration is rather the outcome of political disinclination veiled under the argument of human rights' non-proliferation. In any case, all theoretical objections concerning the right's conceptual ambiguity and its complex character dwindled after the reports by Nowak and the ISWG,[9] which highlighted the existing gaps in the victims' rights to legal protection and the need for a separate prohibition on disappearance.

Still, the Convention's drafters did not avoid addressing the proliferation-fragmentation dilemma; this time, though, the question was whether the establishment of a new monitoring body dealing *per se* with disappearances was an essential condition for the Convention, or if it was preferable to pass this task over to the HRC. Nowak argued that the creation of a new monitoring body would have limited results, since effective functioning would depend on how many states would recognize its competence, a condition which did not apply to the HRC, whose membership is by definition wider. This observation did not counter the objections expressed by the majority of delegations, and the option of introducing a separate monitoring mechanism prevailed.[10] In retrospect, Nowak proved correct: since the Convention came into force, few countries have accepted the jurisdiction of the Committee on Enforced Disappearance (hereinafter CED), with the result that the right's conventional protection has been considerably reduced.[11]

Overall, the existence of the right against enforced disappearance was not called into question during the Convention's drafting, and its establishment was a unanimous decision. Therefore, Art. 1 provides for a non-derogable right not to be subjected to enforced disappearance. The right's nature and dimensions have attracted little theoretical analysis until now, and so they remain essentially unexplored. In this regard, a thorough analysis of the right's special features, as well as of the demarcation of the good protected by it, is essential for its evaluation in the context of the international human rights regime.

---

[8] Waldron (2010), p. 273; Waldron (1999), p. 129.

[9] UN Doc E/CN.4/2002/71, paras 97–102; UN Doc E/CN.4/2004/59, para 170(a).

[10] UN Doc E/CN.4/2002/71, para 102; UN Doc E/CN.4/2004/59, paras 149, 165, 171.

[11] So far, sixteen out of thirty-seven states parties have declared according to Arts 31 and 32 that they recognize the CED's competence. Low attendance, combined with the CED's narrow mandate *ratione temporis* (Art. 35(1), provides that the CED is competent to examine communications only for disappearances which commence after the entry into force of the Convention) render it counterproductive. Consequently, the CED has not managed to alleviate the growing workload of the UNWGEID, which continues to process an immense number of complaints every year. Retrieved March 22, 2023, from http://www.ohchr.org/EN/HRBodies/CED/Pages/CEDIndex.aspx.

3.1.1 Art. 1(1): The Genetics of the Right

The right not to be subjected to enforced disappearance is a negative right, a feature which is evident in the first instance by its syntax. A grammatical interpretation indicates that Art. 1(1) introduces a general prohibition addressed to the Convention's parties not to apply the practice of enforced disappearances to all persons, either nationals or foreigners ("anyone"). Accordingly, the provision sets out an additional layer of protection of the private sphere, which must not be disrupted by state authorities. In other words, the individual (the subject of the right) can demand that the government will not implement enforced disappearance practices against them, and that the state has the correlating duty to refrain from such practices.

This pattern, where the pair "individual-claim" mirrors the pair "state-duty", refers directly to the Hohfeldian classification of human rights. More specifically, Hohfeld has identified four categories of human rights, the first of which is claim-rights. These are the rights which imply the existence of a subject (right-holder) and at least one duty-bearer (either the state or other individuals); the right's protection depends on the duty-bearer's abstention from interfering within the subject's field of protection.[12] For Hohfeld, claim-rights are the only rights *stricto sensu*, because they entail clear duties.[13] Claim-rights correlate to a "perfect [moral and legal] duty"[14] not to interfere with those rights. Within this framework, the right against disappearance qualifies as a claim-right, as individuals may raise their claim not to be forcefully disappeared vis-à-vis the pertinent governmental authorities.[15]

Nevertheless, this analysis carries with it Hohfeld's judicial background, and as such it applies only in a strict judicial context. Therefore, it seems that in the Hohfeldian scheme, justiciability is the safest criterion for categorizing claim-rights, which are ultimately synonymous with enforceable rights.[16] From this angle, then, Hohfeld's theory has little value for enforced disappearance, since it moves away from the previous judicial solutions which address practices of enforced disappearance in the absence of a corresponding legal right (that is, the accumulation of established rights breaches). Accordingly, the existence of a claim-right passes through the positivist test and a claim-right can only be a legal right. This means that a right does not exist if it is not stipulated as such in a legal document. The positivist

[12] Hohfeld (1917), pp. 710–770. *See* also, Keeton (1926–1927), p. 47.

[13] Brown (1999), p. 105.

[14] Kant (2010), pp. 39, 68.

[15] The notion of correlative rights and duties has been rejected by many human rights theorists, on the grounds of oversimplification. Joseph Raz, among others, does not approve of the general rule of correlativity, although he accepts that rights ground duties. Raz does not, however, probe into rights which generate duties for the state, such as general prohibitions which beget for the state a duty to refrain from any interference. His analysis revolves primarily around relations between individuals and their conflicting interests, which create multilayered legal correlations. Therefore, he adopts a more relativist approach; he forms his conclusions on an *ad hoc* basis and rejects standardized schemes, like the Hohfeldian. Raz (1986), p. 189.

[16] Addo (1997), pp. 9–10.

test requires norms to be written and specific. In other words, customary norms, whose content is not specifically stipulated, do not pass the test.[17] This juridical analytic view is also endorsed by Roscoe Pound, who characterizes claim-rights as "significant legal institutions".[18] Thus, the theory of claim-rights may apply only to the Convention's states parties, or to those states which have expressly proclaimed the right not to be subjected to enforced disappearance at a constitutional level. Yet, although this restrictive interpretation of the Hohfeldian theory considerably reduces its field of application, it does not minimize the classification's theoretical value or the categorization of the right on disappearances among claim-rights.

Furthermore, it is not only Hohfeld's theoretical framework according to which the right not to be subjected to enforced disappearance can be found at the central core of human rights protection. The right's negative formulation ("no one shall be subjected to..."), in conjunction with the right-holder's absolute and categorical interest in creating a firewall against state authorities that prevents authorities from performing disappearance practices on them (a personal sphere of protection), should place it systemically among our most familiar civil liberties,[19] or at least at the heart of our first-generation rights.[20] Certainly, though, this categorization is hard to sustain, for it neglects the historical ancestry of civil liberties,[21] most of which precede the UDHR and have a pre-nineteenth-century origin.[22] Despite the historical inconsistencies that the acknowledgment of a "freedom from enforced disappearance" may entail, the right's nature and its protective scope converge in this categorization, i.e. freedom from disappearances.

Committing an enforced disappearance entails at least the endangerment of the victim's physical integrity and mental health, demands ultimate allegiance to the captor, and results in the victim's alienation from any social or legal structure. These perils suffice to establish an individual's reasonable interest in protecting themselves from disappearance. They have an interest in avoiding the extreme pain and suffering caused by enforced disappearance. In this respect, when such compelling individual interests also involve strong moral underpinnings, they lay the foundations for the emergence of a right. Particularly for civil liberties, individual interests are innate to human nature, and unchallenged morality serves as a threshold for a

[17] Randall (1925), p. 87.

[18] Pound (1915), p. 101.

[19] Waldron (1993), p. 7.

[20] Vasak (1977), p. 32.

[21] The terms "civil liberties" and "first-generation rights" will be used interchangeably in the present study, although "first-generation rights" comprise both civil liberties and political rights. The same applies to the terms "liberty" and "right", although this simplification does not overlook the fact that the distinction between the terms condenses the divergent theories into the inherent or legal substance of human rights, while "liberties" are considered to be by default incompatible with the concept of duties. Osiatyński (2009), pp. 5–6.

[22] Glendon (2004), p. 6.

prospective norm. That is, "human interest" alongside "moral nature" are the constituents of a human rights norm.[23]

This general concept has partly been endorsed by the drafters of the UDHR,[24] and further advanced by several liberal human rights theorists. Jeremy Waldron, among other contemporary theorists, perceives first-generation rights as those evoking "images of autonomy, rational agency and independence",[25] rendering their protection vital for the right-holder's well-being or material satisfaction. For Waldron, the distinguishing feature of civil liberties, a feature which prioritizes the need for their protection compared with the other human rights, is the sense of the extra "urgency" they bear.[26] Urgency denotes the recognition of the objectivity that must be ascribed to all civil liberties equally, a notional objectivity that stems from the "agent-neutral" moral principles on which they are built.[27] Civil rights are free from moral relativity or diffusion, whereas morality is an "independent variable".[28] This means that civil rights are not dependent on the right-holder's personal interests and perceptions, and are not subject to positional interpretations.[29] Consequently, although they are the rights of the individual, they are not individualistic rights.[30] Hence, urgency evolves to take on the additional qualitative characteristic of civil liberties, both morally and factually. It serves as the moral shield in the rhetoric of civil liberties, justifying the need to protect them (*in abstracto* protection). It then turns into a fact when a particular right of the holder is breached and the latter seeks protection (*in concreto* protection). Clearly, this argument relies on an essential tautology in which morality and urgency are interlocked. From this perspective, first-generation rights turn into a self-fulfilling moral prophecy.

According to this analysis, the pronouncement and recognition of civil liberties depends on the interplay between individual self-interest, moral objectivity, and

---

23 Donnelly (2003), p. 14.

24 Glendon (2004), p. 19.

25 Waldron (1993), pp. 7, 11.

26 ibid p. 13.

27 ibid pp. 170, 173; cf Sen (1982), p. 33.

28 Gewirth (1980), p. 6. The term is used by Gewirth to encapsulate David Hume's argumentation on moral judgment. For Hume, morality precedes reason (rationality) both conceptually and chronologically. This precedence warrants moral objectiveness and/or moral universality. Thus, "the rules of morality [...] are not conclusions of our reason, independent from any personal considerations [considerations of the individual]". Hume (1896) Book III, Part I, Sect I. Ronald Dworkin assents, although his argumentation is sensibly different. Dworkin (2006), p. 128.

29 cf Raz (1986), p. 187; Sen (1982), pp. 33–35.

30 John Tasioulas offers an alternative reading on the moral objectivity of human rights. He suggests that the fact that human rights serve the interests of their holders does not deprive them of the objectivity requirement, simply because "each human being enjoys a valuable status in virtue of their membership of a species characterized by a series of distinctive capacities, including capacities for thought, deliberation and action". Human rights share by definition the common denominator of being human, or, in the words of Tasioulas, "all human beings are [...] equally human [and thus] this valuable status is possessed by each in equal measure". This means that individual capacities and interests are attributed to the person, but are owed to the species. Tasioulas (2013), p. 6.

urgency of protection. This threefold test corresponds to Alan Gewirth's perception of human rights. Gewirth defines human rights as "personally oriented, normatively necessary, moral requirements", further pointing out that morality and normativity are unavoidably intertwined.[31] Their combination is the equivalent of the Waldrian "morally-neutral principles" (referred as "moral objectivity"), whereas "urgency of protection" reflects the Gewirthian "necessary requirements" (as follows on from the abridgment of the phrase "normatively necessary, moral requirements"). The common factor linking these doctrinal approaches is the endeavor to preclude a relativized-based reading of human rights that could challenge the absolute character of the right-holder's protection. Individual protection is accordingly the decisive element around which both theories revolve; it emerges as the genuine purpose of human rights' existence, their underlying rationale. It is a protection-oriented teleological interpretation (or else what Gewirth names a "normative moral interpretation"[32]) by which the right not to be subjected to enforced disappearance qualifies by way of induction as a civil liberty.[33]

More specifically, enforced disappearance poses such threats to the individual that its moral foundations are immune to relativistic interpretations. Regardless of the particular conditions that a disappearance involves, the practice aims in principle at stripping the individual from any human quality they bear and rendering legal institutions void. Apart from the violation of legal norms, the breaching of self-evident morally objective values like life and liberty and the practical abolishment of the right to justice and freedom from torture mean that enforced disappearance deserves urgent safeguarding because it despises the philosophy of rights itself, making the rule of law inaccessible to the victim, or otherwise taking away from the person the right to have rights.[34] Indeed, enforced disappearances have "reshaped our understandings" of well established human rights.[35] In this respect, if the right-holder's protection is adopted as the most appropriate interpretative tool for human rights discourse in general, then the characterization of the right not to be subjected to enforced disappearance as a "freedom" is certainly consistent with the international human rights regime.

However, the theoretical classification of the right against enforced disappearance as a civil right does not automatically presume its systemic incorporation into the international human rights regime. Given the lack of any explicit reference to it in the International Bill of Human Rights, this can only come through the interpretative connection of the right to the principle of human dignity, the principle which

[31] Gewirth (1984), p. 2.

[32] Gewirth (1980), pp. 156, 280.

[33] The connection between human rights and morality is not a given. It is just one doctrinal approach (expressed by Gewirth among others), according to which human rights ought to have a moral background to guarantee their importance. This "traditionalist account" of human rights has received strong criticism, as it is not deemed sufficient to identify a comprehensive list of human rights. Raz (2010), pp. 322–327.

[34] Kesby (2012), p. 144.

[35] Donnelly (2003), p. 58.

permeates the established international human rights regime. That is why and how the commission of enforced disappearance amounts to a severe violation of human dignity.

3.1.2 Dignitarian Aspects of Enforced Disappearance

The conceptual proximity of the right against disappearance to human dignity is obviously uncontroversial as well as logical; at the same time, it is *prima facie* legally unfounded. Apart from the historical absence of reporting enforced disappearances either in the UDHR or the ICCPR (as the phenomenon had not yet received international attention by the time they were concluded), the absence of reference to human dignity both in the provisions of the Convention on Enforced Disappearance[36] and in its preambulatory clauses, although a minor weakness of the Convention, makes the notional connection between dignity and disappearance initially problematic. This omission is particularly intriguing, taking into account the Convention's use of "structural loans" from other UN human rights instruments (like the CaT), where mentions of the rights in question in association to human dignity are commonplace. In addition to these, Art. 1(1) of the 1992 Declaration explicitly proclaims that "any act of enforced disappearance is an offence to human dignity".[37] This terminological discontinuity between the Convention and the UDHR does not negate the intrinsic link between disappearances and dignity, in fact it renders their joint interpretation as the only pathway. Evidently, this approach depends on the necessary condition that human dignity is the cornerstone of the UDHR, which therefore justifies taking a short digression to explore its meaning and role within the international human rights regime.

Human dignity is unquestionably the starting point of the modern (post-UN) human rights discourse, as it captures the critical shift from natural to legal law, or, better, the latter's acceptance of nature as the inceptive source of human rights.[38] Thus, references to it in the UDHR signify the drafters' attempts to bridge the different legal traditions; as such, human dignity is the "minimum yardstick" of human rights law[39] "by virtue [of human beings] common humanity".[40] In this dignitarian reading of human rights, human dignity embodies at least three key functions: it is

---

[36] On the grounds of precision, Arts 19(2) and 24(5)(c) of the Convention employ the term "human dignity" only to arrange particular issues, and it is not related to the right against disappearances *per se*.

[37] 1992 Declaration, Art. 1(1).

[38] Glendon (1999), p. 12.

[39] The phrase "minimum yardstick" was first used by the ICJ to highlight the importance of Common Article 3 of the four Geneva Conventions of humanitarian law in general, and it became a common characterization thereafter. *Military and Paramilitary Activities in and against Nicaragua (Nicaragua v USA)* (Merits) [1986] ICJ Rep 14, 113–114, para 218.

[40] Brown (1999), p. 107.

the *causa* of human rights existence; (a) it is a prerequisite of their functioning; (b) and it propels the development and flourishing of human nature (c). Regarding the first two functions, it is simultaneously the source of human rights and their protective scope. In other words, human beings have and claim rights due to dignity,[41] and conversely the protection of human rights is intended to safeguard them,[42] revealing an axiomatically circular relation between them. Accordingly, in the context of the well-known chicken-egg scenario, human dignity is both the egg and the chicken. Beyond this, the first two propositions presuppose that human dignity is inherent to human beings, who therefore seek "a life of dignity" through human rights protection.[43] In turn, the inherent nature of dignity provides a degree of objectiveness to the rather indeterminate content of the term, first because it connotes that human dignity is a natural and thus inalienable virtue, and second because it adds a moral nuance to its meaning. In this framework, dignity's inherent nature is employed to establish a standardized and uncontroversial language of human rights, sometimes setting aside its progressive aspect.

This progressive attribute that human dignity carries is emphasized by the third function mentioned above. Indeed, human dignity cannot be confined to a standard-content approach, for otherwise it would prevent any potential improvement of people's moral maturity. Hence, dignity's natural interpretation is deficient if "the intervention of [human] thought and reflection" is not incorporated therein.[44] That is, commonly accepted notions produced by human experience attain a natural protective sheath. In this natural-empirically oriented understanding, human dignity "is concerned with what human beings might become not what they have been historically or 'are' in some scientifically determinable sense",[45] rejecting human nature's perceived immutability.[46] Dignity is the driving force behind human possibility, aiming at human flourishing;[47] consequently, morality (which guarantees its inherent objectivity) has evolved to become "a distinct, independent dimension of [...] experience".[48] Empiricism as expressed in terms of human possibility produces a

---

[41] Osiatyński (2009), p. 189.

[42] Dworkin (1977), p. 199.

[43] Donnelly (2003), p. 14.

[44] Hume (1896) Book III, Part II, Sect I.

[45] Donnelly (2003), p. 23.

[46] Boucher (2009), pp. 75, 93.

[47] The coexistence of human nature and human possibility (flourishing) appears plainly in the American Declaration of Independence, which states that "men are [...] endowed by their Creator with certain unalienable Rights, that among these are Life, Liberty and the pursuit of Happiness". Although human rights are endowed on humans by their Creator (that is, the metaphysical expression of human nature, corresponding to the term "human dignity" in positivistic terms), humans are engaged in the pursuit of happiness, and moreover have a right to it (human flourishing as a matter of human intervention in their nature). The pursuit of happiness has long been seen as a phrase which promotes a utilitarian understanding of human rights, although "its most fundamental point is to recognize and honor the inherent worth of every human being". Dworkin (2006), p. 90; The Unanimous Declaration of the Thirteen United States of America 1776 (US) preamble.

[48] Dworkin (2006), p. 128.

dynamic interpretation of human dignity, and therefore human rights, yet without challenging its inherence in human nature; further, it attempts to reconcile the empirical and natural approaches to human rights law.

The debate on and various interpretative approaches to the functions of human dignity under consideration attest to its significance for the international human rights regime. As a result, the International Bill of Human Rights rests on a "dignity-based language of rights" which necessitates a joined-up analysis of human rights and dignity.[49] In particular, as regards the right not to be subjected to enforced disappearance, it remains to explore the links between its protective scope and human dignity—i.e. why and how committing an enforced disappearance violates human dignity—in order to justify the emergence of the norm and its doctrinal incorporation in the UDHR.

Although it might seem uncontroversial to point out the differences between enforced disappearances and other forms of suffering, it is quite difficult to positively determine the distinct ways in which enforced disappearances trample on human dignity. At this point, Susan Marks and Andrew Clapham's *International Human Rights Lexicon* contributes significantly to our understanding of the norm, suggesting that enforced disappearances trap the disappeared in the condition of "bare life".[50] The concept of "bare life" was introduced in Giorgio Agamben's *Homo Sacer* as a constitutive element of the expanding trend of sovereign exception and within the broader context of the changing structure of sovereignty. Agamben rereads and juxtaposes the Aristotelian terms *bios* and *zoē*, locating "bare life" in between.[51] It is a state where the sovereign alienates the man both from *physis* and *nomos*, depriving him of his natural activities and separating him from the regular juridical order respectively.[52] "Bare life" is an intermediate situation between life and death; the sovereign suspends every human activity and decreases the victim's life to minimum biological functions. Agamben's theory of "bare life" is founded on the example of WWII captives who were treated as guinea pigs in the Nazi concentration camps (the so-called *Versuchpersonen* or VPs). In his description of the life conditions of the "experimental subjects", he mentions that:

> They were persons sentenced to death or detained in a camp, the entry into which meant the definitive exclusion from the political community. Precisely because they were lacking almost all the rights and expectations that we customarily attribute to human existence, and yet were still biologically alive, they came to be situated in a limit zone between life and death, inside and outside, in which they were no longer anything but bare life. [...] Like the fence of the camp, the interval between death sentence and execution delimits an extratemporal and extraterritorial threshold in which the human body is separated from its

[49] Glendon (1999), p. 8.

[50] Marks and Clapham (2005), pp. 121–122.

[51] Agamben's theory of "bare life" received criticism for misinterpreting the Aristotelian nexus of *bios* and *zoē*. Among his critics, Jacques Derrida holds that for Aristotle *bios* and *zoē* are not contradictory notions but are discernible and complementary; hence, the concept of "bare life" rests on false premises. Derrida (2009).

[52] Agamben (1998a), p. 90.

normal political status and abandoned, in a state of exception, to the most extreme misfortunes.[53]

Clearly, concentration camps remove any human quality from their detainees. First, the victims are deprived of any legal protection, or potential protection ("no rights or expectations"), since the camps are spaces of juridical exception meant to extinguish *nomos*. Second, and most important, concentration camps literally remove detainees from the political communities to which they belong ("exclusion from the political community"); they constitute a forced form of political exile within the territorial boundaries of the political community. For Agamben, such a removal from political life impinges on the victims' nature (*physis*). The equation of participation in political life with man's nature fully aligns with the Aristotelian definition of the human being as a *physei politikon zōon* (a political animal by nature), predestined to form part of a *polis* (political community).[54]

Agamben suggests that being reduced to a "bare life" is a process of dehumanization that can be analyzed in two aspects: victims not only experience excessive suffering but are also excluded from political life. "Bare life" overturns the underlying assumption of human rights theory that "all human beings [are] citizens of some kind of political community", and therefore can proceed with the certainty that "if the law of their country [does] not live up to the demands of the Rights of Man, they [are] expected to change them, by legislation in democratic countries or through revolutionary action in despotism".[55] Captives in concentration camps have recourse neither to the first nor the second option, as human rights are subrogated by the captors' absolute power; a perspective which directly points to the political dimension of human rights. Astonishingly enough, Agamben does not associate the "bare life" concept with the phenomenon of enforced disappearance, particularly in the form it took in Latin America, where, during the rise of totalitarianism, secret detention facilities did not differ at all from WWII concentration camps. He only draws an interesting parallel between the Nazi paradigm and the Yugoslav war practices. These scattered references to the former Yugoslavia do not provide a comprehensive report but highlight certain aspects of ethnic cleansing only. As a result, they do not demonstrate that disappearances were a deliberate governmental policy.[56]

From this perspective, the "bare life" concept epitomizes Hannah Arendt's analysis on the notions of totalitarianism and violence, echoing to a great extent her insights and descriptions.[57] In fact, although Arendt's work cannot reasonably be

---

[53] ibid p. 159.

[54] Aristotle, *Politics*, Book A, Chapter 2, 1253a, 3–4.

[55] Arendt (1973), p. 293.

[56] Agamben (1998b), p. 176.

[57] The similarities between Arendt's and Agamben's main patterns are noticeable. For example, Agamben defines "bare life" as "sacred life [...] political life [...] a life that may be killed, which is politicized through its very capacity to be killed", whereas Arendt remarks that "the world found nothing sacred in the abstract nakedness of being human", also emphasizing the prevalence of the political status of humans over their existence itself. Agamben (1998a), pp. 88–89; Arendt (1973), p. 299.

said to refer to enforced disappearance (given that it precedes the phenomenon's emergence and crystallization), her narration on the extermination of the victims of Nazism is not far from the numerous testimonies on disappearance, and thus almost performs a predictive function. She mentions that "the camps are meant not only to exterminate people and degrade human beings, but also serve the ghastly experiment of eliminating [...] the human personality into a mere thing, into something that even animals are not".[58] Both Agamben's and Arendt's analyses of the lives lived in concentration camps offer a vivid visualization of the lives of the disappeared, even though the link between the two practices is not self-evident. The concept of "bare life" (or of lives lived only at the captors' discretion) explains, better than anything else, how enforced disappearance violates human dignity. The violation is twofold: the disappeared are forcefully expelled from the society they belonged to, and they cease to exist in it because their fate is kept unknown (alienation from their *physis*); hence, they are no longer the subject of human rights, since they are literally and metaphorically situated outside the protection of the law (alienation from *nomos*). This simultaneous alienation from *physis* and *nomos* constitutes the reduction from *bios* to *zoē* that deprives the disappeared of a life of dignity. Following this proposition, enforced disappearance is more than a "threat"[59] to a person's inherent dignity, it is its annihilation.

3.1.3 Political Aspects of Enforced Disappearance

Two issues arise from the application of "bare life" to enforced disappearance. First, "bare life" has a distinct and prominent political dimension. In Agambenian terms, it is "authentically political",[60] a potential outcome of the "politicization of life" (the so-called "biopolitics"—the politics of *bios*).[61] For Arendt, too, life in concentration camps is the deliberate political choice of the sovereign, an attempt to cease any form of existing or potential opposition.[62] Therefore, if the phenomenon of enforced disappearance is an expression of "bare life", it remains to spot the political ramifications of the right not to be subjected to enforced disappearance. Second, the reducing of *bios* to *zoē*, and particularly the alienation from *physis* and *nomos*, constitutes such a severe violation of human dignity that it questions the very essence of humanity. Again, there is an inescapable tautology: human dignity is a human feature; vice versa, a life without dignity is not worth living for a human being. Following this argument, those exposed to a "bare life" are forcefully deprived of their inherent quality as a subject of human rights (they are "outside the protection

[58] Arendt (1973), p. 438.

[59] Shue (1980), pp. 17–34.

[60] Agamben (1998b), p. 106.

[61] ibid pp. 120–122.

[62] Arendt (1973), p. 436.

of the law" according to Article 2 of the Convention). Alienation from *nomos* (*nomos* conceived not in positivist terms, nor as a legal reality, but as the socially established means to provide protection) throws up the perpetual philosophical question of who is the subject of human rights (human rights "subjectivity").[63] Hence, it is worth exploring whether enforced disappearance does endanger human rights subjectivity (recognition as a person before the law). Or do the disappeared have rights?

Moving to the first issue, "bare life's" political content is indisputable. It is the choice of the sovereign to abruptly cut the links of the individual from the political community, the arbitrary political exclusion of those deemed dangerous or unwelcome. In this regard, "bare life" is the ultimate measure to guarantee domestic tranquility in the hands of the sovereign. Although Agamben does not confine "bare life" to totalitarian regimes, his thought directly implies certain democratic deficits, picturing forms of "total domination" as being within the sovereign's jurisdiction (politics over *bios*);[64] this partly diverges from Arendt's fixed context, in which such political exclusion is a method of suppression of totalitarian rule ("totalitarian domination").[65] The typology of the right against enforced disappearance proper does not condition its existence on particular political circumstances, by which a prerequisite would render the right's field of protection precarious. Politicizing enforced disappearance has never been an option for the drafters of the Convention, even though the perpetrating of disappearances presupposes a settled state policy.[66] However, even outside the conventional frame, the characterization of disappearances as political acts was attempted only by those states practicing them with the view to relegating their significance and keeping the international community outside their internal affairs.[67]

---

[63] The term "subjectivity" is consciously preferred to "subjectivation" (or "subjectivization" or "subjectification"). The two notions differ because "subjectivity" is the status of being a human-rights holder, whereas "subjectivation" stands for the social processes and political mechanisms that dictate the prevalent philosophy that human-rights holders succumb to—close to indoctrination. Besides, "subjectivity" has long been employed in human rights literature, while "subjectivation" has received philosophical elaboration in principle. The latter is the English version of the Foucauldian terms "*subjectivation*" or "*assujettissement*"; that is, "the influence of normalizing power on individuals, which in turn 'produces' or 'fabricates' subjects". Harrer (2005), p. 79. Apart from Michel Foucault, Jacques Rancière elaborated the term recently in his study on the subject of human rights. For Rancière, human beings are not endowed with human rights by virtue of their nature; instead, human rights possession is filtered through the political community, and therefore "the rights of Man are not the rights of a single subject" but are a process of political indoctrination. Rancière (2004), p. 302. Accordingly, the notion of "subjectivation" is far from the traditional dignitarian understanding of human rights, as its existence depends on the acts and decisions of a higher collective subject, the political community. As such, the Rancièrian view does not coincide with Foucault's regarding the emergence of the right against enforced disappearance, although it may well elucidate the actual situation which the disappeared confront.

[64] Agamben (1998b), p. 120.

[65] Arendt (1973), p. 438.

[66] UN Doc A/HRC/7/2, para 26.

[67] Egeland (1982), pp. 192–194.

Thus, the issue at stake is not whether enforced disappearances are associated with certain political regimes, but whether they are a sign of governance deficiency or political immaturity when they form governmental policy. The wording points directly to modern manifestations of the phenomenon, where disappearances are used by long-established democracies as alleged anti-terrorist tools to the benefit of society and do not occur strictly within the totalitarian context, in which case Arendt's model would suffice. On such occasions, disappearances are purged in the name of national security, and they are not easily conceivable as a state terror policy, first because terror is not directed at the citizens of the country that applies them, and second because most often the victims are transferred outside the state's jurisdiction (the "not in my backyard" doctrine). From this perspective, intimidation is tolerable, since it is directed against state enemies, leaving the population satisfied or untouched. What is more, the boundaries between exclusion and inclusion zones (the disappeared and the rest) are indiscernible; given that the victims are aliens, they are politically and territorially remote from the rest of the community. Nonetheless, enforced disappearances remain a policy of "exportable" state terror[68] designed to bring the victim under "total domination", matching both the Agambenian definition of what is a "camp" as well as the concept of "bare life". Agamben observes that:

> The camp as dislocating localization is the hidden matrix of the politics in which we are still living, and it is this structure of the camp that we must learn to recognize in all its metamorphoses, into the *zones d'attentes* of our airports and certain outskirts of our cities.[69]

This allows us to emphasize the dynamic interpretation these terms require. Apparently, the policy of enforced disappearances is implemented by democratic governments under the pretext of public order and national security, a fact which reveals the shortcomings of modern democracies.

However, the application of Agamben's theory of "bare life" is necessarily limited to enforced disappearances that include state involvement. Enforced disappearances carried out by non-state actors do not match the theory, irrespective of whether they entail state complicity or not (depending on the governmental authorities' willingness or ability to prevent their occurrence). Put simply, the less the sovereign is involved in the practice, the less "bare life" is a successful explanatory formula for disappearances. Inevitably, enforced disappearances arising between social groups (crime syndicates, clans etc.) are placed outside the "bare life" frame, despite their undoubted implications for exposing structural and political flaws.

The second political issue involving enforced disappearances is the glaring reality that the disappeared are placed outside the protection of the law (the Agambenian alienation from *nomos*). The Convention addresses this matter in Article 2[70] in the light of disappearances' constitutive elements. Under Article 1, the right against disappearance emerges as a hyper-right, whose violation entails not only the breach

---

[68] Agamben (2001), p. 45.

[69] Agamben (1998b), p. 114.

[70] *See* Chap. 2.

of a series of civil rights but also the dispossession of all rights, such as political rights. Taking this into consideration, enforced disappearance is the ultimate contemporary example of Agamben's bipolarity between zones of rights and zones of no-rights, bringing into being the murky reality of "bare life".[71] The UNWGEID confirms the accuracy of the concept of "bare life" and states that "while deprived of his/her liberty [the disappeared] is denied any right under the law, and is placed in a legal limbo, in a situation of total defenselessness". Technically, the victim then becomes a 'non-person'.[72]

The UNWGEID essentially reiterates the terminology introduced by the IACtHR in its recent jurisprudence,[73] further drawing a link between the right not to be subjected to enforced disappearance and the right to juridical standing. The latter is recognized as such on a regional level only,[74] and there is no corresponding reference to it either in the International Bill of Human Rights or in the ECHR. Nonetheless, apart from regional jurisprudence, the connection between these two norms is recorded at the international level too, since it is explicitly mentioned in Article 1(2) of the 1992 Declaration. Notwithstanding the different legal formulations, the above correlation demonstrates that the prohibition of enforced disappearance is a *de facto* precondition for the enjoyment (if not the existence) of the corpus of civil liberties; or, to put it simply, the disappeared are not the subjects of human rights. Ascertaining this contravenes the axiom of natural law theory, according to which individuals cannot lose their quality as subjects of human rights, even when their rights are not respected or when there are no legal remedies to restore the violation of them, because rights are attached to personhood.[75] Thereafter, political exclusion cannot beget human rights exclusion: to wit, there cannot be a state of no-rights, or a case of de-subjectivity.

In this sense, Rancière's theory on the subject of human rights (despite the fact that it has no common element with natural law theories), is particularly striking since it also rejects rightlessness. For Rancière, human rights are an epiphenomenal aspect of politics, a standpoint that dictates the preponderance of human rights subjectivation over the concept of subjectivity. In this respect, humans are nothing but the subjects of politics, and rights are a fabrication of the political subject.[76] Yet, Rancière perceives subjectivation as a one-way process, due to the power that politics carries; hence there is no reverse course allowing for the de-subjectivation of

[71] Kesby (2012), p. 130.

[72] UNWGEID. General Comment on the right to recognition as a person before the law in the context of enforced disappearances. Retrieved March 22, 2023, form http://www.ohchr.org/Documents/Issues/Disappearances/GCRecognition.pdf.

[73] *Anzualdo Castro v Peru*, Inter-American Court of Human Rights Series C No 202 (22 September 2009) paras 56, 59, 87–88.

[74] According to Article 3 of the IACHR, "every person has the right to recognition as a person before the law'; likewise, Article 5 of the African Charter on Human and People's Rights reads: "every individual shall have the right [...] to the recognition of his legal status".

[75] Weinreb (1992), pp. 297, 301.

[76] Rancière (2004), p. 302.

humans, even when they are deprived of their fundamental rights. That is, "the subjects of [...] rights are the very people who lack the qualification and 'status' to hold rights. Rights are held by those who, though lacking all qualifications to do so, take them, claim, and enact them".[77] The Rancièrian view emphasizes the non-discriminatory function of subjectivation; rights are a tool for politically powerless groups, and useful particularly for those deprived of those rights. As such, human rights are what you make of them. Following this reasoning, human rights are constrained within the tight limits of the rights of vulnerable groups (rights of women, children etc.). It is only these groups that correspond to the Rancièrian collective political subject—the subject of the rights of Man. Furthermore, according to this scheme, claiming a right is far more crucial than its enjoyment, inasmuch as a claim bears proof of the right's existence.

These contemplations concerning the subject of human rights are not congruent with the issue of enforced disappearance. According to Rancièrian theory, a right's existence is dependent upon its subjects' claims, and it is not a matter of protection. Yet, this observation presupposes that the physical integrity of the agents themselves is not jeopardized and their claims can reach society. In the event of enforced disappearance, there is no such possibility that the victim can successfully claim the right's existence, given that the victims are entirely under their captors' power, placed outside the protection of the law. This view falls short of preserving a life with dignity for the victim (that is, the good protected by the right), even after claiming the right's existence.[78] Moreover, Rancière, as well as the aforementioned dignitarian approaches, does not recognize the process of de-subjectivation: Rancière because he founds his doctrine on the axiom of non-rightlessness, and the dignitarians because they have evolved around the law notion of subjectivity. In this context, both approaches do not substantiate the de-subjectivation which takes place during enforced disappearance.

Revealingly, the combination of the dignitarian and political aspects of enforced disappearance leads to the paradoxical application of subjectivity and de-subjectivation at the same time. Indeed, these two approaches will be used concurrently with regards to disappearances, precisely because the phenomenon obliterates the very concept of "the subject of human rights". Adopting a de-subjectivation reasoning is possible only because the prohibition on enforced disappearance must be characterized as a civil right, thereby verifying the prohibition's value. In other words, the prohibition on enforced disappearance shields the agent's subjectivity, posing a legal barrier to the potential victim's de-subjectivation. As indicated above, the good protected by the right against disappearance is a life with dignity, which in these terms is translated into the avoidance of de-subjectivation. That is, the severity of an enforced disappearance renders life with dignity synonymous with the prevention of de-subjectivation.

---

[77] Kesby (2012), p. 121.

[78] Osiatyński (2009), p. 191.

3.1.4 Enforced Disappearance as a Civil Right Violation

The recognition of an autonomous right by the CPED is radical in terms of the phenomenon's confrontation and the noteworthy advancements made in the international human rights regime. The prohibition on enforced disappearance bears the features of a civil liberty, or of any other similar classification where the individual element is foremost. Still, apart from the individual aspects of enforced disappearance, the right has definite political ramifications inasmuch as it entails an explicit state policy. This fact, alongside the intentional alienation of the victim from *nomos*, gives a particular political dimension to the right, which might well obscure the right's characterization as civil. However, the right against disappearance is not hybrid, but rather is a hyper-right, whose violation entails the victim's inability to effectively protect a series of their rights.[79] From the victim's perspective, the prohibition on disappearance bears a predominantly individual value. In turn, the political aspects seem subordinate, since they cannot be immediately assessed by the victim when a disappearance occurs.[80] Put simply, it is practically impossible for the victims of a disappearance to perceive themselves as political subjects in the first instance, putting aside anything related to their basic subsistence. The captor's sovereign power over the victim is the element which infringes human dignity, rather than the potential peril to the victim's life. All in all, the right not to be subjected to enforced disappearance is a blatant violation of human dignity and tests its inviolability. This violation reaches the limits of dehumanization and threatens human rights' inalienability.[81]

The right's stipulation in the 2007 Convention is critical for the completion of the international human rights regime in general, mostly because it throws light on perennial questions regarding its foundations. The recognition of the right reconceptualizes notions like human and moral nature, so far as it renders their dynamic—or at least non-static—interpretation imperative. The prohibition on disappearance provides strong evidence of the fact that human possibility has developed the notions

---

[79] According to the settled jurisprudence of the IACtHR, an enforced disappearance is a "pluri-offensive" right, because it involves "multiple violations of several rights". *Radilla-Pacheco v Mexico*, Inter-American Court of Human Rights Series C No 209 (23 November 2009) paras 139–140; *Torres Millacura v Argentina*, Inter-American Court of Human Rights Series C No 229 (26 August 2011) para 95.

[80] In the present analysis, the term "civil" is presented as the opposite of "political" and is associated with the term "individual". The ultimate purpose of this schema is to prioritize the individual consequences (that is, for the human being as a living organism) of a disappearance over the political ones. In this context, the civil character of the right preponderates over its political aspects. Yet, the pronouncement of a civil right presupposes a person's recognition as a citizen by the sovereign, and therefore the term "civil" consists of at least one political decision, the subject's acceptance as a citizen. As a matter of fact, it is doctrinally inconsistent to separate these two groups of rights. In addition, both civil and political rights are considered individual rights, rather than collective rights. Thus, the concept of civil rights is subsumed under that of individual rights, which is broader.

[81] Donnelly (2003), p. 10.

of human and moral nature over the course of many years. This means that the culture of human rights is developmental in form,[82] and human rights are nothing but institutions reflecting the maturity of people and law.[83] The phenomenon of enforced disappearance is an occasion where human possibility turns into an example of human perversity, as the perpetrators invent an appalling way to infringe on other people's human dignity. From this perspective, the legal response to disappearances "emerge[d] from the concrete experiences [and] suffering of real human beings", and this reflects "a process of social learning".[84]

Consequently, the occurrence and recognition of the right not to be subjected to enforced disappearance is not a sign of proliferation, but rather testimony to the new ways invented by humans to cause human suffering and to harm human dignity. Hence, it is argued that the prohibition on enforced disappearance shall be reckoned an integral part of the "irreducible core of human rights", which until recently was considered *numerus clausus*.[85] This short catalogue of human rights consists of the right to life, as well as prohibitions of slavery and torture and the right not to be subject to *ex post facto* application of law.[86] These rights share the common ground of human inviolability or against people being treated "as the living instruments of others", deprived of their ability to be the autonomous owners of their own lives, a consideration which describes why such violations require absolute legal responses.[87]

Even though the above summaries aim primarily at the right's classification in the human rights regime, they raise the issue of a possible internal hierarchy of human rights.[88] Already, references to the irreducible core of human rights, to fundamental or hyper-rights, have laid the ground for a hierarchical construction among human rights according to their subject matter. However, a rights hierarchy has been rejected repeatedly by the international community, to avoid the creation of a multi-speed human rights regime. The Proclamation of Teheran as well as the Vienna Declaration on human rights turned spotlights on the indivisibility and interdependence[89] of human rights, attempting to establish the conception of human rights equality within the UN. Most often, theory interprets hierarchical evaluations as a barrier to an integrated human rights approach, conflicting with indivisibility, at

[82] Boucher (2009), p. 249.

[83] Pound (1915), p. 102.

[84] Donnelly (2003), p. 58.

[85] *Anzualdo Castro v Peru*, Concurring Opinion of Judge Sergio García Ramírez, para 3.

[86] Meron (1986), p. 11.

[87] Lee (2005), pp. 81, 83.

[88] Donnelly observes correctly that natural law theorists experience the "widespread tendency to view natural rights claims as being in some sense absolute" and they eventually "adopt a positivist theory of rights"; he renounces "absoluteness" measurements of human rights, suggesting that they cannot reconcile with the natural law proposal that depends solely on morality claims that are non-receptive to rankings. Donnelly (1982), p. 395.

[89] Final Act of the International Conference on Human Rights (Proclamation of Teheran). (Teheran 22 April–13 May 1968). UN Doc A/Conf.32/41, op clause 13; UNGA. (12 July 1993). Vienna Declaration and Programme of Action. UN Doc A/Conf.157/23, op clause 5.

least regarding the rights' subject-matter.[90] Yet, the concepts of indivisibility and hierarchy are not opposing;[91] on the contrary, the violation of a hyper-right, like the prohibition of disappearance, directly involves the breach of a series of rights. From this stance, not only do the two concepts not clash, they are complementary. Finally, in this content-based hierarchy scheme, the right against disappearance is to be found among the list of core rights; it is a subsistence right which determines the enjoyment of the remaining human rights.

3.2 Art. 1(2): The Prohibition of Derogation

Art. 1(2) essentially intensifies the absolute character of the right against enforced disappearance, as it furnishes the right with a prohibition of derogation. It provides that "[n]o exceptional circumstances whatsoever, whether a state of war or a threat of war, internal political instability or any other public emergency, may be invoked as a justification for enforced disappearance". Thereby, states parties' capacity to invoke a state of emergency or any kind of political convulsion as an excuse to perform acts of enforced disappearance is discarded. This phrasing has previously been adopted by the 1992 Declaration (Art. 7), albeit as a non-binding instrument. This provision is a duplicate of Art. 2(2) of the CaT, which renders the prohibition on torture a non-derogable right, using the exact same wording. These two provisions introduce unconditional prohibitions of derogation from the respective rights they refer to, and for this reason they are correctly typified as the strictest non-derogable clauses. Consequently, Art. 1(2) advances the system of protection against disappearances, because it excludes all and any circumstances ("no exceptional circumstances whatsoever") which may be used as grounds for disappearances.[92]

The mere fact itself, that the terminology from the 1992 Declaration to the 2007 Convention remains intact, is indicative of the drafters' commitment to the non-derogable character of the right and the subsequent will of states parties to be bound by it.[93] In the flux of negotiations over the Convention's drafting, there has been almost no hesitation about the norm's non-derogable character, since it has time and again been affirmed by international and regional documents and by international

[90] Eide and Rosas (1995), pp. 15–16.

[91] Shelton (2002), pp. 302–303; Meron (1986), p. 21.

[92] The majority of international instruments give examples of which circumstances are perceived to be exceptional and so justify derogation. The terms vary, and thus the ECHR provides for a "public emergency threatening the life of a nation", the IACHR speaks of an "other emergency that threatens the independence or security of a State Party", whereas the ICCPR requires a "time of public emergency which threatens the life of a nation". Despite these terms' abstractness, they eventually became states' escape clauses, as states attempted to relativize them when the life of a nation or the security of a state is in peril, thus legitimizing derogations whose necessity is questioned. Accordingly, the language of the CaT and the CPED guarantees individual protection through its indeterminacy ("no exceptional circumstances whatsoever"). Gross and Ní Aoláin (2006), p. 257.

[93] UN Doc E/CN.4/2004/59, para 170(a); UN Doc E/CN.4/2003/71, para 26.

and even domestic jurisprudence. As well as the 1992 Declaration, the Inter-American Convention on disappearance also prohibits the commission of enforced disappearance when exceptional circumstances occur, and outlaws any methods which conceal the whereabouts and health conditions of the detained individual.[94] This provision is quite detailed and seems thorough at first sight, as it not only rules out the commission of the exceptional case of disappearances but also outlines which guarantees should be met so that traces of the detained are not lost. In this respect, this article attempts to determine the distinctive features of a disappearance, which means the concealment of a victim's fate or whereabouts. However, by setting guarantees for this element only, it opens the door to a fragmented approach to enforced disappearance, thus leaving space for harsh interrogation techniques or mistreatment of the detained victims.

3.2.1 Jurisprudential Affirmations of Non-derogability

Besides these early demonstrations of international instruments, jurisprudence has examined the norm's non-derogable quality more systematically. The HRC first suggested that enforced disappearance is a rule that is non-receptive to derogation.[95] In *Ann Maria Garcia Lanza de Netto et al v Uruguay* of 1980, it held that

> the Covenant (art. 4) does not allow national measures derogating from any of its provisions except in strictly defined circumstances, and the Government [of Uruguay] has not made any submissions of fact or law to justify such derogation. Moreover, some of the facts referred to above raise issues under provisions from which the Covenant does not allow any derogation under any circumstances.[96]

Two basic conclusions follow from this passage: first, the HRC perceives Art. 4 as an exception to the body of the Covenant, reserves a narrow interpretation of it, and demands that states parties produce proof of fact or law concerning the necessity of

---

[94] IACFDP Art. X.

[95] The HRC had received many complaints dealing with the practice of enforced disappearance by the time of the Uruguayan regime in the 70s. Yet, it had mistakenly treated these communications as incommunicado detentions as a result of the international community's inexperience with the phenomenon of enforced disappearances. Consequently, any mentions of derogation cannot be directly linked to disappearance, although they essentially refer to it. *Ilda Thomas & Hiber Conteris v Uruguay*, HRC (1985). UN Doc CCPR/C/25/D/139/1983, para 7.5; *Sergio Ruben Lopez Burgos v Uruguay*, para 11.6; *Alba Pietraroia & Rosario Pietraroia v Uruguay*, HRC (1981) UN Doc CCPR/C/12/D/44/1979, para 14; *Esther Soriano de Bouton v Uruguay*, HRC (1981) UN Doc CCPR/C/12/D/37/1978, para 12; *Luciano Weinberger Weisz & Ismael Weinberger v Uruguay*, HRC (1980) UN Doc CCPR/C/11/D/28/1978, para 14; *Alberto Grille Motta v Uruguay*, HRC (1980) UN Doc CCPR/C/10/D/11/1977, para 15; *William Torres Ramirez v Uruguay*, HRC (1980) UN Doc CCPR/C/10/D/4/1977, para 17; *Miguel A Millan Sequeina v Uruguay*, HRC (1980) UN Doc CCPR/C/10/D/6/1977, para 14.

[96] *Ann Maria Garcia Lanza de Netto et al v Uruguay*, HRC (1980) UN Doc CCPR/C/9/D/8/1977, para 15.

human rights derogations. Hence, the HRC underscores the procedural prerequisites set by Art. 4. Second, the HRC affirms the proximity of enforced disappearance to non-derogable rights, although it identifies it only as a complex practice and not as a norm. The important feature of this paragraph is that it carries the first evidence of a doctrinal connection between enforced disappearance and Art. 4(2), which expressly mentions which rights are non-derogable under the ICCPR. So far, and especially after the Convention's entry into force, the HRC has not offered an unequivocal connection between enforced disappearance and the non-derogable core of the Covenant. In the recent disappearance case of *Yubraj Giri v Nepal*, the HRC stated with respect to the detainees' mistreatment that "while it is not separately mentioned in the list of non-derogable rights, in article 4 paragraph 2, this norm of general international law is not subject to derogation".[97] The HRC did not endorse the author's claims, according to which "the prohibition against enforced disappearance is absolute and cannot be derogated from under any circumstance".[98] Overall, the HRC's jurisprudence leaves the question of the norm's non-derogability unresolved, since it does not place it among the non-derogable rights of Art. 4(2) as a general rule of international law.

In contrast, the IACtHR has adopted a more open stance on this issue, declaring the truth of the norm's non-derogability. In the renowned case of *Goiburú et al v Paraguay*, the IACtHR held that "the prohibition of [forced disappearance] is a non-derogable provision of international law or *jus cogens* [because] it is deemed to harm essential values and rights of the international community".[99] This verdict illustrates the progress made by the IACtHR; the Inter-American Court has gradually accepted that the right not to be subjected to enforced disappearance itself is a non-derogable rule, whereas in previous judgments it only agreed that the practice of enforced disappearance violates a series of rights from which no derogation is tolerated. More specifically, the IACtHR has been advocating that "serious human rights violations such as torture, extrajudicial, summary or arbitrary execution and forced disappearance, all of them prohibited because they violate non-derogable rights recognized by international human rights law".[100] This evolution may largely be attributed to Judge Trindade, who systematically supported in his concurring opinions that enforced disappearance constitutes a non-derogable rule of international law, pointing to the prohibition's originality.[101]

---

[97] *Yubraj Giri v Nepal*, HRC (2011) UN Doc CCPR/C/101/D/1761/2008, para 7.9.

[98] ibid para 5.4.

[99] *Goiburú et al v Paraguay*, paras 93, 128.

[100] *Barrios Altos v Peru*, Inter-American Court of Human Rights Series C No 75 (14 March 2001) para 41; *Trujillo-Oroza v Bolivia*, Inter-American Court of Human Rights Series C No 92 (27 February 2002) para 106; *Almonacid-Arellano et al v Chile*, Inter-American Court of Human Rights Series C No 154 (26 September 2006) para 112; *Tiu Tojín v Guatemala*, para 53; *Ibsen Cárdenas & Ibsen Peña v Bolivia*, Inter-American Court of Human Rights Series C No 217 (3 May 2010) para 12.

[101] *Barrios Altos v Peru*, Concurring Opinion of Judge Cançado A.A. Trindade, paras 10–11; *Almonacid-Arellano et al v Chile*, Concurring Opinion of Judge Cançado A.A. Trindade, para 15.

Apart from the categorical affirmation that enforced disappearance is a prohibition not to be derogated from, "no matter the conditions of each State",[102] the IACtHR further examined what this dictum entails and determined its content. In this sense, the Inter-American Court views that a state's failure to investigate allegations of enforced disappearance under the pretext of an internal armed conflict amounts to violating a non-derogable norm;[103] obviously it remains indifferent whether the state has formally declared itself to be in a state of emergency. As a result, any attempts to avoid or reject responsibility for enforced disappearance or the need to punish the commission of it, either by not investigating a reported case or by enacting amnesty laws and provisions on prescription, are equal to derogation.[104] Given its immense experience of disappearance cases, the IACtHR realized that the prohibition is "an inexcusable abandonment of the essential principles on which the Inter-American System is based",[105] and therefore construed non-derogability as a legal concept in the service of ensuring the culprits' punishment. By extending the prohibition's non-derogable character to the states-parties' positive duty to investigate both the disappearance allegations and their potential ensuing efforts to secure a state of impunity for the perpetrators, the IACtHR aimed at and succeeded in rendering its judgments effective for alleviating the victims' suffering.

Unlike the IACtHR, the jurisprudence of the remaining regional human rights courts is not so constructive concerning the right's non-derogable character. Although the ECtHR had the opportunity to positively pronounce that enforced disappearance is not permissible in cases of any kind of emergency, it merely repeated that the right to life and the prohibition on torture are non-derogable; not that it had ever acknowledged the right's autonomous character. Even in cases where the respondent states declared districts to be in emergency conditions for months or years, so as to curtail the enjoyment of human rights, and where they performed *inter alia* enforced disappearance, the European Court's jurisprudence remained cumbersome.[106] Likewise, the ACHPR's scant references to disappearances could

[102] *Anzualdo Castro v Peru*, para 199.

[103] *Río Negro Massacres v Guatemala*, para 227.

[104] *Barrios Altos v Peru*, para 41; *La Cantuta v Peru*, Inter-American Court of Human Rights Series C No 162 (29 November 2006) para 152; *González Medina & Family v Dominican Republic*, Inter-American Court of Human Rights Series C No 240 (27 February 2012) paras 126–127; *The Massacres of El Mozote and Nearby Places v El Salvador*, para 281.

[105] *Radilla-Pacheco v Mexico*, para 139.

[106] *Tahsin Acar v Turkey*, App no 26307/95 (ECtHR 8 April 2004) paras 186–188, 209; *Mahmut Kaya v Turkey*, paras 27, 110, 112; *Bazorkina v Russia*, paras 129, 139. The "Turkish cases" make the most of the ECtHR's jurisprudence regarding disappearance in times of emergency, although none has been dealt with as a disappearance case. In most of these cases, the Strasbourg Court emphasized the arbitrariness of the victims' detention and seemed to apply a lower threshold to human rights standards to Turkey, because it did not consider Turkey to be a well-established democratic society. Ní Aoláin (2007), pp. 69–74.

not contribute to the norm's development.[107] Nevertheless, jurisprudence paved the way for the conventional stipulation of the right's non-derogable character. Hence, Art. 1(2) was a momentous, yet anticipated, provision of the CPED.

3.2.2 The Legal Aftermath of the Right's Non-derogable Character

Art. 1(2) has a tangible function within the conventional framework: it sets a parallel absolute obligation for states-parties not to violate the right of Art. 1(1). This means that Art. 1(2) supplements the right expressed in the first paragraph by establishing a mirror obligation to the prohibition. The non-derogation clause follows the stipulation of the right and precedes the definition of enforced disappearance; although its placement is *prima facie* insignificant, it is in line with the complex nature of the practice of disappearances. Otherwise, in cases where the placement was opposite and the non-derogability clause followed the definition, misinterpretations as to the aspects of disappearance covered by the prohibition of derogation would be possible, even likely. Such possibilities would not be far-fetched considering the precedent of the CaT, where the placement of provisions is intended to differentiate between the derogation status of torture and that of cruel, inhumane or degrading treatment, the latter of which is permissible in a state of emergency.[108] This approach is at variance with enforced disappearance offences, which require a complex state practice. In other words, if derogations were permitted for at least one of the definition's elements, then the CPED would be of minimum value to victims.

The absoluteness of states-parties' obligation not to commit disappearances under any circumstances, renders reservations about Art. 1 inadmissible. Reservations about this provision would be impermissible anyway, because they do not pass the traditional object and purpose test of the VCLT.[109] Additionally, the CPED expressly mentions states-parties' ability to submit a reservation regarding its arbitration procedure (Art. 43); consequently, the omission of similar references from the treaty body denotes the drafters' intention to preclude the submission of

---

[107] *Commission Nationale des Droits de l'Homme et des Libertés v Chad*, Comm no 74/92 (ACHPR 1995) paras 4, 21; *Malawi African Association et al v Mauritania*, Comm nos 54/91, 61/91, 98/93, 164–196/97, 210/98 (ACHPR 2000) paras 84, 144.

[108] The diverse derogation status of torture and ill-treatment has been of great concern to the Committee against Torture, which has rightly pointed that there is no clear line between ill-treatment and torture, and that most often the former facilitates the latter. To bypass this handicap, which by definition diminishes the CaT's field of protection and therefore its success, the Committee against Torture opted for a *contra legem* interpretation of the CaT (characterized as dynamic) and held that "the prohibition of ill-treatment [is] likewise non-derogable under the Convention and its prevention [is] an effective and non-derogable measure". Committee against Torture. (24 January 2008). General Comment No. 2, Implementation of Article 2 by States Parties. UN Doc CAT/C/GC/2, para 3.

[109] VCLT, Art. 19(c).

reservations from all other articles. Apart from the VCLT tests, there is no safe criterion to ascertain the legality of reservations, nor can "an automatic correlation between reservations to non-derogable provisions"[110] be inferred. More specifically, a conventional norm's non-derogability does not preclude a state-party's ability to submit a reservation.[111] The particularity of human rights treaties, though, where states-parties undertake responsibilities concerning persons within their jurisdiction and not towards the remaining parties, conditions their success—among others—of states-parties' least possible reservations.[112] In this framework, reservations about non-derogable human rights seem absurd, and pose "a heavy onus" on states-parties concerning their justification.[113] The relationship between derogability and reservations with respect to international human rights treaties is tentatively supported by theory,[114] as well as by jurisprudence.[115] The Inter-American Commission on Human Rights has interpreted non-derogable human rights in light of VCLT Art. 19(c), and considers them to be the purpose and object of human rights treaties. It has therefore supported the idea that "a reservation […] designed to enable a State to suspend any of the non-derogable fundamental rights must be deemed incompatible with the object and purpose of the [respective] Convention and, consequently, not permitted by it".[116] The HRC not only espoused this reading of non-derogable rights, but further broadened it by reaching the conclusion that "some provisions are non-derogable exactly because without them there would be no rule of law".[117] Accordingly, the rule that "non-derogability entails non-reservation" was gradually shaped in international literature.

Although this rule is not doctrinally well-founded in treaty law, it was adjusted to become the main point of interest of human rights treaties: namely, the greatest possible protection of individuals, or else the maximum and unconditional degree of state commitment. From this perspective, it may well be argued that Art. 1(2) creates absolute obligations for states-parties and allows for no reservations. Apart from this, the right's non-derogable character indicates a sort of a hierarchical

---

[110] HRC. (4 November 1994). Issues relating to reservations made upon ratification or accession relating to reservations made upon ratification or accession to the Covenant or the Optional Protocols Thereto, or in relation to Declarations under Article 41 of the Covenant. UN Doc CCPR/C/21/Rev.1/Add.6, para 10.

[111] Schabas (2008), p. 901.

[112] Redgwell (1997), pp. 404–405.

[113] UN Doc CCPR/C/21/Rev.1/Add.6, para 10.

[114] Shelton (2002), pp. 315–316; Redgwell (1997).

[115] The ICJ early in 1951 took the position that reservations in human rights treaties reflect states-parties' intention to derogate from the rule under consideration. It stated that "the parties [to a Convention] intended to derogate from that rule by admitting the faculty to make reservations thereto". *Reservations to the Convention on the Prevention and Punishment of the Crime of Genocide* (Advisory Opinion) [1951] ICJ Rep 15, 24.

[116] Inter-American Commission on Human Rights (8 September 1983). Restrictions to the death penalty (Arts. 4(2) and 4(4) of the American Convention on Human Rights). Advisory Opinion' Series A No 3, OC-3/83, para 61.

[117] UN Doc CCPR/C/21/Rev.1/Add.6, para 10.

supremacy in the human rights system, a pattern which keeps reappearing in the present analysis through references to the "irreducible core of human rights", or the characterization of the prohibition on disappearance as a "hyper-right". Thereat, a potential connection between non-derogability and the right's normative value is worth exploring.

3.2.3 Non-derogability and Hierarchical Supremacy

The idea of a human rights hierarchy is not a novelty; instead it "reflects the quest for a normative order" which would integrate legal and moral features in the international human rights regime.[118] This notion infers a natural law approach to human rights, prioritizing rights deemed to be ingrained in human dignity. This view, though, is largely thought to lack objectivity. In this context, non-derogability stands as an objective criterion for the hierarchical classification of human rights, at the same time merging natural law implications and positive law requirements. Non-derogable rights are absolute, in the sense that they are a restraint of state practice; they are bound conventionally by norms which are not subject to limitation clauses, reservations or denunciations. As a matter of fact, they form a "hierarchical pinnacle" in the international human rights treaty regime.[119] On these grounds, the so-called "irreducible core of human rights" is not a list formulated solely on a subject matter basis; rather, it consists of the four rights which are non-derogable under the ICCPR, the ECHR and the IACHR (bearing in mind that the ACHPR does not contain a derogation clause).[120] The shared feature of non-derogability, combined both with the highest level of international and regional acceptance, converts these rights into universal norms.

Although the right not to be subjected to enforced disappearance belongs, in terms of substance, to the "irreducible core of human rights" (as explained above), it does not qualify for this superior group of rights within the hierarchy of positive law. The right against disappearance stands alone in the international human rights regime, formally acknowledged only within the Convention's limits. Accordingly, the right's non-derogable character has not reached a point of universal acceptance. The right's absence from the International Bill of Human Rights and from the regional human rights treaties is historically explained; nevertheless, this absence impedes the norm's systemic integration within the hierarchical elite of human rights. A contradictory scheme emerges: on the one hand, the substantive features of the right against disappearance place it at the epicenter of the human rights regime, while on the other hand, its omission from the basic rights treaties lowers its position in the alleged pyramid of human rights. This paradox is most obvious in the

---

[118] Meron (1986), p. 21.

[119] Shelton (2002), pp. 313, 316, 330.

[120] Meron (1986), p. 11; Hartman (1981), p. 15.

context of the UN legal order: the stipulation of the right in the UN Convention does not entail its inclusion in the decisions of the HRC. Even though the ICCPR and the CPED are drafted in under the auspices of the UN, their ratification status prevents a unified approach to the phenomenon of enforced disappearance. All in all, a strictly positivist approach is not empirically open to the daunting challenges of human rights. It renders "the irreducible core of human rights" stagnant; a concept unable to adjust to contemporary state practices or current threats to human dignity.

3.3 Art. 1: Foundational, But Non-inclusive

It is a truism that the formulation of a norm on enforced disappearance and its conventional stipulation has been long awaited. In this way, the provision of a non-derogable prohibition on disappearance has been a manifest success, and fundamental for the conclusion of the 2007 Convention. Art. 1 is the core of the CPED, without which a legal instrument could not exist. Except for the apparent positive effects on the struggle against the phenomenon of disappearance, the recognition of an autonomous norm leads to the completion of the international human rights regime. The right is palpable evidence of an evolutionary stand towards human rights; it signifies a regime ready to assimilate the experience of human ferocities directed against human beings and to adapt its norms accordingly. Still, the conventional affirmation of the prohibition against enforced disappearance is of limited value. The norm is experiencing a *sui generis* legal isolation, because it binds only states-parties to the Convention. Therefore, its legal impact extends to, and depends on, the number of states that ratify the CPED. Given the present number of states-parties of the Convention, it is doctrinally impossible to draw any connections between Art. 1 and the provision's normative supremacy. In the conventional context, no-one can support the idea that the prohibition against enforced disappearance is an obligation owed to the international community (*erga omnes* obligation) or that it is a peremptory norm (*ius cogens*). The right's universal recognition relies on the number of states-parties to the Convention, a condition which diminishes its potential. For this reason, it is critical to examine if the right not to be subjected to enforced disappearance transcends treaty limits, and if there is a customary rule prohibiting enforced disappearance.

3.4 The Sources of Human Rights and the Right Against Enforced Disappearance: "New Wine into Fresh Wineskins [...] Both Preserved"[121]

So far, four general theses on human rights can be inferred from the analysis on the right not to be subjected to enforced disappearance: human rights are natural rights (1); natural rights are strong moral claims (2); natural law is empirically open, and thus natural rights are evolving norms (3); and subsistence rights are hierarchically supreme due to the moral values they embody (4). Most importantly, the said theses reveal two particular implications for the sources of human rights. To begin with, natural law (*jus naturae*) is perceived to be a source of human rights law, and furthermore the features of morality and evolvability attributed to natural rights emphasize the prominence of custom as a source of human rights law. These assertions neither challenge the sources of international law nor call for their reconfiguration; certainly, though, they explain why the discussion about the application of international law sources on human rights cannot become obsolete.

Provided that the doctrinal consistency of international law sources' theory is a major priority, then counting natural law among the sources is definitely not a safe choice. On the other hand, if the key interest is in affording a solid explanation for the ontology of human rights law, then considering natural law as a legal source is deemed necessary. One of the propositions set out above is that human rights are natural rights, which further implies that human rights law can only be explained through a natural law approach (thesis 1). Although an in-depth examination of natural law exceeds the scope of this study, a few remarks are needed.

Natural law pertains to "rules of law that have an inherent and necessary validity [...] whenever a rule of law is found which could not be other than it is, could not *not* exist, and does not require to be accounted for or justified in terms of any other rule, it is a rule of natural law".[122] This divine validity of natural law is the ontological foundation of human rights law. Human rights law, as a separate field of general public international law, is unique because it conflicts with the traditional subject of public international law, the state. Rights have been created as an antidote to the misuse or flaws of sovereignty,[123] and as such human rights first took on the form of concessions by the sovereign. Human rights law reestablishes the human being at the center of legal tradition. As Philip Allott states, "law is a product of the total social process of the society of which it is the law";[124] it is a gift of civilization in the name of humanity.[125] Similarly, law, the notion of the sovereign state, reflects (at

---

[121] Matthew 9:17.

[122] Fitzmaurice (1958), p. 164.

[123] Henkin (1995/1996), p. 31.

[124] Allott (1990), p. 254.

[125] Tomuschat (2008), p. 12.

least ideally) the will and aspirations of the society by which it is constructed. Recalling the Vattelian system, Allott maintains that

> "since nations are composed of men [...] who before the establishment of civil society lived together in the state of nature, such [...] sovereign States must be regarded as so many free persons living together in the state of nature". And the reified abstractions inhabiting the international state of nature are not fictions. They are persons.[126]

In this framework, *jus naturae* is the inherent limit of the sovereign state, and human rights law is one of its primary forms of expression. Accordingly, human rights are natural because they cannot be other than that, since human beings are entitled to human rights because of human dignity. Assenting to that scheme, one cannot deny the impact of natural law on the content of rights, and must subsequently recognize that natural law is a material source of human rights.[127] As a material source it is not added to the list of Art. 38 of the ICJ Statute, which encapsulates the formal sources of public international law; rather, it fuels them, providing raw material for the creation of legal norms.[128]

No matter how reasonable the connection between natural and human rights law seems at first blush, it has unavoidable legal repercussions for human rights. First, the common feature of human dignity due to people's nature, and their consequent entitlement to human rights, renders rights universal. To sustain this view, we need to distinguish between natural law as the bedrock of human rights, and the characterization of every right as natural and thus universal. The former recognizes human nature, and subsequently natural law, as the central tenet of human rights, and the *raison d'être* of human rights law as a field of international law in general, while the latter elevates every human right to a natural claim. That is, although all human rights carry the feature of universality—given that all human beings might equally claim them—not each and every right reaches the status of a universal norm. This intermediate position appears by itself to be a compromise in the application of the natural law on human rights; it breaks the sequence between human nature and universality by proposing that the universality of human nature does not equally encompass the legal claims it generates. Quite the contrary: the claim that nature

---

[126] Allott (2002), p. 58.

[127] Perceiving natural law as a material source of public international law is probably a moderate view, balancing the two theoretical positions. From one point of view, natural law is "the ultimate source of any rule" and operates "directly as a formal source of law" alongside the sources of Art. 38 ICJ Statute, further compensating for the absence of "normal legislative and judicial organs" in the international legal system. Fitzmaurice (1958), pp. 166, 168. Yet, it can be as equally well explained that natural law is "the expression of dictates of morality" in international law, and as such it is the precursor of the "general principles of law, [which are] the principles arrived at by way of comparison, generalization and synthesis of rules of law in its various branches [...] common to various systems of national law, [subject] to municipal jurisprudence". Lauterpacht (1970), pp. 46, 74, 358. From this angle, the general principles of law recognized by civilized nations (Art. 38(1)(c)) are the formal codification of natural law, which eventually is little more than good morals.

[128] Despite the particularities of human rights law, it consists in part of general public international law, and they have both their sources in common, rendering recourse to Art. 38 ICJ Statute inevitable.

begets rights is reinforced by admitting human rights' classification (thesis 4), depending on an ethical hierarchy of the moral claims these rights comprise (thesis 3). The natural explanation of rights is a *prima facie* aberration from the strict positivist reading of legal claims, even though it accommodates their hierarchical ranking pursuant to their content, or so-called "substantive validity".[129] Although several criteria for the classification of rights are proposed, there is dearth of principles explaining their hierarchy, particularly due to the long-existing hesitancy of theory to prioritize legal claims.

Thus, the natural explanation of rights is a safe hierarchy test, lying far from the "idealistic" understanding of law often attributed to it.[130] Most importantly, this approach detaches human rights from the state-centric design of the sources of international law. In particular, it disengages rights from the concept of an extensive and uniform state practice which will eventually beget a customary norm or will gradually give rise to a conventional rule. In other words, if consent and state behavior are the decisive elements in the formation of rules (conventional and customary respectively), natural law partly shifts this focus of attention to content evaluation regarding human rights norms. In this light, consent is readily granted for minor claims which do not entail explicit duties for the state, whereas state practice is by definition contestable for critical human rights matters.[131] Going in this direction, measuring rules by substantive validity diminishes the consensual and behavioral foundation of legal norms, whilst it provides for the necessary flexibility to explain the formulation of human rights rules. In this respect, states' promptness to ratify legal instruments which stipulate vague rules resulting in obligations veiled with uncertainty does not conform with the "substantive validity" test of norms. For example, this proposition is verified by the popularity of instruments which only require states to commit to the prospective amelioration of living standards, compared with the unpopularity of those which aim at shielding the individual vis-à-vis state powers.[132] The same applies to a greater extent to the formation of customary norms, where state practice rarely tallies with *opinio juris*. All in all, the above follow on from the idea that natural rights are "ultimately superior to the state itself, [a concept which further constitutes] the continuous thread in the historical pattern of legal and political thought".[133] Evidently, deciphering human rights through natural law challenges the even application of the principal formal law sources to human rights, since it curtails the influence of treaty law and questions the relevance of custom.

[129] d'Aspremont (2011), pp. 96–97.

[130] ibid p. 100.

[131] Rancière (2004), p. 302.

[132] Henkin (1979), p. 227.

[133] Lauterpacht (1950), p. 80.

3.4.1 *Human Rights and the Repositioning of Treaty Law and Custom*

In general terms, treaty law is considered "a barrier [...] to the realization of human values",[134] given that its key element is consent, the ultimate expression of sovereignty. Thus, consent renders treaties "a mode of state practice".[135] Certain eminent scholars have moved even further to "rule out conventions as a source of human rights law" since they "only bind the states that signed them [and therefore they] deprive human rights law of its universality".[136] This makes a strong case, as treaty law is consent-dependent; yet it is only half the truth, because it does not take into account the fact that treaty law might evolve into a source of custom, or, conversely, crystallize into an already existing customary law.[137] Nonetheless, according to Louis Henkin,

> human rights treaties continue to increase, a reflection of the system's steady drift toward human values. It is a reflection, too, of the new sensitivity of states and of the state system to pressures leading to consent. It is perhaps the only instance of a new body of international law born and grown in response to an idea, to public opinion - domestic and international opinion.[138]

From this angle, two characteristics may be inferred for the application of treaty law to human rights. First, the production of treaty norms cannot but remain a slow and inflexible process, due to the formality of the process and the required consent. Hence, treaty law often struggles to catch up with national developments in the field of human rights.[139] Second, human rights treaties are not utterly estranged from morality: their drafting indicates the focus of the international community, and reflects public opinion's awareness on particular issues. Despite their systemic inadequacy for the promotion of human rights law, they are meaningful—even from a

134 Henkin (1995/1996), p. 31.

135 D'Amato (1995/1996), p. 91.

136 ibid p. 52; *see* also, Simma and Alston (1988–1989), p. 82.

137 *North Sea Continental Shelf Cases (Federal Republic of Germany v Denmark; Netherlands)* [1969] ICJ Rep 3, 40, para 63.

138 Henkin (1995/1996), p. 36.

139 Louis Henkin notices that human rights treaties most often reflect improvements in domestic legislation or are part of a *quid pro quo rationale*, which allows the sovereign to promote other interests. His point of reference is the third Restatement, which provides that "there may be non-conventional human rights law in addition to that which it was prepared to recognize and restate at the time, and that more such law would doubtless come". The American example, though, is exceptional. Furthermore, Henkin was the Chief Reporter of the American Law Institute for the third Restatement; accordingly, he had the ability to draw analogies and point out discrepancies between the American and the international legal order. However, explaining human rights treaties through domestic analogy is not always possible. Enforced disappearance is not included in the American constitution; likewise, genocide, or torture, which have long been stipulated in international documents, do not appear in many states' relevant instruments. Ibid 37–38; Restatement (third) of the Foreign Relations Law of the United States (ALI 1987) para 702; D'Amato (1995/1996), p. 54.

symbolic perspective—as they incorporate human values. Accordingly, although the CPED's success relies typically on the number of ratifications, in essence it epitomizes public opinion's anguish over, and struggle against, enforced disappearance. Besides, the CPED's delay in coming into force confirms the state's anxiety concerning disappearance.

At the same time, the CPED's temporal placement suggests that it will crystallize into customary law, while the possibility that the Convention will gradually evolve into a custom will be rejected. Had the CPED appeared at the beginning of the legal debate over enforced disappearance, this view would ignore the legal impact of previous regional attempts and the UN's efforts to establish the right, and it would have resulted in the Convention's systemic isolation. However, if the CPED is now at the crucial stage of legal proceedings regarding the phenomenon, then the possibility that it will codify existing customary rules remains an option.

3.4.1.1 Preliminary Observations on Customary Law

Identifying a customary prohibition of disappearance is an intricate procedure, which first requires someone to take a stand on custom generally as a source of international law, and furthermore to elaborate on its application to human rights law. It is widely asserted that custom provides for the flexibility necessary to international law, compared to treaty-making. For this reason, "ascertainment of customary international law does not hinge on any standardized pedigree [...] it eschews formal ascertainment and follows a fundamentally non-formal ascertainment pattern".[140] This anomaly specific to customary patterns is interwoven with the difficulty of detecting custom's constitutive elements in differing circumstances.

Customary law is akin to a plain recipe consisting of two ingredients: state acts and statements in *opinio juris* evidence.[141] The definitional queries arising from the two components' combination have long occupied international theory. The co-existence of state practice and *opinio juris* for the establishment of a norm presupposes that state actions are coupled with states' simultaneous belief that they are legally obliged to act accordingly. This practically renders the creation of new norms impossible, since a shift in state practice erases the previous proper legal conduct. In this framework, custom could be defined as a sort of "collective delusion" of states (a figment of the collective imagination),[142] a norm which binds states before it becomes legal. Because of such theoretical oddities, the descriptive force of customary law is overestimated over its normative force. To avoid custom from being rejected entirely, one needs to concentrate on the source's empirical character

[140] d'Aspremont (2011), p. 163.
[141] Lowe (2007), p. 38.
[142] Kammerhofer (2004), p. 553.

and to spot "the magic ingredient of the formula [which is] time".[143] James Crawford uses the metaphor of coffee to explain custom: the older the blend, the better the coffee.[144]

In the absence of a strict pattern taxonomy, repetition standardizes practices which will progressively develop into customary norms. In addition, it allows for the eventual reconciliation of custom's two components. Yet, this perspective renders custom a highly empirical process—that is, behaviors legalized through repetition—while it does not necessarily validate custom's normative character. Anthropologically, customary international law is empirical, because it provides evidence of what public opinion suspects is morally correct, and subsequently what states consent to, as a legal norm (inductive reasoning). In essence, *opinio juris* is a sociological term, contingent on state consent for its legal affirmation.[145] Thus, *opinio juris* is a novel and unique parameter in the law of international sources, facilitating the interplay between society and law. Given that it is not a purely legal concept, it creates confusion in several cases. Hence, it is reasonably characterized as "an interloper of recent origin" in international law.[146]

Overall, the empirical perception of customary law does not delve into the content of the rule. Although the temporal element might well couple custom's two components, it subjects *opinio juris* to state practice. The test of repetition robs *opinio juris* of its sociological aspect and transforms it into a wider form of state practice. After all, repeating behavior (*opinio juris*) and state practice are the same. Consequently, "consent or at least non-dissent remain foundational to custom",[147] and *opinio juris* has a subordinate role in the creation of international law norms. The empirical approach neither offers a theoretical solution to international custom in general nor suffices to explain human rights customary rules in particular.

3.4.1.2 Customary Human Rights: A Deductive Process

The concept of customary human rights is inherently problematic, because the formation of a customary human right rule is inhibited by state practice. When it comes to human rights custom, states fulfill a double role. First, they are the founders of norms, whose violation they are responsible for. Unless the international community reaches the sphere of utopia, where states become the defenders of human

[143] Crawford, J.R. (23 May 2014). The identification and development of customary international law. British International Law Association, 1. Retrieved March 22, 2023, from http://www.google.gr/url?sa=t&rct=j&q=&esrc=s&source=web&cd=1&ved=0CB8QFjAA&url=http%3A%2F%2Fwww.ila-hq.org%2Fdownload.cfm%2Fdocid%2FBC985B09-ACEA-4356-AD31C90620705001&ei=1p9xVJK3AdPjaoGkgrAI&usg=AFQjCNFUoRnjms2d6141Aoiq_ucrCBANzQ&bvm=bv.80185997,d.d2s.

[144] Crawford, J. Foundations of International Law, LLM oral classes, Cambridge 2009–2010.

[145] Crawford (2014), p. 12.

[146] ibid p. 7.

[147] Henkin (1995/1996), p. 36.

rights, the birth of customary human rights is irreconcilable with state practice. Second, human rights claims are built on strong moral beliefs, which implies that *opinio juris* (in its sociological aspect) is cardinal for these norms. Evidently, "a realistic inquiry should demonstrate that [the two elements of custom] clash or create tensions", even if they are interconnected.[148] In this respect, customary human rights are like a patient who is on crutches because one of their legs has been amputated due to gangrenous ulcers (the infected part being the controversial state practice). On the other end of the scale, due to state practice's defective role in the formation of customary human rights, these claims are built on strong moral beliefs. Thus, *opinio juris* substitutes for the lack of consistent state practice.

The conflict between the two constitutive elements of custom can only be resolved through a deductive process, which places more importance on normative statements than on the empirical investigation of state practice. In effect, this implies that the authority of customary human rights derives from international normative beliefs outside law. Moving in this direction, the dictum of ICJ in the *Nicaragua* case was a major breakthrough in the deductive theory of customary law: not only did the Court emphasize an *opinio juris* for the identification of a customary norm, it also rationalized its existence through its breaches. The ICJ minimized as far as possible the significance of state practice.[149] More specifically, the Court held that

> for a rule to be established as customary, the corresponding practice must [not] be in absolutely rigorous conformity with the rule. In order to deduce the existence of customary rules, the Court deems it sufficient that the conduct of States should, in general, be consistent with such rules, and that instances of State conduct inconsistent with a given rule should generally have been treated as breaches of that rule, not as indications of the recognition of a new rule.[150]

Unlike empirical theory, which aims at establishing an inner bond between them, the ICJ admits that custom's two components do not always coexist (this first proposition takes the form of an actual observation). Secondly, it deems this disruption normal: legal norms are frequently violated by states, meaning that any such inconsistencies between state conduct and *opinio juris* are verifications of such a breach. Precisely because of the failure to ascertain formal customary norms', irregularities in state practice are the only means to identify infringements. This further implies that *opinio juris* is unalterable compared to state conduct. Although they are both forms of state policy, the former is less susceptible to fluctuations than the latter. Finally, the Court concludes that if the establishment of a rule entails potential breaches, then the occurrence of breaches points to the existence of the rule. This third thesis is perilous, as it affirms the rule by tracking its violations, and reduces

---

[148] Paust (1995/1996), p. 149.

[149] The ICJ demonstrated its tendency to explore the existence of customary rules alongside conventional ones early on in its *Continental Shelf* judgment, where it applied the deductive method, even though it did not expressly mention it. *Continental Shelf (Libyan Arab Jamahiriya v Malta)* [1985] ICJ Rep 113 29–30, para 27.

[150] *Military and Paramilitary Activities in and against Nicaragua* [1986] para 186.

custom to its breaches.[151] This legal construct "differs from traditional customary law in fundamental respects. Traditional customary law was not made; it resulted".[152]

The Court's deductive methodology relies on the necessary assumption that *opinio juris* enjoys a "sacred immunity", which is attainable only for certain rules. In an effort to classify which norms conform to the deductive approach, theory accentuates the sociological aspect of *opinio juris*. *Opinio juris* is assessed in terms of the widespread expectation and demand that a community has for a particular norm.[153] Unavoidably, the content of the norm undergoes the test of objective morality, or else the morals of public opinion. Similarly, public protest, or the "intensity and depth of the attitudes of condemnation" of a specific state conduct, is indicative of the breach of a—not necessarily legally binding—rule.[154] In this framework, the subjective element of customary law is subject to public scrutiny instead of state consent. In this broad sense, *opinio juris* is shaped by the actors of international law as well, and it may also embody general principles of law, recognized either on a national or an international level; as a result, customary law becomes a highly decentralized law. Of course, this view severely downgrades the concept of state sovereignty, while it has definitely not been endorsed by the ICJ. The Court's reasoning did not extend outside the realm of law, although it asserted the intrusion of sociological features in the establishment of customary law by tracing *opinio juris*' passage into soft law.

The ICJ perceives UNGA Resolutions as an expression of *opinio juris*;[155] a realistic rather than a groundbreaking view. It acknowledges that states are more eager to manifest something that is considered morally imperative by signing non-binding legal documents than to accept legal obligations. The Court highlights this moderate position on the divergence in states' behavior regarding binding and non-binding legal documents. Soft law becomes a means of "national self-criticism [which is] necessary to preserve meaningful human rights".[156] In this respect, soft law is an intermediate expression of *opinio juris*, resting between its sociological aspect and a purely consent-based treatment of it. Yet, the application of *opinio juris* from the angle of soft law cannot truly attest which customary norms fall under the deductive process.

Frederic Kirgis' reading of the *Nicaragua* judgment decodes the deductive approach based on two points. Firstly, it is noted that emphasis on *opinio juris* concerns the restrictive rules of customary international law, because "when the stakes are not as high, [the international community has] not been as quick to find

---

[151] Kelly (2000), p. 477. Kelly submits that the ICJ exceeds the limits of its jurisdiction, as it does not verify the existence of customary law, but creates one.

[152] Henkin (1995/1996), p. 37.

[153] Paust (1995/1996), p. 151.

[154] Simma and Alston (1988–1989), p. 92.

[155] *Military and Paramilitary Activities in and against Nicaragua* [1986] paras 188, 264.

[156] Gunning (1991), p. 216.

restrictive customary rules".[157] Restrictive rules contain prohibitions on states, whereas permissive rules regulate state conduct positively. Therefore, state practice that runs contrary to a restrictive rule is most probably a breach of it, while state practice that has an inconsistent approach to permissive norms might reveal intent to create a new norm. In turn, *opinio juris* is most critical concerning restrictive rules, which are more unlikely to change. Secondly, Kirgis also understands custom as a two-ingredient recipe, and adds that there is no standard quota connecting them; that is, the significance of state practice and *opinio juris* varies among customary norms, according to their content. Hence, customary norms are located on an abstract sliding scale in line with the weight of state practice or *opinio juris* respectively. Kirgis advocates that

> [o]n the sliding scale, very frequent, consistent state practice establishes a customary rule without much (or any) affirmative showing of an *opinio juris*, so long as it is not negated by evidence of non-normative intent. As the frequency and consistency of the practice decline in any series of cases, a stronger showing of an *opinio juris* is required. At the other end of the scale, a clearly demonstrated *opinio juris* establishes a customary rule without much (or any) affirmative showing that governments are consistently behaving in accordance with the asserted rule.[158]

Although the *Nicaragua* judgment pertains to the prohibition of the threat or use of force, the deductive approach, as well as Kirgis' sliding scale, is mostly employed in the verification of customary human rights and humanitarian law. More specifically, civil rights constitute a typical example of restrictive norms, since they impose on states the negative obligation to refrain from any action that would intervene in the individual's sphere of personal interests. As such, negative rights are placed at the end of the sliding scale, where a "clearly demonstrated *opinio juris*" outweighs the requirement of consistency in state practice.

In the case of customary human rights, *opinio juris* prevails over state practice not only because of the ethical values it encapsulates, but because the states which perpetrate the relevant norm do not defend their conduct as legal; instead, they deny it on factual grounds.[159] The prohibition of torture is, among others, a commonly referenced example of this behavior. It is a restrictive rule with strong moral ramifications and an *opinio juris* with solid foundations. Although it has been formally defined, the customary character of the norm has been the subject of discussion in international theory and adjudication, especially when the existing legal framework is not applicable. In this event, states accused of torture do not admit to such a behavior, even if they are bound by a formal legal obligation. Their choice to deny the commission of torture demonstrates their efforts to avoid public detestation and raise international awareness on this issue. In this way, these states cannot claim that they object to the existence of the customary rule, even if their conduct contravenes it. For instance, the ICTY, in its *Furundžija* judgment, adopted this course of

---

[157] Kirgis (1987), p. 148.

[158] ibid p. 149.

[159] Simma and Alston (1988–1989), p. 92.

thinking when applying the ICJ's *Nicaragua* rationale to the prohibition on torture.[160] The deductive approach regarding the prohibition on torture had been endorsed by the US judiciary even earlier, in 1980. In the *Filartiga v Peña-Irala* judgment, the American court stated that "the fact that the prohibition of torture is often honored in the breach does not diminish its binding effect as a norm of international law".[161]

To summarize, the recognition of civil rights as norms of customary value is possible only by applying the deductive approach. This method resolves conflicts arising between state practice and *opinio juris*, and corresponds to the moral normativity of these rights. It is true that the deductive customary human rights law is a law which was "made, purposefully, knowingly [and] willfully",[162] rendering it susceptible to criticism. Nevertheless, it is a law needed to enrich the international community with fundamental values. Therefore, the deductive approach is harmonized with natural law theory. As Hersch Lauterpacht observes: "we cannot hope to understand adequately the law of nature unless we disabuse our minds of the idea that it has been exclusively, or predominantly, speculative, deductive, and fanciful; that it has been divorced from experience".[163] That is, natural law is what we make out of it, hence it is deductive, as it serves to establish the founding principles on which the international community lies.

3.4.1.3 The Customary Rule of Enforced Disappearance

According to the above analysis, the prohibition on enforced disappearance ought to qualify as a customary human right, for there is a clearly demonstrated *opinio juris* resulting from the fact that states in their official statements deny practicing disappearance. Even states which repeatedly violate the rule deny any involvement and responsibility for the disappeared.[164] It seems clear that, due to enforced disappearance's classification as a civil right, the deductive approach is the solely applicable approach, taking into consideration the norm's regular breaches and the lack of a concrete state practice.

Consequently, it is unlikely that we can sustain the idea that the customary rule of enforced disappearance can be explained through the empirical process. Apart from the inconsistencies in state practice, a consent-based *opinio juris* would inevitably locate the origin of a customary prohibition at the time of the CPED's signature or entry into force. According to the empirical approach, not only does the Convention constitute a formal ascertainment of the norm, but it expresses the joint maturity of state practice and *opinio juris* concerning the prohibition of

[160] *Prosecutor v Furundžija (Judgement)* ICTY IT–95–17/1–T (10 December 1998) para 138.

[161] *Filartiga v Peña-Irala* (30 June 1980) 630 F2d 876, 884.

[162] Henkin (1995/1996), p. 37.

[163] Lauterpacht (1950), p. 98.

[164] Kyriakou (2012), p. 432.

disappearance. Alternatively, it is proposed that the prohibition of disappearance should be placed slightly earlier, at the time the ICC Statute, which entered into force in 2002. Antonio Cassese seems to espouse the empirical approach and notes:

> with respect to this crime [enforced disappearance] the ICC Statute has not codified existing customary law but contributed to the crystallization of a nascent rule, evolved primarily out of treaty law (that is, the numerous treaties on human rights prohibiting various acts falling under this heading), as well as the case law of the Inter-American Commission and Court of Human Rights, in addition to a number of UN General Assembly resolutions. These various strands have been instrumental in the gradual formation of a customary rule prohibiting enforced disappearance of persons.[165]

Cassese recognizes only the contribution of soft law to the formation of a customary rule; he does not consider it an expression of *opinio juris* but believes it to be the rule's inception. Thus, the ICC Statute reveals the origin of the customary prohibition with regards to its criminal aspects.[166] Under both scenarios, the establishment of customary enforced disappearance follows the norm's late integration into binding legal documents, either in 2002 or in 2010.

At the other extreme, if *opinio juris* can be detected in any formal public statement, irrespective of whether we can identify the statement's bearer as a subject of international law, then the nascence of the customary prohibition dates back to 1985, when the FEDEFAM drafted a proposed convention on enforced disappearance, annexed to the UNWGEID's annual report.[167] Apart from the definition provided, this draft convention characterizes disappearance as an offence which should be prohibited. The draft convention, alongside its annexation to a UN document, demonstrates the shared awareness of NGOs and international organizations on the phenomenon, which in turn bears proof of a shared *opinio juris*. The FEDEFAM draft convention marked a critical point in the recognition of a customary prohibition, because it provided for a definition of the norm. In the case of enforced disappearance, the norm's customary birth relies inevitably on its definition, taking in mind its proximity to other norms, and also its complexity. The concern which arises, though, is whether the draft convention may lead to the customary prohibition on disappearance when it proclaims only the illegality of the offence. The criminal offence of disappearance falls systemically under the right against disappearance; it is the central obligation ensuring the right's acceptance. In this respect, there is no practical advantage if one distinguishes between the customary prohibition of the offense and the customary recognition of the right (which consists of a prohibition). Furthermore, the draft convention provides that the systematic performance of

---

[165] Cassese (2008), p. 113.

[166] Protection from enforced disappearance is falls under three regimes: when practiced systematically it is a crime against humanity, enjoying the protection of international humanitarian law; its criminal aspect is protected under the ICC Statute; it is also a general human rights prohibition. It is therefore argued that there are three distinct norms of enforced disappearance, each of which has attained customary status at different points. Sarkin (2012), pp. 550–551.

[167] UN Doc E/CN.4/1985/15 para 42, Annex III, Arts I, II.

disappearances is a crime against humanity, thus conferring a sense of normativity on the offence.[168]

Moreover, if the broadest possible approach regarding *opinio juris* is chosen, there are more sources that certify its existence concerning disappearance. For example, the customary value of enforced disappearance has been maintained by the US courts in the *Filartiga* and *Forti v Suarez-Mason* judgments.[169] In its *Filartiga* judgment the US Court of Appeals upheld that "the sources from which customary international law is derived [are] the usage of nations, judicial opinions and the works of jurists".[170] Moving a step further, the District Court found in the *Forti v Suarez-Mason* case that "plaintiffs have met their burden of showing an international consensus as to the status and content of the international tort of "causing disappearance"",[171] and it overturned the previous ruling according to which "the requisite degree of international consensus which demonstrates a customary international norm" of enforced disappearance "did not exist".[172]

Finally, the third, intermediate approach detects *opinio juris* in soft law manifestations of a universal character. It is a moderate position which safely locates customary enforced disappearance at the 1992 Declaration, which establishes the widest possible consensus as far as the norm, its definition, and its wrongfulness are concerned. The ICRC relies as well on the UN Declaration to verify the existence of customary enforced disappearance. Although it is primarily concerned with the systematic practice of disappearance, which constitutes a crime against humanity, the ICRC affirms the customary norm, and concludes that "any enforced disappearance is a violation of international humanitarian law and human rights law".[173] Therefore, it recognizes a general customary norm of enforced disappearance by applying the deductive method, and does not distinguish between humanitarian law and human rights.

Irrespective of when the emergence or establishment of customary enforced disappearance might be placed, there is no doubt that there was an intensification of international attempts to prove existence of the norm between 1985 and 1992. Hence, the seed of customary enforced disappearance existed long before the CPED's entry into force, and it may be safely argued that the customary norm had

[168] ibid, Annex III, Art X.

[169] Lillich (1995–1996), pp. 5–6; *see* also, Paust (2009), p. 371.

[170] *Filartiga v Peña-Irala* (1980) 884.

[171] *Forti v Suarez-Mason* (25 July 1988) 694 FSupp 707, 709.

[172] *Forti v Suarez-Mason* (6 October 1987) 672 FSupp 1531, 1543. Unlike the American courts, the IACtHR has not examined thoroughly the existence of customary enforced disappearance, probably due to its long tradition of adjudicating disappearance cases, its adoption of a solid rationale regarding the norm's existence, and its early enactment of a regional disappearance treaty. The IACtHR implied the existence of customary disappearance by virtue of the customary prohibition of arbitrary detention or imprisonment. This reference stands alone and is not indicative of the IACtHR's approach to enforced disappearance. *Osorio Rivera & Family Members v Peru*, Inter-American Court of Human Rights Series C No 274 (26 November 2013) para 120.

[173] ICRC (2005a), p. 343.

been established by 1992. Unlike the empirical approach, the deductive approach manages to incorporate all efforts made by the international community to recognize the norm by broadening the notion of *opinio juris*. Thus, it takes a more realistic view with respect to states' compliance with international law, which has proved instrumental for human rights.[174]

3.4.1.4 The Content of Customary Enforced Disappearance

The affirmation of customary enforced disappearance raises the question of possible dissimilarities between its content and the protective ambit of the conventional rule. Because of the right's complex character, any discrepancy between the two rules revolves inevitably around disappearance's components. In particular, customary enforced disappearance cannot escape the definitional debate regarding the perpetrators' intent to put the victim outside the protection of the law. Since the deductive approach aims at lessening states' consent in favor of *opinio juris*, deductive customary disappearance cannot normally require that the perpetrators' intentional behavior exists throughout the stages of a disappearance. Contrary to the ICC's definition and the stance of several states, a deductive approach to customary enforced disappearance, or a human rights approach to custom, ought to perceive the victim's isolation from legal protection as the practice's outcome. That is, a pro human rights methodology for the establishment of the customary norm automatically broadens the content of the latter. This interpretation is more relevant to enforced disappearance, as it lacks sufficient legal basis in practical terms because it is impossible to spot *opinio juris* regarding this element of the definition in the documents which are taken into consideration when the deductive approach is applied. Nonetheless, the fact that this view is espoused by the IACtHR, alongside Nowak's position, somehow legitimizes this approach.[175]

In conclusion, it is worth mentioning that the ICRC considers states' positive obligation to investigate enforced disappearance to be part of the customary law norm as well. The ICRC's course of thinking about the customary duty to investigate disappearance is ambiguous, for it employs recurrent jurisprudential pronouncements (made mostly by the ECtHR) to establish the customary duty of investigation.[176] Although it replaces both elements of custom with jurisprudence, the ICRC's analysis is theoretically consistent. Even though civil rights generate primarily negative obligations for the state, they comprise positive—mirror—obligations; civil rights call for states to preserve them, by investigating their alleged breaches. As a result, this analysis lies within the CPED's limits and finds its basis in Art. 12(1), even if it is not in doctrinal conformity with the principles of customary law.

[174] Sarkin (2012), pp. 547–548.

[175] *See* Chap. 2.

[176] ICRC (2005b), pp. 2098–2102.

Overall, customary human rights most often express the expectation of the international community for the realization of already formally ascertained rights. As such, customary human rights are "recognizably conjoined in the ongoing social process" and are literally what we make of them.[177] Thereafter, customary enforced disappearance ought to be a norm wider than the conventional, in terms of protection for the victims. The human rights approach to custom echoes to some public opinion: it is open to international actors insofar as the subjects of international law allow it. Customary enforced disappearance should respectfully echo the anguish and anxiety a disappearance causes, a feature which cannot be legally stipulated. Besides its broader protective scope, *ratione materiae*, customary enforced disappearance is not circumscribed by the number of the CPED's member-states.[178] Accordingly, the establishment of a customary norm is a paramount *ratione personae*, since it binds all states, irrespective of their accession to the CPED or to relevant regional documents. In this respect, customary human rights is universal international law.[179] This proposition, though, depends on the hypothesis that the rule of customary enforced disappearance does not tolerate persistent objectors. The norm's incompatibility with persistent objectors can only be explained by an alleged normative supremacy, which indicates that it has attained *jus cogens* status.

3.4.2 On Peremptory Human Rights

Any attempt to maintain that an international law rule is peremptory is at the very outset doomed, or at least precarious, due to doctrinal and theoretical dissent regarding its substance and relationship with the sources of international law. Although a comprehensive explication of the *jus cogens* concept is beyond the scope of this analysis, a few key remarks are needed. The concept of *jus cogens* is founded on three interrelated propositions: *jus cogens* is neither a formal nor a material source of international law, it is rather a meta-norm (a); *jus cogens* forms part of the natural explanation of human rights (b); and *jus cogens* emanates from customary norms (c). These propositions are unavoidably cyclical: they are more a doctrinal choice than a matter of proof.[180] Thus, in the present analysis, they are predefined for reasons of consistency.

The first proposition is the least controversial, and almost unanimously accepted. The attribute of peremptory norms relates to their qualitative maturity, and denotes universal acceptance by the international legal order. In this framework, peremptory norms are described as "meta-norms",[181] a characterization which is subject to a

177 Paust (1995/1996), p. 150.

178 Trindade (2012), p. 511.

179 D'Amato (1995/1996), p. 73.

180 Paust (1995/1996), p. 155.

181 D'Amato (1995/1996), p. 57.

two-fold interpretation. Firstly, they have a temporal meaning: *jus cogens* norms signify the evolving nature of certain rules, which eventually become cardinal to the international community. Consequently, this temporal aspect implies the ephemerality of *jus cogens* norms. Paust attempts to reconcile the ephemerality with the ultimate normative supremacy of *jus cogens* and maintains that:

> As all other principles and norms of general international law, they may be modified [...] they can be modified by changing patterns of expectation and behavior, some of which may be reflected in or conditioned through time by treaties. It is not the norm of custom, thingified, or the treaty, thingified, which modifies (at least directly), but rather the patterns of expectation and relevant behavior which underlie previously identifiable peremptory norms. [...] No human law is likely to be so eternal or so certain a guarantee to save us from ourselves. Yet knowing this, one can understand the actual strength of customary jus cogens and recognize that these who make claims about the inclusion of certain norms into the matric of peremptory norms are actually participating in an effort to shape attitudes and, perhaps, human behavior.[182]

Paust's reading of *jus cogens* points at the overwhelming impact of human nature on human law. In this respect, Paust's approach coincides with the observation that enforced disappearance is the result of human perversity, a norm which emerged as a response to an advanced method of violating human dignity. Nevertheless, peremptory norms are qualitatively equipped with maximum objectivity, which in turn renders them peremptory.

The second meaning of "meta-norms" relates to their enhanced qualitative power: *jus cogens* rules are imperative because of their content. This element is particularly important on a symbolic level, given there is no established test to verify which norms are peremptory. As a result, *jus cogens* remains in most cases a theoretical characterization, the most powerful tool a scholar possesses to indicate a rule's importance. From this angle, D'Amato notices correctly that

> *jus cogens* is an asset, enabling any writer to christen any ordinary norm of his or her choice as a new *jus cogens* norm, thereby in one stroke investing it with magical power. Nor does it appear to be a limit to the number of norms that a writer may promote to the status of supernorm.[183]

The legal construction of *jus cogens* is overestimated as it lacks precision concerning its origin and creation; furthermore, its hierarchical relationship with conventional or customary norms is unclear. Although it pertains to core values of the international community, as expected, it remains an intangible concept which cannot serve its mission and furnish norms with an extra layer of protection. Both writers implicitly suggest that if there are well-established customary human rights norms, then *jus cogens* is of limited value in the field of human rights. The concept's usefulness relates mainly to the irreconcilability of *jus cogens* norms with the existence of persistent objectors.

The second and third propositions are determined by the very essence of human rights law. Bearing in mind that only customary rules are universal human rights

[182] Paust (1991), pp. 84–85.

[183] D'Amato (1990), pp. 1–2.

norms, peremptory norms can only occur in the development of customary rules. From this perspective, peremptory human rights norms are customary rules enjoying enhanced double guarantees regarding *opinio juris*. In addition, such norms refer to rights which are fundamental to human nature; "*jus cogens* [bears] a willifying characteristic [it] is clearly an attribute of natural law [acknowledging] unwritten standards of behavior as a primary source of law".[184] Hence, the common denominator between natural law and *jus cogens* norms is their alleged substantive preeminence. Although natural law is synonymous with human nature, the legal construction of *jus cogens* does not necessarily add to human rights protection. On the contrary, it is often considered unreliable, because of its deficient legal explanation.[185] Most often, a norm is outlined as *jus cogens*, either because it creates obligations *erga omnes*, or on account of its non-derogable character.[186] Yet, inductive reasoning is not appropriate to decode the essentials of *jus cogens*, for it merely describes its two main attributes.[187]

In general terms, the *jus cogens* concept remains obscure. A prudent definition of peremptory norms focuses on the fact that they are

> founded on community interests and characterized by the prohibition against disposing over certain rights, be it to one's own disadvantage or to the detriment of others who are not in a position to provide effectively or their protection themselves, such as peoples, groups or individuals.[188]

In this respect, *jus cogens* seems to be the *ultimum refugium* for the protection of the defenseless, a guarantee of the international protection of all those who lack international legal standing, as they cannot be considered subjects of international law. Consequently, an effective *jus cogens* concept "has to bind the state both in its treaty relations and with respect to acts of the legislature, executive and judiciary", and be available for individuals to access in their domestic legal order.[189] Kadelbach's

---

[184] Parker and Neylon (1989), p. 419.

[185] The difficulty in defining and demarcating *jus cogens* rules has been highlighted as well, during their conventional stipulation. Although the drafters of VCLT consented with regards to the substantive supremacy of *jus cogens* rules, this was not enough to explain the effects these rules would entail. Therefore, it was submitted during the plenary meeting of the Conference preceding the Convention's adoption that the "emergence of rules having the character of *jus cogens* is comparatively recent, while international law is in process of rapid development. The Commission considered the right course to be to provide in general terms that a treaty is void if it conflicts with a rule of *jus cogens* and to leave the full content of this rule to be worked out in State practice and in the jurisprudence of international tribunals". There was widespread uncertainty at the Conference, which still surrounds the concept of *jus cogens*. This is the reason why Art. 53 VCLT is not considered to crystallize existing customary international law, and it is thus argued that there is a fine line between conventional and customary *jus cogens*. United Nations Conference on the Law of Treaties. (First & Second Sessions Vienna, 26 March–24 May 1968 & 9 April–22 May 1969). UN Doc A/CONF.39/11/Add.2, 67.

[186] Brunnée (2010), p. 454.

[187] Ragazzi (1997), p. 48; Kadelbach (2006), p. 30.

[188] Kadelbach (2006), p. 35.

[189] de Wet (2004), p. 100.

proposed explanation is human-rights oriented, built upon the argument that *jus cogens* is the final barrier to the misuse of international law by sovereign states;[190] a rationale similar to that of universal customary human rights rules. Accordingly, theory must be thoroughly dedicated to recognizing those few norms which are peremptory, to preserve their qualitative uniqueness. After all, the fundamental values of the international community are nothing but the basics of human nature. The natural explanation of *jus cogens* points out the rather obvious intrinsic relationship between peremptory norms and human rights; that is, although the concept is vague and "a detailed inventory of the contents of the box is difficult to draw, it is nevertheless hard to deny that human rights are contained within it".[191] Human rights law benefits from the concept of *jus cogens*, at least on a doctrinal level.

3.4.2.1 A Peremptory Enforced Disappearance

The difficulty of proving that a customary norm, or a right in particular, has attained peremptory status remains challenging, and international tribunals have been extremely hesitant in attributing this status to any rule of international law. In the case of the right against enforced disappearance, its peremptory character may be inferred by way of analogy from the *jus cogens* status of the prohibition on torture.[192] However, this reasoning is not an option in the present analysis, where a comparison between the right against disappearance to any other norm would deprive the former of its autonomous character.

The jurisprudence of the IACtHR is instrumental on this point. In the case of *Goiburú et al v Paraguay* the Court adjudicated that the right not to be subjected to enforced disappearance is a *jus cogens* norm. Although the factual background of the case does not differ significantly from the other disappearance incidents that were brought before the Court, the IACtHR carefully chose this case to declare the norm's peremptory status. The case refers to the illegal arbitrary detention, torture and enforced disappearance of Agustín Goiburú Giménez and three other persons by Paraguayan state agents between 1974 and 1977. It is worth noting that there is no link between the disappearances of the four applicants, except that they were committed by the Stroessner regime. The most critical aspect in these disappearances is that the perpetrating state collaborated with the intelligence forces of

[190] Kadelbach (2006), p. 34.

[191] Bianchi (2008), p. 491.

[192] *Prosecutor v Furundžija*, paras 153–157. The IACtHR, in numerous cases concerning enforced disappearance, has affirmed the *jus cogens* status of the prohibition on torture. The Court found states responsible for *jus cogens* violations regarding the torture suffered by the disappeared victims. Although this approach is to the detriment of the norm of enforced disappearance, on a doctrinal level it reveals a continuous trend to affirm the absolute character of the prohibition of disappearance. *Blake v Guatemala*, para 15; *Maritza Urrutia v Guatemala*, para 92; *Gómez-Paquiyauri Brothers v Peru*, Inter-American Court of Human Rights Series C No 110 (8 July 2004) paras 76, 112, 128; *Tibi v Ecuador*, para 143.

neighboring countries to capture the victims; the so-called "Operation Condor". This was the network of national security' agencies that were active during the 1970s in the Southern Cone countries, with the mission to exterminate any alleged enemies of the regimes.[193] According to expert witnesses, "Operation Condor" was based on the shared ideological basis of the dictatorial regimes of the Southern Cone. These regimes promoted "the national security doctrine [...] which allowed them to consider leftist movements as common enemies, whatever their nationality".[194] Consequently, victims could not escape the danger of disappearance even if they fled to a neighboring country.

In this framework, Goiburú and his family sought shelter in Argentina in order to slip away from the Paraguayan authorities. Still, he was abducted by Argentinian agents and transferred to detention facilities in Paraguay. He managed to escape from captivity and returned to Argentina, where he was abducted for the second time after a few years. His fate has remained unknown since then, although it is assumed he was executed while disappeared according to the relevant files. The same course of events is thought to have applied more or less to the other three applicants, i.e. the victims' disappearances involved the intelligence agencies and/or diplomatic personnel of at least two countries. The Court identified the situation as a "systematic practice of "State terrorism" at an inter-State level".[195] It determined that an "illegal relationship [was] established between the Governments and intelligence services"[196] of the Southern Cone countries, and held that Paraguay bore "aggravated international responsibility" for the victims' disappearances. Contrary to the general rules of state responsibility, the fact that the victims' abduction was committed by agents of another country, outside Paraguayan territory, was not considered to diminish Paraguay's responsibility.[197] It was most probably the element of trans-border disappearance which impelled the Court to engage the idea of the *jus cogens* status of enforced disappearance, also taking into account that the respondent state acquiesced almost entirely to the claims raised by applicants. Instead of limiting its jurisdiction to determining the appropriate reparations and costs, the IACtHR decided to continue its evaluation of the case,

---

[193] Operation Condor involved the intelligence services of at least six countries overall, Argentina, Bolivia, Brazil, Chile, Uruguay and Paraguay, and the number of the disappeared victims is estimated to have been 30,000. Scovazzi and Citroni (2007), pp. 180–181.

[194] *Goiburú et al v Paraguay*, para 56.

[195] ibid, para 72.

[196] ibid, para 65.

[197] The concept of "aggravated international responsibility" received severe criticism by Judge Sergio García Ramírez, who mentioned in his separate opinion that "'aggravated' responsibility does not exist, and neither does 'attenuated' responsibility, because simple responsibility (without considerations of intensity or nuance) implies the possibility or need 'to respond' for certain acts owing to legal evidence of attribution that links specific conduct to a particular person who must respond for it juridically by the establishment of certain consequences". Ibid, Separate Opinion of Judge Sergio García Ramírez, para 4.

> [b]earing in mind its responsibility to ensure the optimum protection of human rights and given the nature of the instant case, [and considered] that delivering a judgment in which the truth of the facts [...] are determined, is a way of contributing to preserve the historical memory, to make reparation to the victims' next of kin and to help avoid a repetition of similar acts.[198]

Therefore, the exploration of enforced disappearance's peremptory status was most definitely a conscious decision made by the Court.[199]

The IACtHR found that "the prohibition of the forced disappearance of persons and the corresponding obligation to investigate and punish those responsible has attained the status of *jus cogens*".[200] It relied on two elements: first on the gravity of the offence of a disappearance, and second on the preamble of the IACFDP, which provides that the forced disappearance of persons violates numerous non-derogable and essential human rights. The reasoning offered by the Court was short and insufficient, because it used the attribute of non-derogability to induce the norm's *jus cogens* status; then it equated peremptory and non-derogable rules and reduced the former to the latter.[201] It remains unclear whether the IACtHR referred to the peremptory status of the conventional or customary prohibition on disappearance, since the ruling mentions both legally binding and non-legally binding instruments as sources of law regarding enforced disappearance. Therefore, it does not delineate the exact content of the peremptory norm, given that the existing definitional divergences render customary enforced disappearance as being broader than conventional.[202] Further, the IACtHR does not justify the grounds on which enforced disappearance is a peremptory norm. The only indication of justification is the association of enforced disappearance with the victim's deprivation of any form of judicial protection, which forms a peremptory rule as well.[203] In his separate opinion, Judge Trindade explored how the substantial content of *jus cogens* is expanded by the addition of the prohibition on disappearance. Thus, he argued that enforced disappearance violates "the right to access to justice *lato sensu* [and] the right to full jurisdictional assistance".[204] Trindade's approach balanced juridical necessities with

[198] ibid, para 53.

[199] Sporadic references to the peremptory status of the prohibition on disappearance had been made by the IACtHR from 2003, yet without any doctrinal elaboration. *Juridical Condition and Rights of the Undocumented Migrants (Advisory Opinion)*, Inter-American Court of Human Rights Series A No 18 (17 September 2003) para 69.

[200] *Goiburú et al v Paraguay*, para 84.

[201] ibid, para 128.

[202] Trindade's specific opinion was clear-cut. He suggested there is a customary prohibition on disappearance which has attained a peremptory status. Trindade (2009), p. 13. *See* also, Trindade (2011), pp. 27–47. Trindade's view on peremptory norms coincides with that of Casesse, who holds that only international judicial courts are vested with the power to determine which norms have attained a peremptory status, and further accepts that such an investigation refers only to customary rules. Yet, his general perception regarding the creation of customary rules is far more restrictive. Cassese (2012), pp. 164–165.

[203] *Goiburú et al v Paraguay*, para 131.

[204] ibid, Separate Opinion of Judge A.A. Cançado Trindade, para 66.

theoretical requirements. It has already been mentioned that enforced disappearance results in placing the victim outside the protection of the law; it creates a state of "legal limbo" which intensifies the victim's vulnerability. This breach of the disappeared's human dignity corresponds in judicial terms to a denial of access to justice. Trindade was very accurate when referring to a "*lato sensu* access to justice": the right to justice is the closest legal basis on which the peremptory status of enforced disappearance may be founded without question at the same time as the prohibition's autonomous character.[205]

3.4.2.2 A Peremptory Enforced Disappearance?

The question whether the right not to be subjected to enforced disappearance is a peremptory norm is not receptive to an answer, due to the ambiguity surrounding the concept of *jus cogens*. The *jus cogens* status of the right against disappearance is more of a scientific decision, rather than a doctrinal reality subject to proof. In this framework, if one accepts: that the right against disappearance is a civil liberty (a); that it is a natural right attached to the core of human dignity (b); and that there is a customary prohibition on disappearance (c), then there is already a consolidated field of protection, and the peremptory status of the norm does not confer an extra layer of protection. On the other hand, an affirmation of disappearance's *jus cogens* character elevates symbolically the prohibition to a super-norm. As a result, a peremptory enforced disappearance depends on the writer's conception and expectations towards the international legal order in general. If the international community is interested in

> a humanized (or even truly humanist) *ordre public* in which the public or general interest fully coincides with the prevalence of human rights – what implies the recognition that human rights constitute the basic foundation, themselves, of the legal order, at international and national levels. Underlying the concept of *jus cogens* is the *jus naturalist* thinking, which lead to peremptory norms as from the assertion and acknowledgment of ethical values which seek to benefit humankind as a whole.[206]

The prohibition on disappearance definitely forms a part of this.

Jurisprudence

ICJ

Continental Shelf (Libyan Arab Jamahiriya v Malta) [1985] ICJ Rep 113.

---

[205] Trindade (2012), p. 535.

[206] *Miguel Castro Castro Prison v Peru*, Inter-American Court of Human Rights Series C No 181 (2 August 2008), Concurring Opinion of Judge A.A. Cançado Trindade, para 155.

Military and Paramilitary Activities in and against Nicaragua (Nicaragua v USA) (Merits) [1986] ICJ Rep 14.
North Sea Continental Shelf Cases (Federal Republic of Germany v Denmark; Netherlands) [1969] ICJ Rep 3.
Reservations to the Convention on the Prevention and Punishment of the Crime of Genocide (Advisory Opinion) [1951] ICJ Rep 15.

ICTY

Prosecutor v Furundžija (Judgement) ICTY IT–95–17/1–T (10 December 1998).

IACtHR

Almonacid-Arellano et al v Chile, Inter-American Court of Human Rights Series C No 154 (26 September 2006).
Anzualdo Castro v Peru, Inter-American Court of Human Rights Series C No 202 (22 September 2009).
Barrios Altos v Peru, Inter-American Court of Human Rights Series C No 75 (14 March 2001).
Gómez-Paquiyauri Brothers v Peru, Inter-American Court of Human Rights Series C No 110 (8 July 2004).
González Medina & Family v Dominican Republic, Inter-American Court of Human Rights Series C No 240 (27 February 2012).
Ibsen Cárdenas & Ibsen Peña v Bolivia, Inter-American Court of Human Rights Series C No 217 (3 May 2010).
Juridical Condition and Rights of the Undocumented Migrants (Advisory Opinion), Inter-American Court of Human Rights Series A No 18 (17 September 2003).
La Cantuta v Peru, Inter-American Court of Human Rights Series C No 162 (29 November 2006).
Miguel Castro Castro Prison v Peru, Inter-American Court of Human Rights Series C No 181 (2 August 2008), Concurring Opinion of Judge A.A. Cançado Trindade.
Osorio Rivera & Family Members v Peru, Inter-American Court of Human Rights Series C No 274 (26 November 2013).
Radilla-Pacheco v Mexico, Inter-American Court of Human Rights Series C No 209 (23 November 2009).
Torres Millacura v Argentina, Inter-American Court of Human Rights Series C No 229 (26 August 2011).
Trujillo-Oroza v Bolivia, Inter-American Court of Human Rights Series C No 92 (27 February 2002).

ECtHR

Tahsin Acar v Turkey, App no 26307/95 (ECtHR 8 April 2004).

ACHPR

Malawi African Association et al v Mauritania, Comm nos 54/91, 61/91, 98/93, 164–196/97, 210/98 (ACHPR 2000).

Commission Nationale des Droits de l' Homme et des Libertés v Chad, Comm no 74/92 (ACHPR 1995).

National Courts

Filartiga v Peña-Irala (30 June 1980) 630 F2d 876.

Forti v Suarez-Mason (25 July 1988) 694 FSupp 707.

Forti v Suarez-Mason (6 October 1987) 672 FSupp 1531.

UN Documentation

UNGA

UNGA. (12 July 1993). Vienna Declaration and Programme of Action. UN Doc A/Conf.157/23.

United Nations Conference on the Law of Treaties. (First & Second Sessions Vienna, 26 March–24 May 1968 & 9 April–22 May 1969). UN Doc A/CONF.39/11/Add.2, 67.

Final Act of the International Conference on Human Rights (Proclamation of Teheran). (Teheran 22 April–13 May 1968). UN Doc A/Conf.32/41.

ECOSOC

UN Doc E/CN.4/2004/59.

UN Doc E/CN.4/2003/71.

UN Doc E/CN.4/2002/71.

UN Doc E/CN.4/1985/15.

HRC

Yubraj Giri v Nepal, HRC (2011) UN Doc CCPR/C/101/D/1761/2008.
HRC. (4 November 1994). Issues relating to reservations made upon ratification or accession relating to reservations made upon ratification or accession to the Covenant or the Optional Protocols Thereto, or in relation to Declarations under Article 41 of the Covenant. UN Doc CCPR/C/21/Rev.1/Add.6.
Ilda Thomas & Hiber Conteris v Uruguay, HRC (1985). UN Doc CCPR/C/25/D/139/1983.
HRC. (30 April 1982). General Comment No. 06: The Right to Life (Art. 6).
Retrieved March 22, 2023, from http://www.ohchr.org/EN/HRBodies/CED/Pages/CEDIndex.aspx.
Alba Pietraroia & Rosario Pietraroia v Uruguay, HRC (1981) UN Doc CCPR/C/12/D/44/1979.
Alberto Grille Motta v Uruguay, HRC (1980) UN Doc CCPR/C/10/D/11/1977.
Esther Soriano de Bouton v Uruguay, HRC (1981) UN Doc CCPR/C/12/D/37/1978.
Ann Maria Garcia Lanza de Netto et al v Uruguay, HRC (1980) UN Doc CCPR/C/9/D/8/1977.
Luciano Weinberger Weisz & Ismael Weinberger v Uruguay, HRC (1980) UN Doc CCPR/C/11/D/28/1978.
Miguel A Millan Sequeina v Uruguay, HRC (1980) UN Doc CCPR/C/10/D/6/1977.
William Torres Ramirez v Uruguay, HRC (1980) UN Doc CCPR/C/10/D/4/1977.

Miscellaneous

Committee against Torture. (24 January 2008). General Comment No. 2, Implementation of Article 2 by States Parties. UN Doc CAT/C/GC/2.
UN Doc CCPR/C/21/Rev.1/Add.6.
UNWGEID. General Comment on the right to recognition as a person before the law in the context of enforced disappearances. Retrieved March 22, 2023, from http://www.ohchr.org/Documents/Issues/Disappearances/GCRecognition.pdf.

OAS Documentation

Inter-American Commission on Human Rights (8 September 1983). Restrictions to the death penalty (Arts. 4(2) and 4(4) of the American Convention on Human Rights). Advisory Opinion' Series A No 3, OC-3/83.

National Documentation

Restatement (third) of the Foreign Relations Law of the United States (ALI 1987).
The Unanimous Declaration of the Thirteen United States of America 1776 (US) preamble.

Online Sources

Crawford, J.R. (23 May 2014). The identification and development of customary international law. British International Law Association, 1. Retrieved March 22, 2023, from http://www.google.gr/url?sa=t&rct=j&q=&esrc=s&source=web&cd=1&ved=0CB8QFjAA&url=http%3A%2F%2Fwww.ila-hq.org%2Fdownload.cfm%2Fdocid%2FBC985B09-ACEA-4356-AD31C90620705001&ei=lp9xVJK3AdPjaoGkgrAI&usg=AFQjCNFUoRnjms2d6141Aoiq_ucrCBANzQ&bvm=bv.80185997,d.d2s.

References

Books

Agamben G (1998a) Homo Sacer: sovereign power and bare life (trans: Heller-Roazen D). Stanford University Press

Allott P (1990) Eunomia, new order for a new world. Oxford University Press

Allott P (2002) The health of nations, society and law beyond the state. Cambridge University Press

Arendt H (1973) The origins of totalitarianism: new edition with added prefaces. Harcourt

Aristotle, Politics, Book A, Chapter 2, 1253a

Boucher D (2009) The limits of ethics in international relations: natural law, natural rights, and human rights in transition. Oxford University Press

Cassese A (2008) International criminal law, 2nd edn. Oxford University Press

d'Aspremont J (2011) Formalism and the sources of international law, a theory of the ascertainment of legal rules. Oxford University Press

Derrida J (2009) In: Lisse M et al (eds) The beast & the sovereign: vol I (trans: Bennington G). Chicago University Press

Donnelly J (2003) Universal human rights in theory & practice, 2nd edn. Cornell University Press

Dworkin R (1977) Taking rights seriously. Harvard University Press

Gewirth A (1980) Reason and morality. Chicago University Press

Gross O, Ní Aoláin F (2006) Law in times of crisis, emergency powers in theory and practice. Cambridge University Press

Hume D (1896) In: Selby-Bigge LA (ed) A treatise of human nature (first published 1739). Clarendon Press, Book III

ICRC (Henckaerts J-M, Doswald-Beck L eds) (2005a) Customary international humanitarian law, volume I: rules. Cambridge University Press

ICRC (Henckaerts J-M, Doswald-Beck L eds) (2005b) Customary international humanitarian law, volume II: practice – parts 1 & 2. Cambridge University Press

Kant I (2010) The critique of practical reason (Th. Kingsmill Abbott E.d & tr., first published 1778). Pennsylvania State University
Kesby A (2012) The right to have rights. Oxford University Press
Lauterpacht H (1950) International law and human rights. Steven & Sons
Lauterpacht H (1970) In: Lauterpacht E (ed) International law, collected papers, vol I, the general works. Cambridge University Press
Lowe V (2007) International Law. Oxford University Press
Marks M, Clapham M (2005) International human rights lexicon. Oxford University Press
Osiatyński W (2009) Human rights and their limits. Cambridge University Press
Ragazzi M (1997) The concept of international obligations erga omnes. Oxford University Press
Raz J (1986) The morality of freedom. Oxford University Press
Schabas W (2008) War crimes and human rights: essays on the death penalty, justice and accountability, Cameron May
Scovazzi T, Citroni G (2007) The struggle against enforced disappearance and the 2007 United Nations Convention. Martinus Nijhoff Publishers & VSP
Shue H (1980) Basic rights, subsistence, affluence, and U.S. foreign policy, 2nd edn. Princeton University Press
Tomuschat C (2008) Human rights, between idealism and realism, 2nd edn. Oxford University Press

Articles

Addo MK (1997) Does Hohfeld still matter? Bracton Law J 29:7–12
Agamben G (2001) On security and terror (trans: Zehle S). Frankfurter Allgemeine Zeitung
Alston P (1984) Conjuring up new human rights: a proposal for quality control. Am J Int Law 78(3):607–621
Bianchi A (2008) Human rights and the magic of *jus cogens*. Eur J Int Law 19(3):491–508
Brunnée J (2010) The prohibition on torture: driving *jus cogens* home? Am Soc Int Law Proc 104:454–457
D'Amato A (1990) It's a bird, it's a plane, it's jus cogens! Connecticut J Int Law 6(1):1–6
D'Amato A (1995/1996) Human rights as part of customary international law: a plea for change of paradigm. Georgia J Int Comp Law 25(1&2):47–98
de Wet E (2004) The prohibition of torture as an international norm of *jus cogens* and its implications for national and customary law. Eur J Int Law 15(1):97–122
Donnelly J (1982) Human rights as natural rights. Hum Rights Q 4(3):391–405
Donnelly J (1986) International human rights: a regime analysis. Int Organ 40(3):599–642
Dworkin R (2006) Objectivity and truth: You'd better believe it. Philos Public Aff 25(2):87–139
Egeland J (1982) Political disappearances - a challenge for humanitarian law. NordiskTiddskriftInt'lRet 51:189
Gewirth A (1984) The epistemology of human rights. Soc Philos Policy 1(2):1–24
Glendon MA (1999) Foundations of human rights: the unfinished business. Am J Jurisprud 44(1):1–14
Glendon MA (2004) The rule of law in the Universal Declaration of Human Rights. Northwest Univ J Int Hum Rights 2:2–19
Gunning IR (1991) Modernizing customary international law: the challenge of human rights. Virginia J Int Law 31(2):211–248
Harrer S (2005) The theme of dubjectivity in Foucault's lecture series *L'Herméneutique du Sujet*. Foucault Stud 2:75–96
Hartman JF (1981) Derogation from human rights treaties in public emergencies: a critique of implementation by the European Commission and Court of Human Rights and the Human Rights and the Human Rights Committee of the United Nations. Harv Int Law J 22(1):1–52
Henkin L (1979) International instruments for the protection of human rights. Acta Juridica 1979:224–235

Henkin L (1995/1996) Human rights and state "sovereignty". Georgia J Int Comp Law 25(1&2):31–46
Hohfeld WN (1917) Fundamental legal conceptions as applied in judicial reasoning. Yale Law J 26(8):710–770
Kammerhofer J (2004) Uncertainty in the formal sources of international law: customary international law and some of its problems. Eur J Int Law 15(3):523–553
Keeton GW (1926–1927) Hohfeld's fundamental juristic conceptions. Hong Kong Univ Law J 1(1):46–51
Kelly JP (2000) The twilight of customary international law. Virginia J Int Law 40(2):449–544
Kirgis FL Jr (1987) Custom on a sliding scale. Am J Int Law 81(1):146–151
Kyriakou N (2012) The *International Convention for the Protection of All Persons from Enforced Disappearance* and its contributions to international human rights law, with specific reference to extraordinary rendition. Melbourne J Int Law 13(1):424–461
Lee J (2005) Human dignity and inviolability, the absolute prohibition on torture. UCL Jurisprud Rev 12:80–94
Lillich RB (1995–1996) The growing importance of customary international human rights law. Georgia J Int Comp Law 25(1&2):1–30
Meron T (1986) On a hierarchy of international human rights. Am J Int Law 80(1):1–23
Parker K, Neylon LB (1989) *Jus cogens*: compelling the law of human rights. Hastings Int Comp Law Rev 12(2):411–464
Paust J (1991) The reality of *jus cogens*. Connecticut J Int Law 7(1):81–86
Paust JJ (1995/1996) The complex nature, sources and evidences of customary human rights. Georgia J Int Comp Law 25(1&2):147–164
Paust JJ (2009) Civil liability of Bush, Cheney, et al. for torture, cruel, inhuman, and degrading treatment and forced disappearance. Case West Reserve J Int Law 42(1&2):359–388
Pound R (1915) Legal rights. Int J Ethics 26(1):92–116
Rancière J (2004) Who is the subject of the rights of man? South Atl Q 103(2/3):297–310
Randall HJ (1925) Hohfeld on jurisprudence. Law Q Rev 41(1):86–94
Redgwell CJ (1997) Reservations to treaties and Human Rights Committee General Comment No.24(52). Int Comp Law Q 46(2):390–412
Sarkin J (2012) Why the prohibition of enforced disappearance has attained *jus cogens* status in international law. Nordic J Int Law 81(4):537–584
Sen A (1982) Rights and agency. Philos Public Aff 11(1):3–39
Shelton D (2002) Hierarchy of norms and human rights: of trumps and winners. Saskatchewan Law Rev 65(2):301–332
Simma B, Alston P (1988–1989) The sources of human rights law: custom, jus cogens, and general principles. Aust Yearb Int Law 12:82–108
Tasioulas J (2013) Human rights, legitimacy, and international law. Am J Jurisprud 58(1):1–26
Trindade AAC (2009) *Jus cogens*: the determination and the gradual expansion of its material content in contemporary international case-law. XXXV Curso de Derecho Internacional (General Secretariat of the OAS 2009)
Trindade AAC (2012) Enforced disappearances of persons as a violation of *jus cogens*: the contribution of the jurisprudence of the Inter-American Court of Human Rights. Nordic J Int Law 81(4):507–536
Vasak K (1977) A 30-year struggle: the sustained efforts to give force of law to the Universal Declaration of Human Rights. UNESCO Courier 30(1):29–32
Waldron J (1993) Liberal rights, collected papers 1981-1991. Cambridge University Press
Waldron J (1999) What is a human right? Universals and the challenge of cultural relativism. Pace Int Law Rev 11(1):107–162
Waldron J (2010) Inhuman and degrading treatment: the words themselves. Can J Law Jurisprud 23(2):269–286

Book Chapters

Agamben G (1998b) The camp as Nomos of the modern (D. Heller-Roazen tr.). In: de Vries H, Weber S (eds) Violence, identity and self-determination. Stanford University Press, pp 106–118
Brown C (1999) Universal human rights: a critique. In: Dunne T, Wheeler NJ (eds) Human rights in global politics. Cambridge University Press, pp 103–127
Cassese A (2012) For and enhanced role of *jus cogens*. In: Cassese A (ed) Realizing utopia, the future of international law. Oxford University Press, pp 158–171
Eide A, Rosas A (1995) Economic, social and cultural rights: a universal challenge. In: Eide A et al (eds) Economic, social and cultural rights, a textbook. Martinus Nijhoff
Fitzmaurice G Sr (1958) Some problems regarding the formal sources of international law. In: van Asbeck FM et al (eds) Symbolae Verzijl. Martinus Nijhoff, pp 153–176
Kadelbach S (2006) Jus cogens, *obligations* erga omnes *and other rules – the identification of fundamental norms*. In: Tomuschat C, Thouvenin J-M (eds) The fundamental rules of the international legal order, jus cogens and obligations erga omnes. Martinus Nijhoff Publishers, pp 21–40
Mulgan RG (1968) The theory of human rights. In: Keith KJ (ed) Essays on human rights. Sweet & Maxwell, pp 13–29
Ní Aoláin F (2007) The individual right of access to justice in times of crisis: emergencies, armed conflict, and terrorism. In: Francioni F (ed) Access to justice as a human right. Oxford University Press, pp 57–93
Raz J (2010) Human rights without foundations. In: Besson S, Tasioulas J (eds) The philosophy of international law. Oxford University Press, pp 321–338
Trindade ACC (2011) The expansion of the material content of *jus cogens*: the contribution of the Inter-American Court of Human Rights. In: Spielmann D et al (eds) La Convention Européenne des Droits de l' Homme, un instrument vivant – Mélanges en l'honneur de Chr.L. Rozakis. Bruylant, pp 27–47
van Boven T (2010) Categories of rights. In: Moeckli D et al (eds) International human rights law. Oxford University Press, pp 173–188
Weinreb LL (1992) Natural law and rights. In: George RP (ed) Natural law theory, contemporary essays. Oxford University Press, pp 278–308

Chapter 4
The Scope of Truth and Reparation

4.1 The Right to the Truth: A Key Aspect of the CPED

The conclusion of the CPED owes largely to the efforts made by the relatives of the disappeared to know the truth regarding their fate and whereabouts. As soon as the phenomenon of disappearance spiraled in Latin America and other regions of the world, the victims' next of kin sought to reveal the truth regarding the circumstances under which disappearances occurred. This endeavor originated naturally from the anguish and anxiety that a disappearance causes to the relatives of the victim, and thereby it was a sensible and realistic claim, free of any legal content. In this respect, searching for the hidden truth surrounding disappearances occurred before the stipulation of what constitutes the pattern of enforced disappearances, and long before the legal assessment of the phenomenon. In general terms, the need to know the truth about the disappeared was the societal reaction to the phenomenon. It was this inherent need of the victims' relatives to learn the truth and challenge the concealment of their fate which led to the failure of those regimes intent on spreading terror among the population through disappearances. Truth holds a central role in the fight against disappearance. Its recognition as a human right is just an acknowledgement of the efforts made by civil society to combat the phenomenon of enforced disappearance. As a result, the right to the truth is only one aspect of the notion of truth, which embodies human beings' ontological needs.

4.1.1 On the Notion of Truth

The notion of truth, and the determined pursuit of human beings to find it, has received significant attention in the philosophical field, primarily because it is perceived both as an ontological concept and as a matter of ethics. Although the

I. Pervou, *The Right not to Be Subjected to Enforced Disappearance*,
https://doi.org/10.1007/978-3-031-36731-1_4

philosophical explications of truth surpass the scope of the current research, a few remarks are necessary for the comprehensive understanding of the right.

Almost every scientific study on truth begins from the well-known Aristotelian definition that:

> To say that what is is not, or that what is is not, is false; but to say that what is is, and what is not is not, is true; and therefore also he who says that a thing is or is not will say either what is true or what is false. But neither what is nor what is not is said not to be or to be.[1]

In abstract terms, Aristotle's theory of truth requires an agreement between linguistic expressions (what is said) and things (what it is), or else the concurrence of *logos* with inherence.[2] This perception of truth pertains to predications which are not contingent on definitional processes. It is a truth deriving from what it is, and cannot be otherwise, and as such it explains unconditional affirmative propositions. In other words, truth must be simple, or else it does not correspond to what it is. The purity of truth propositions attributes a natural dimension to truth. If truth is simple and pure, it will be natural to human beings. Nonetheless, this natural quality of truth does not absolve reasonable-thinking truth-seekers of the responsibility to search for it. This means that in Aristotelian terms, necessary truth is not equal to self-evident propositions; rather, it requires human input for its revelation. However, truth, because of its definitional objectivity (a proposition is either true or false),[3] reduces a human's personal contribution whether he decides to accept and reveal it or not. In this context, it is suggested that truth involves a moral judgment by the subject, which becomes a moral obligation if the revelation of truth is a choice of the state.[4] Thus, truth necessarily blends reason and morality, without prioritizing one over the other.[5]

Arendt, from the perspective of a political philosopher, seems to adopt a similar position on truth. In *The Origins of Totalitarianism* she mentions that

> [t]he only capacity of the human mind which needs neither the self nor the other nor the world in order to function safely and which is independent of experience as it is of thinking is the ability of logical reasoning whose premise is the self-evident. The elementary rules of cogent evidence, the truism that two and two equals four cannot be perverted even after the conditions of absolute loneliness. It is the only reliable "truth" human beings can fall back upon once they have lost the mutual guarantee, the common sense men need in order to experience and live and know their way in a common world.[6]

Arendt adds two important elements to the definition of truth. First, knowing and seeking the truth are natural qualities of human beings. This means that human beings are able to identify the truth even when they find themselves in extreme conditions, when any sort of social structure has been destroyed. Accordingly, it could

[1] Aristotle, *Metaphysics*, 1011b25.

[2] Ferejohn (1981), pp. 286–287.

[3] Dworkin (2006), pp. 89, 93.

[4] Naqvi (2006), p. 250.

[5] Hume (1896) Book III, Part I, Sect I.

[6] Arendt (1973), p. 477.

be suggested that even the victims of extreme human rights violations, those trapped in a "bare life" scheme, and who are subject to a process of dehumanization by the perpetrators of these violations, still maintain the ability to distinguish between the true and the false. Therefore, recognizing the truth is a primitive human ability. Secondly, because of its reality, knowledge of the truth is common to all human beings; it is a value which provides the foundations for rebuilding a society. Arendt's conception that truth is a quality of the individual, and that its value is realized collectively, echoes the Aristotelian idea of man as a political animal by nature.[7] Since it is common to all, it is a notion destined to be disseminated. Moreover, Arendt proposes that even the perpetrators of truth cannot alienate themselves from it. She holds that

> if the propaganda of truth fails to convince the average person because it is too monstrous, it is positively dangerous to those who know from their own imaginings what they themselves are capable of doing and who are therefore perfectly willing to believe in the reality of what they have seen.[8]

Truth has a two-sided power: it is a means to accomplish social cohesion, by designating the grounds on which a community is built, while it also serves as a weapon of manipulation in the hands of the sovereign who decides to sidestep it.

Arendt's theory relies on the condition that sovereigns tend to disregard truth, to their benefit. This hypothesis is reasonable, given that Arendt analyzes the emergence of totalitarian regimes. She submits that the perpetrators of truth ignore it intentionally, since truth is innate to thought but not to action.[9] Put simply, people's minds are truth-oriented, even when their actions are not. Arendt reshapes the Aristotelian argument on the agreement between what is said and what it is, in political terms: truth expresses the agreement between human thought and public human action. In public life, adherence to the truth is a moral choice, or an obligation owed to society. From this angle, truth presupposes the sovereign's righteousness, which amounts to a claim for justice by the non-sovereign. Conversely, the abandonment of truth by the sovereign equates to injustice, to society's detriment.

The connection between truth and justice is not new. The UN, in its Updated Principles on Impunity, proclaims that the triplet "memory, truth, and justice" is fundamental to humankind.[10] This triplet, though, is the explanation of one notion alone; it could be amended to memory (individual truth), truth (collective truth, or collective memory), and justice (legal truth). This analysis of truth is especially conducive to societies which have suffered gross human rights violations, where memory stands for the experience of the victims or their next of kin (as it appears through the magnifying glass of pain), truth is the accumulation of memories that

---

[7] Cf Aristotle, *Politics*, Book A, Chapter 2, 1253a, 3–4.

[8] Arendt (1973), p. 446.

[9] ibid, p. 9.

[10] CommHR (8 February 2005). Updated set of principles for the protection and promotion of human rights through action to combat impunity. UN Doc E/CN.4/2005/102/Add.1, principles 2, 3, 19–21.

leave their stamp on society as a whole, and justice is the formal acknowledgement of truth. At one end, memory bears a descriptive power, whereas at the other justice carries the prescriptive force of law; seemingly from memory to justice there is a rise in objectivity, which renders justice the most robust confirmation of truth. All three readings of truth carry a moral underpinning; memory is society's moral obligation to the victims, truth is the moral obligation of society to itself, whereas justice is morality through reasoning.[11]

The interrelation between truth and justice was conceptualized well in the presentation of the Chief Prosecutor for the United Kingdom at the Nuremberg Trials. Sir Hartley Shawcross stated:

> Human memory is very short. Apologists for defeated nations are sometimes able to play upon the sympathy and magnanimity of their victors, so that the true facts, never authoritatively recorded, become obscured and forgotten. One has only to recall the circumstances following upon the last World War to see the dangers to which, in the absence of any authoritative judicial pronouncement, a tolerant or a credulous people is exposed. With the passage of time the former tend to discount, perhaps because of their very horror, the stories of aggression and atrocity that may be handed down; and the latter, the credulous, misled by perhaps fanatical and perhaps dishonest propagandists, come to believe that it was not they but their opponents who were guilty of that which they would themselves condemn. And so we believe that this Tribunal, acting, as we know it will act notwithstanding its appointment by the victorious powers, with complete and judicial objectivity, will provide a contemporary touchstone and an authoritative and impartial record to which future historians may turn for truth, and future politicians for warning.[12]

According to these remarks, justice is an authoritative record of truth ("true facts [...] authoritatively recorded") and also of preserving memory ("facts [...] forgotten [...] in the passage of time"). Thus, it might well be argued that the eternal nature of truth is ensured by justice, leading to "a truth through justice" (a broader concept than judicial truth, which relates only to evidence during the process),[13] and thereby "international tribunals [...] are conduits of truth [...] and creators of an 'objective historical record'".[14] Overall, judicial pronouncements of such magnitude, which usually relate to systematic and heinous human rights violations, have a threefold function: they establish historical truth (past), they pay tribute to the truths disclosed before them by punishing the perpetrators and ending their impunity (present),[15] and, finally, they prevent the recurrence of similar events (future). Consequently, in traumatized societies, justice is the least controversial expression of truth.

---

[11] Waldron (2008), pp. 10, 56.

[12] Nuremberg Trial Proceedings, (4 December 1945), 3. Retrieved March 22, 2023, from http://avalon.law.yale.edu/imt/12-04-45.asp.

[13] Naqvi (2006), p. 246.

[14] Gaynor (2012), p. 1260.

[15] Naqvi (2006), p. 247.

4.1.2 An International Entitlement to the Truth

The international legal order started dealing with the notion of truth quite early. The initial reference to the concept of truth is included in the 1974 UNGA Resolution "Assistance and co-operation in accounting for persons who are missing or dead in armed conflicts", where it was held that "the desire to know the fate of loved ones lost in armed conflicts is a basic human need which should be satisfied to the greatest extent possible".[16] This resolution came shortly after the Turkish invasion of Cyprus, which exposed a legal gap in the 1949 Geneva Convention (hereinafter GC) but did not contain any provision for people who remained unaccounted for after the termination of an armed conflict. The UNGA Resolution makes reference to "a need to know the truth": it identifies the human desire to receive information on the fate of loved ones. Although it identifies the legal issue, the reference is timid and descriptive, lacking legal substance. Soon afterwards, the First Additional Protocol to GC (hereinafter AP1) acknowledged this pressing need. In the section for missing and dead persons, it introduces a general principle (Art. 32), according to which

> the activities of the High Contracting Parties, of the Parties to the conflict and of the international humanitarian organizations mentioned in the Conventions and in this Protocol shall be prompted mainly by the right of families to know the fate of their relatives.

Although the provision grammatically stipulates "a right of families to know the fate of their relatives", it is correctly pointed out that it makes it impingent on the parties engaged in a conflict to always keep in mind that their activities might be scrutinized by the families' entitlement to the truth.[17] That is, AP1 insists that it is the warring parties who must take responsibility for truth-seeking concerning the dead and missing, not because of families' desire for the truth.[18] The wording of Art. 32 agrees with this argument: AP1 provides for a "right to know" instead of a "right to the truth".

The difference between the two is considerable, even if they seem identical. In the first instance, the "right to know" indicates a state's obligation to disclose all the information it possesses regarding a dead person, and to further investigate the fate of a missing person. In this case, there is no presumption of wrongful behavior by the state. Even more, if the right to know is strictly limited to the humanitarian context, the opposing party will most probably be responsible for not disclosing a victim's fate. Hence, the parties to a conflict are bound by a reciprocal obligation to collect and impart the relevant information. For this reason, the families of the victims shall not bring their claim to know the truth against their state of nationality, but against the adverse party. A "right to know" is an expression of the right to seek,

---

[16] UNGA Res 3220 (XXIX) (6 November 1974).

[17] Sarigiannidis (2014), p. 34.

[18] HRCouncil (22 March 2010). Progress report of the Human Rights Council Advisory Committee on Best Practices on the issue of missing persons. UN Doc A/HRC/14/42, para 47; Secretariat. (6 August 1999). Observance by United Nations forces of international humanitarian law. UN Doc ST/SGB/1999/13, para 9.8.

receive, and impart information in the context of humanitarian law, or merely the correlative, the state's obligation to inform families regarding the fate of victims during a conflict. In contrast, a "right to the truth" carries a negative connotation. The state's duty to reveal information on the fate of an alleged victim stems from its prior denial or unwillingness to inform the victim's relatives, and it further implies its involvement in erasing the alleged victim's traces.[19]

The contextual differentiation between the two rights (i.e. their systemic classifications as a humanitarian and a human rights law claim respectively) is of minor importance, taking into account that the international community earlier removed the distinction between missing and disappeared persons. Instead, the decisive point in recognizing two separate norms is state complicity regarding a victim's whereabouts. A right to know pertains to people unaccounted for, to a situation where state behavior is initially considered neutral, while a right to the truth concerns the concealment of the victim's fate, indicating a state's wrongful act. Despite this difference, the realization of the two distinct norms is still blurry, as opposite views exist within the UN.[20]

Furthermore, international theory has not formed a settled opinion on whether there are two international law norms, or one norm which attracts different wordings. For this reason, it is usually preferred to speak of a "right to know the truth", to avoid misconceptions.[21] On top of this, and besides the wording of the drafters of the legislation, there are cases hard to characterize under international law, such as those where one cannot clearly determine whether the victims are missing or disappeared, whether the state is responsible for losing their traces or not, or whether there has been a systematic or only occasional practice of concealing their fate. Under these circumstances, any attempt to distinguish between the right to know and the right to the truth is unreasonable.

The example of the Human Rights Chamber for Bosnia and Herzegovina is ideal here. The Chamber's jurisdiction *ratione materiae* concerned applications based on alleged or apparent human rights violations with particular priority given to allegations of especially severe or systematic violations which occurred or continued after

---

[19] HRCouncil. (12 October 2009). 12/12. Right to the truth. UN Doc A/HRC/12/12, preamble. The HRCouncil in its preambulatory clauses states, *inter alia*: "Recalling that a specific right to the truth may be characterized differently in some legal systems as the right to know or the right to be informed or freedom of information". Distinguishing between the two rights is supported as well by the UN High Commissioner for Human Rights, CommHR. (8 February 2006). Study on the right to the truth. UN Doc E/CN.4/2006/91, para 12. However, there are also unfortunate moments as far as the distinction between the two rights is concerned. In the first study, on the principles against impunity, it is noted that the right to the truth refers only to individual claims, whereas the right to know is collective and broader, imposing a duty to remember. This distinction was not espoused by the second study on the principles against impunity. CommHR. (2 October 1997). Question of the impunity of perpetrators of human rights violations. UN Doc E/CN.4/Sub.2/1997/20/Rev.1, para 17; cf UN Doc E/CN.4/2005/102/Add.1.

[20] UN Doc E/CN.4/2005/102/Add.1, principle 2, 4.

[21] Scovazzi and Citroni (2007), pp. 347–360.

the termination of the armed conflict (*ratione temporis*).[22] Although the Chamber was created as a result of an internationalized armed conflict, it dealt with systematic or large-scale human rights violations from a human rights perspective. The Chamber's jurisdictional basis was of course indifferent to those victims who sought a just verdict; nevertheless, it led to definitional legal oddities. The Chamber examined cases of victims whose traces were lost during the armed conflict and who remained unaccounted for in peacetime, thus acknowledging the continuous character of the crime. It dealt with a standardized pattern of enforced disappearances which appeared at a low-scale, occasional level. According to its jurisdiction, the Chamber considered admissible the individual claims of relatives of people for whom there was no official information. In this event, a legal characterization of such cases before the Chamber would be fragile. First, there was no clear or certain threshold that could be established to indicate if the accumulation of these cases of enforced disappearance amounted to a crime against humanity (yet this was only a doctrinal question). Second, since the situation in Bosnia and Herzegovina was characterized as an internationalized armed conflict, the victims of disappearances were considered missing people from a legal standpoint and their next of kin could submit a claim in order to know their fate. Yet this approach did not correspond to the actual circumstances—the situation in Bosnia and Herzegovina was not an archetypical armed conflict—and consequently the Chamber applied the terms "disappeared", "missing", "right to know", and "truth" interchangeably.[23] This terminological irregularity demonstrates the well-established interplay between human rights and humanitarian law, and further the use of the practice of disappearances during armed conflicts.[24] Although the rights to know and to the truth are of marginal significance to the Chamber's case law, its jurisprudence is highly illustrative regarding the potential overlap between the two norms.

Apart from the field of humanitarian law, claims revolving around truth have also been explored in the context of the right to freedom of expression. This is a sensible connection, taking into account that the revelation of truth presupposes the propagation of information. The CommHR, in its resolution on the "right to the truth", acknowledges that "the right to the truth may be characterized differently in some legal systems as the right to know or the right to be informed or freedom of information",[25] whereas jurisprudence affirms that "it is an integral part of freedom of expression to seek historical truth".[26] Truth acquires another meaning through the spectrum of freedom of expression, as it exceeds the value of a pressing inner need. In the preceding analysis, truth (irrespective of the level of complicity in the

[22] Dayton Peace Agreement, General Framework Agreement for Peace in Bosnia and Herzegovina (initialed 21 November 1995, signed 14 December 1995) Annex 6, Art. VIII 2(e).

[23] *Dordo Unković v the Federation of Bosnia & Herzegovina* Human Rights Chamber for Bosnia and Herzegovina CH/99/2150 (9 November 2001) paras 91, 94; UN Doc E/CN.4/2002/71, para 42.

[24] Finucane aptly characterizes the armed conflict in Bosnia and Herzegovina as a "mixed international/noninternational armed conflict". Finucane (2010), pp. 171, 175.

[25] CommHR (20 April 2005). Right to the truth. UN Doc E/CN.4/Res/2005/66, preamble.

[26] *Chauvy et al v France*, App no 64915/01 (ECtHR 29 June 2004) para 69.

perpetrator's behavior) is an insurmountable desire generated by previous human rights violations. It has strong moral implications and has a prominent importance both for individuals and for society as a whole.

In the framework of freedom of expression, truth represents a general quest for information regarding "questions of indisputable public interest in a democratic society";[27] as such, it is subject to the limitations applied to freedom of expression.[28] Truth becomes the truth of the beholder who participates in the public debate; a notion subject to relativity, which serves as a measure of the polyvocality in society. In an attempt to find a fine balance between truth-seeking as a mode of shaping one's personal opinion and a general irrefutable truth which is common to mankind, jurisprudence distinguishes between facts and value-judgments. Accordingly, the ECtHR maintains that "the existence of facts can be demonstrated whereas the truth of value-judgments is not susceptible of proof",[29] and restricts freedom of expression only when speech contravenes clearly established historical facts.[30] For the European Court, only historical truth is uncontested due to its factual background, and, interestingly enough, it reached this conclusion on the subject of the Holocaust. Therefore, "historical facts which [are] a matter of common knowledge, and [are] inescapable and essential for any objective account" cannot become the object of personal considerations as part of public debate, for this would jeopardize historical truth.[31] Consequently, historical truth poses limitats to the right to freedom of expression.

4.1.3 Intermediate Conclusions

So far, it appears that truth is a multidimensional concept in international law. Entitlement to the truth either through humanitarian reasons or in the context of freedom of expression is deemed vital. In both contexts, truth is not an autonomous right that generates enforceable claims for its subject. In the case of humanitarian law, the "right to know (the truth)" imposes the duty on the parties engaged in an armed conflict to investigate and release the information regarding a dead or missing person, whereas in the field of freedom of expression the quest for the "truth" is a term synonymous with the scope of forming personal opinions, as elastic as the various ways in which it can be interpreted, and only historical truth is not receptive to relativity-based explanations. In humanitarian law, the right to know (the truth) involves a measure of alleviation of pain and is a responsibility of the state, while in freedom of expression it derives from the rights to seek and acquire information.

---

[27] *Giniewski v France*, App no 64016/00 (ECtHR 31 January 2006) para 51.

[28] UN Doc E/CN.4/2006/57, paras 86–87.

[29] *Lingens v Austria*, App no 9815/82 (ECtHR 8 July 1986) para 46.

[30] *Giniewski v France*, para 52.

[31] *Lehideux & Isorni v France*, App no 55/1997/839/1045 (ECtHR 23 September 1998) para 46.

Accordingly, the term "right to the truth" is misused, when it should be the term "entitlement to the truth".

The entitlement of the relatives of missing people to the truth after the termination of an armed conflict demonstrates the urgency surrounding the notion of truth, the innate need of people to discover the fate of their loved ones. This urgency and the sorrow of the relatives goes hand in hand with the misconduct of the involved state. The urgent need that people have for the truth concerning their relatives is the concept's characteristic feature, the liaison between the philosophical concept and the realistic conditions which beget an entitlement to the truth. When truth leads to the violation of human rights, and the people who remain unaccounted for are the victims of these violations, truth reaches the threshold of a right. It creates a procedural claim, first to confirm that violations of human rights have taken place and then to administer justice. In this case, the demand for truth meets the functions of the philosophical notion of truth: it contributes to the establishment of a society governed by the rule of law; it preserves historical memory; and it helps in the restoration of peace. Thus, truth is a human need which generates a legal claim for justice. Truth is a mixture of reason and morality which corresponds legally with the right to justice.

Overall, it is suggested that

> the right to the truth derives its legal basis as an enforceable right primarily from two underlying categories of protections [...] (i) A state's failure to disclose the fate of a person in a custody of the state constitutes inhuman treatment with respect to family members and is a continuing violation of applicable protections against such treatment. (ii) A state's failure to adequately investigate and prosecute crimes committed against a person in its custody constitutes a violation of family's right of access to justice.[32]

Indeed, the concealment of a victim's fate aggravates the next of kin's anguish and sorrow, and, if prolonged, amounts to cruel, inhumane, or degrading treatment. The first legal basis is complementary to the second, and not mutually exclusive. Denial of justice is a source of infuriation for the victims' relatives, exacerbating the inhumane treatment they have already been subjected to. In turn, denial of justice alone is a reason for anxiety. In this way, none of the right's two legal bases takes precedence over the other.

The conditions in which the right emerges evoke images of the archetypical enforced disappearance, where concealment of a person's traces coupled with a denial of justice heighten the relatives' suffering. Besides this, the two rights on which the right to the truth depends—the general prohibition on torture, which includes CIDT, and access to justice—are components of the prohibition of disappearance, and appear regularly in court decisions which cannot rely *ratione materiae* on the prohibition on disappearance *per se*. Two considerations follow: first, the phenomenon of disappearances was instrumental in the emergence of the right to the truth, which in turn became a lever for the reaction of civil society against the phenomenon. Second, the right to the truth is unique, because the right-holder and

[32] Groome (2011), p. 177.

the individual who had suffered human rights violations are not one person. The right introduces a shift regarding the traditional perceptions of the subject of human rights and broadens its ambit. These two propositions require assiduous and detailed attention within the context of enforced disappearance.

4.1.4 The Right to the Truth and Enforced Disappearance: Pre-CPED Aspects

The right to the truth is incorporated in Art. 24(2) of the CPED, and it was the first time that it was stipulated in a legally binding document as a right, although it had earlier been recognized by international bodies and in regional jurisprudence.[33] The debate on the inclusion of a right to the truth which preceded the CPED's conclusion illustrates the right's necessity for the victims of disappearance, as well as states' skepticism with respect to the obligations that the right would entail. Despite the fact that the appointed independent expert at the time had outlined the legal gap regarding truth that should be filled by a future binding document,[34] many states objected and proposed that there should be a reference to a commitment by states to supply information on the fate of disappeared persons.[35] Finally, the right's establishment was deemed crucial because truth is foundational to the establishment of a right to reparation.[36] After all, a legally binding document on disappearance could not ignore the notion of truth which had already been framed by jurisprudence.

The HRC as early as 1990 noted that a mother of a disappeared girl had "the right to know what has happened to her daughter. In this respect, she [the victim's mother] too is a victim of the violations of the Covenant suffered by her daughter".[37] In particular, it was held that the mental distress suffered by a victim's mother exposes her to a situation similar to that of torture or CIDT according to Art. 7 ICCPR, even though the HRC did not make a distinction between the two legal terms—to avoid any reference to a differential threshold status.[38] In contrast, the IACtHR's approach to the right to the truth was not that straightforward. In its *Castillo-Páez v Peru* judgment, the Court did not affirm the IACommHR's argumentation on the violation of a right to the truth, since the IACHR did not contain a corresponding provision. It acknowledged that the victim's family had the right to know what happened to the victim and that "it [was] therefore incumbent on the State to use all the means at its

[33] Fact Sheet No.6/Rev/3, 7.

[34] UN Doc E/CN.4/2002/71, para 80.

[35] UN Doc E/CN.4/2004/59, para 78.

[36] ibid, para 138.

[37] *María del Carmen Almeida de Quinteros et al v Uruguay*, HRC (1990) UN Doc CCPR/C/OP/2/1981, para 14.

[38] idem.

disposal to satisfy these reasonable expectations".[39] This approach was either indicative of the IACtHR's reluctance to declare the existence of a new norm or of its bewilderment about how to manage the notion of truth. In any case, the Court proclaimed an entitlement to the truth in a manner similar to that of AP1.

The IACtHR's jurisprudence concerning truth developed gradually. In its *Bámaca-Vélasquez v Guatemala* judgment, although it adjudicated that concealing a victim's fate is equal to CIDT for its next of kin, rendering them also victims of a disappearance, nevertheless it insisted on a state's duty to investigate the truth (instead of a right attributed to the victims) as part of the procedural guarantees that the rights to a fair trial and to judicial protection (Arts 8 and 25 respectively) provide.[40] The most essential aspect of this judgment is that the IACtHR treats truth as a double-edged sword. At a substantive level, the obliteration of truth is a violation of the prohibition on torture, whereas on a procedural level, the same behavior on behalf of the state is translated into a failure to investigate the circumstances under which a victim disappears, resulting in a violation of access to justice. In this way, the Court manages to merge both legal foundations of truth. The Inter-American jurisprudence progressively affirmed that the state's duty to investigate the conditions in which a disappearance occurs is conjoined with the victim's right to the truth,[41] stating that

> the investigation must have an objective and be assumed by the State as its own legal duty, not as a step taken by private interests that depends upon the initiative of the victim or his family or upon their offer of proof.[42]

The leap forward in the Court's jurisprudence was made in the case of *Anzualdo Castro v Peru*, when it was held that

> the content of the right to the truth [is] to inform the relatives of the fate of the victims and, if they were killed, the location of their remains [...] it is considered that the relatives of the disappeared victims are victims of the phenomena of forced disappearance, by which they are entitled to have the facts investigated and the responsible prosecuted and punished. The Court has recognized the right to the truth of relatives of victims of serious human rights violations is framed within the right to access to justice.[43]

The IACtHR offered a comprehensive definition of the right to the truth and mapped its content, its right-holders, and its systemic reliance on the right to access to justice.[44] The Court's progressive understanding of truth runs parallel to the international developments in combating disappearance: by 2009, when this judgment was

[39] *Castillo-Páez v Peru*, paras 85, 90.

[40] *Bámaca-Vélasquez v Guatemala (Merits)*, para 165, 182(e). *See* also, *Barrios Altos v Peru*, para 48.

[41] *La Cantuta v Peru*, para 224.

[42] *Velásquez-Rodríguez v Honduras (Merits)*, para 177.

[43] *Anzualdo Castro v Peru*, para 118.

[44] Regarding the dependence of truth, the Inter-American jurisprudence settled on the right to access to justice after the IACtHR rejected truth claims established on the right to freedom of expression. *Pueblo Bello Massacre v Colombia*, paras 219–220.

issued, the CPED was already open to signature, while a number of actions within the UN concerning truth had been carried out.[45]

The ECtHR followed a convoluted course in the realization of the notion of truth within the framework of disappearances. For the Court, the entitlement of the victims' relatives to the truth is subsumed by the right to an effective remedy (Art. 13). Truth is the set of information regarding investigations for the alleged victims that will be disclosed to victims' next of kin. More specifically, in the case of enforced disappearance:

> the notion of an effective remedy for the purposes of Article 13 entails, in addition to the payment of compensation where appropriate, a thorough and effective investigation capable of leading to the identification and punishment of those responsible and including effective access for the relative to the investigatory procedure [...] Seen in these terms the requirements of Article 13 are broader than a Contracting State's procedure obligation under Article 2 to conduct an effective investigation.[46]

The Court acknowledged that enforced disappearance creates an environment of uncertainty, which obliges the responding state to guarantee that the relatives receive information on the investigatory procedure to the maximum possible extent. This is the reason it distinguishes between the state's duty to investigate an alleged violation of the right to life (Art. 2) and an alleged enforced disappearance. The provision of adequate information to the victims' relatives is a criterion for the effectiveness and promptness of the investigations conducted; [47] either that, or investigations must be genuine and thorough.[48] Thereby, state must guarantee to follow correct procedure to find the truth. Although the ECtHR does not proclaim a right, or even entitlement, to the truth, it acknowledges the grievous harm that a disappearance entails, and raises the threshold of the right to an effective remedy when victims are killed or reported missing "as a result of the use of force by agents of the State".[49]

However, the Court regularly employs a scheme determining the respondent state's positive obligation to investigate an alleged violation when the violation at stake is complex and involves more than one right. This legal construction is not applied to truth claims alone, but to all alleged breaches that require the state's cooperation in the verification of the surrounding facts. Accordingly, the ECtHR's approach to truth becomes problematic for two reasons. First, because the term "truth", as such, does not appear in the Court's decisions, and references to it must be inferred from the context. Truth claims are cloaked under the duty to investigate, hence they are difficult to detect. Second, the connection of truth with the duty to

---

[45] In the meantime, the Permanent Council of OAS voted in a resolution concerning assistance being given to the relatives of the disappeared, affirming their right to the truth. OAS Permanent Council. (23 May 2005). Persons who have disappeared and assistance to members of their families. OEA/Ser.G, CP/CAJP.2278/05/rev.4, op clauses 6, 8.

[46] *Kaya v Turkey*, para 107; *El-Masri v FYROM*, Joint Concurring Opinion of Judges Tulkens, Spielmann, Sicilianos and Keller, para 4.

[47] *Timurtaş v Turkey*, para 97.

[48] *Kurt v Turkey*, Partly Dissenting Opinion of Judge Matscher.

[49] *Cyprus v Turkey*, App no 25781/94 (ECtHR 10 May 2001) para 131.

investigate as a violation of a stipulated ECHR right restricts truth substantially. In the Court's view it seems to be merely a procedural guarantee, or, more precisely, a matter of evidence.

The ECtHR delivered a historic judgment on enforced disappearances in 2009, shortly before the CPED's entry into force. In the case of *Varnava et al v Turkey*, it acknowledged that "a disappearance is a distinct phenomenon, characterized by an ongoing situation of uncertainty and accountability in which there is a lack of information or even a deliberate concealment and obfuscation of what has occurred."[50] Despite this conclusion, and although the ECtHR took into account the relevant practice of the remaining international and regional bodies concerning disappearance, still it confounded expectations, since it did not recognize the right or entitlement of the victim's next of kin to the truth. The Court held that there is an enhanced procedural obligation to investigate an alleged enforced disappearance under ECHR Art. 2, which consists of the duty to find the victim's remains and to identify and prosecute the perpetrators of the unlawful acts committed.[51]

Clearly the ECtHR's jurisprudence on enforced disappearance and truth is in disarray because of the lack of a coherent basis determining the state's duty to investigate. According to the above analysis,[52] in some cases the Strasbourg Court bases the state's obligation to investigate on Art. 13, distinguishing between the state's duty to trace the victim and its duty to release information to the victim's next of kin. In this event, the ECtHR leaves an open window for the relatives' entitlement to the truth, while in the *Varnava* judgment it establishes the duty to investigate in Art. 2 alone. Consequently, it promotes the idea of a victim-centered duty to investigate and finds it unnecessary to examine alleged violations of Art. 13.[53] Practically, in *Varnava* the Court does not recognize an entitlement to the truth; the duty to investigate a disappearance fully outweighs the relatives' entitlement to access the investigatory procedure.[54] On a doctrinal level, the duty to investigate is single, and its legal basis shall not affect the applicant's claims. However, in these cases, applicants submit claims on behalf of the disappeared, and also for the suffering they have experienced themselves because of the disappearance. As a result, an entitlement to the truth under Art. 13 ECHR must be acknowledged alongside the state's duty to track the victim's traces in order for the Court to guarantee full and adequate redress to the victim's relatives. Further, this opinion has been endorsed by PACE,

[50] *Varnava et al v Turkey*, App nos 16064/90 et al (ECtHR 18 September 2009) para 148.

[51] ibid, para 145.

[52] *Kaya v Turkey*, para 107.

[53] *Varnava et al v Turkey*, para 231.

[54] Following the *Varnava* judgment, the ECtHR has been progressively restricting relatives' entitlement to the truth in opposition to the state, particularly when an international body is in charge of the investigative procedure. The ECtHR rejects both sides' claims regarding state ineffectiveness in locating and identifying the missing person's corpses, since the Committee on Missing Persons in Cyprus (CMP) has the mandate to conduct these investigations. *Emin (Mustafa) et al v Cyprus*, App no 59623/08 (ECtHR) para 38; *Charalambous et al v Turkey*, App no 46744/07 (ECtHR) para 61.

which has concluded that the right to the truth is "a right to be informed of the fate of [the] disappeared relatives",[55] which presupposes "the recognition of close relatives as victims in their own right".[56]

The ambiguities in the European jurisprudence about truth were resolved soon after the CPED's entry into force, and an incredible shift in the Court's reasoning was recorded. Although there is no evidence that the CPED was a powerful factor triggering the development of the European case-law, it marked a turning point whose influence certainly extends to regional jurisprudence.

4.1.5 The CPED's Right to the Truth and the Victim Status

The explicit provision of a right to the truth in Art. 24(2), as well as references to it in the preamble, is classified among the CPED's pros, particularly because there was no corresponding provision either in the IACFDP or in the 1992 Declaration. Thereby, the CPED's contribution with respect to the international acknowledgment of truth is twofold: on the one hand, it provides a formal ascertainment of the entitlement to the truth, upgrading it to a human right, while on the other hand it determines who the right-holders are in Art. 24(1).

In the first strand of the analysis, regarding the right's content, the UNWGEID's relevant general comment is enlightening. Although the UNWGEID's "General Comment on the Right to the Truth in Relation to Enforced Disappearance" has the 1992 Declaration as a point of reference, it nevertheless offers a crucial and detailed study on the right's status and substance. Clearly there is an contradiction: the UNWGEID analyzed the aspects of the right to the truth through the lens of the 1992 Declaration, which does not proclaim a right to the truth,[57] while it issued this general comment on August 2010, only a few months before the Convention's entry into force. Moreover, it may well be suggested that the general comment genuinely interprets Art. 24(2), since it takes notice of, and capitalizes on, the documents concerning the elaboration of the CPED; besides, in the absence of an authoritative interpretation by the CED this general comment offers the most complete insight into the theme.[58] According to the general content, four elements epitomize the right's content: it is a restorative (a), procedural (b), and absolute (c) right, which poses a heavy evidential threshold on the duty-bearer (d).

[55] PACE. (3 October 2005). Enforced disappearances. Res 1463 (2005), op clause 10.2.

[56] PACE (3 October 2005). Enforced disappearances. Res 1719 (2005), op clause 2.2.

[57] The closest equivalent of a right to the truth in the 1992 Declaration is found in op. clause 13.

[58] It is worth noting that one of the main causes of the UNWGEID's creation was the anguish and sorrow of the victims' families. UN Doc A/Res/35/193, preamble. The UNWGEID does not aim to punish perpetrators, or provide victims with reparations or compensation; rather, it focuses on ascertaining the truth, to further alleviate the suffering of victims' relatives. Consequently, the UNWGEID's mandate is founded on the concept of truth.

First, the right to the truth has a restorative character: it is intended to administer justice and serves a means of non-recidivism, so as to repair an existing violation of the prohibition on disappearance. Consequently, the right to the truth shall be "clearly distinguished from the right to information, and in particular the right of the relatives [...] to obtain information on a person who is deprived of his liberty".[59] The protective scope of the right to the truth does not extend to people deprived of their liberty in general; instead, it requires the victim's deprivation of liberty and the subsequent concealment of their fate to exist cumulatively. The right to information develops a function counter to the right to the truth: its role is to prevent the concealment of the fate of detainees. From this perspective, relatives' entitlement to information, or, better, detainees' right to communication, safeguards detainees against a potential abuse of power by their guards.[60] Thereat, prolonged *incommunicado* detentions breach detainees' right to communication, while they increase the risk of a disappearance. The CPED provides for a right to communication as well (Arts 17(3) and 18(1)), in the form of an obligation placed on its member-states with the purpose of eliminating the phenomenon's occurrence. Hence, the two rights are distinguished from each other on a temporal level and with regards to the victim's status (disappeared and detainee respectively).

Second, the right to the truth is a procedural right[61] (*status activus processualis*): the state's obligation to take all necessary steps in order to trace a victim requires the establishment of pertinent mechanisms which will enable the state to fulfill its obligation. In turn, the relatives' right relies on the existence of these mechanisms, otherwise they cannot be informed of the investigatory procedure. The right's enjoyment demands the state's input in the form of institutional mechanisms; this is the reason why the terms "duty to investigate" and "right to the truth" appear sometimes interchangeably in international practice.

Third, the right to the truth is absolute: "not subject to any limitation or derogation. No legitimate aim, or exceptional circumstances, may be invoked by the State to restrict this right".[62] The absolute character of the right to the truth cannot be directly inferred either by the 1992 Declaration or by the CPED; hence, the UNWGEID applies a dynamic interpretation of the right. The right's absolute character is justified by the anguish and sorrow an enforced disappearance causes to the victim's relatives and their powerlessness vis-à-vis state mechanisms; in turn, their

[59] UNWGEID. General comment on the right to the truth in relation to enforced disappearance, para 2. Retrieved March 22, 2023, from http://www.ohchr.org/Documents/Issues/Disappearances/GC-right_to_the_truth.pdf.

[60] The term "right to information" is inappropriate, as it refers to the legitimate interest of a detainee's next of kin to be informed of the detention conditions. The term "right to communication" is more accurate, since there is the paradigm of the Third Geneva Convention (GC3) relative to the treatment of prisoners of war (Arts 70–71, 123). The right to communication of prisoners of war is of a preventive character, aiming at the reduction of missing persons (GC3 Arts 109–119), likewise in human rights law.

[61] UNWGEID, General Comment on the Right to the Truth in Relation to Enforced Disappearance, para 3.

[62] ibid, para 4.

suffering amounts to torture or CIDT, which are non-derogable prohibitions.[63] This connection between the prohibition on CIDT and the right to the truth is sensible in the context of the 1992 Declaration, which does not proclaim an autonomous prohibition on disappearance. Instead, it incorporates the perception of that time, understanding enforced disappearance as a complex practice which violates a series of norms simultaneously but does not function as an autonomous norm itself. Thus, this course of reasoning is obsolete within the CPED's scheme. Besides, the concept of CIDT attracts conflicting arguments as far as its non-derogable character and content are concerned.[64] Nonetheless, the UNWGEID's understanding of the right to the truth as a non-derogable norm is correct, taking into consideration the absolute quality of the prohibition against disappearance alongside truth's supplementary character. That is, the right to the truth carries the features of the prohibition on disappearance, since the occurrence of the former requires the violation of the later, and because its scope of application is to secure the prohibition's judicial enforcement.[65] In the CPED's framework, the right to the truth is a legal remedy to the violation of the right against disappearance.[66]

Fourth, the right to the truth entails specific obligations for states. Their duty to investigate is ongoing, and fulfilled if the victims' traces are tracked or if their fate and whereabouts are determined by presumption. In any event, the investigatory procedure is considered successful only if its results satisfy the victim's next of kin by shedding light on their disappearance.[67] The UNWGEID underlines that the duty to investigate is procedural and not an obligation to secure a result. That is, the state is required to prove that it has taken all necessary steps to find the victim, but not to actually uncover the course of their suffering or to locate their remains. In the most probable scenarios, that the victim does not reappear or their corpse remains undiscovered, the state bears the burden to prove that it has exhausted all available means at its disposal to trace the disappeared. Nevertheless, the absolute character of the right to the truth is mitigated, given that states' duty to investigate is imperfect.[68]

On the whole, the right to the truth is a dividing line between lawlessness and justice; between the breach of the right against disappearance and the ensuing plea

---

[63] ibid.

[64] *Öcalan v Turkey*, App no 46221/99 (ECtHR 12 May 2005) para 179–183; *Ireland v the United Kingdom*, App no 5310/71 (ECtHR 18 January 1978) para 65; *Lawless v Ireland (n 3)*, App no 332/57 (ECtHR 1 July 1961) paras 19–20, 22; cf *Caesar v Trinidad & Tobago*, Inter-American Court of Human Rights Series C No 123 (11 March 2005) para 97; *Lori Berenson-Mejía v Peru*, Inter-American Court of Human Rights Series C No 119 (25 November 2004) para 100.

[65] Apparently, the right lacks an autonomous character, on account of its dependence on the prohibition against disappearance. Cf. Scovazzi and Citroni (2007), p. 359; CommHR, Study on the Right to the Truth, para 42.

[66] Sarigiannidis (2014), p. 36.

[67] UNWGEID, General Comment on the Right to the Truth in Relation to Enforced Disappearance, para 5.

[68] The general principle of a mirror correlation between rights and duties is overturned, as there is no exact correlation between the absolute right to the truth and the duty imposed on states to investigate the victims' fate. Cf. Raz (1986).

for justice by the victims' families in order to honor the victims' memory. For them, the inability to reach the truth is equivalent to a *damnatio memoriae*. Art. 24(2) of the CPED, written with the intent to reduce the number of victims of disappearances, reflects the sad reality that the phenomenon of disappearance persists. From the moment a disappearance occurs, the exercise of the right to the truth aims at detecting the disappeared, but its primary focus is to bring relief to their next of kin, thus circumscribing the proliferation of victimization. Except for the stipulation of the right *per se*, the CPED determines the right-holders of the right in Art. 24(1).

Art. 24(1) of the CPED provides that for the purposes of the Convention, a victim is a "disappeared person and any individual who has suffered harm as the direct result of an enforced disappearance". The CPED's definition of the victims of enforced disappearance is quite broad: apart from the disappeared, anyone who has suffered as a result of the committed disappearance is characterized as a victim (broadly, *locus standi in judicio*). The definition extends to the victim's relatives, as well as to any individual affected by the disappearance, irrespective of family or legal ties with the victim. It is only necessary to demonstrate a causal link between the harm suffered and the occurrence of the disappearance. Practically, witnesses, human rights defenders, journalists[69] or members of NGOs and associations who undertake activities in the field of disappearance can be considered victims under Art. 24(1), depending on the factual specific peculiarities of each case. From a procedural perspective, if someone proves direct harm stemming from an enforced disappearance, then their applications claiming alleged violations of the norm submitted to judicial organs shall be considered admissible *ratione personae*. This definition is aligned with the UN Declaration of Basic Principles of Justice for Victims of Power and Abuse of Power, which in 1985 acknowledged three major categories of victims. It provided that victims are

> persons who, individually or collectively have suffered harm, including physical or mental injury, emotional suffering, economic loss, or substantial impairment of their fundamental rights, through acts or omissions that are in violation of criminal laws operative within Member States, including those laws proscribing criminal abuse of power [a,] or acts or omissions that do not yet constitute violations of national criminal laws but of internationally recognized norms relating to human rights [b, and finally victims are also] the immediate family or dependants of the direct victim and persons who have suffered harm in intervening to assist victims in distress or to prevent victimization [c].[70]

These definitions are founded on two key axes. First, someone's characterization as a victim presupposes the existence of a rule and an alleged perpetrator, irrespective of the legal order that stipulates the rule. Second, the UN distinguishes between direct and indirect victims when evaluating "the degree of proximity of the source of victimisation".[71] In this respect, the Declaration distinguishes between direct and

---

[69] UNGA. (21 February 2014). The safety of journalists and the issue of impunity. UN Doc A/Res/68/163, op clause 2.

[70] UNGA. (29 November 1985). Declaration of Basic Principles of Justice for Victims of Crime and Abuse of Power. UN Doc A/Res/40/34, Annex Arts 1, 18, 2.

[71] Rombouts and Vandeginste (2000–2003), p. 94.

indirect victims only to determine their position vis-à-vis the target of the violation, and does not evaluate the extent of their suffering. The UNGA promotes a victim-centered approach, where the initial target of the violation and the perpetrator's intent are immaterial to one's characterization as victim; victimization is an actual situation, and a legal assessment confirms their suffering and regulates their treatment. Evaluation does not measure suffering but subsequent treatment. For this reason, those who are harmed in an attempt to "prevent victimization" are considered victims as well, although they are outside the perpetrators' sphere of abuse.

Embracing this philosophy, the IACtHR considers the relatives of the disappeared victims as victims themselves, and presumes their suffering by virtue of the occurrence of the disappearance alone.[72] In so doing, it shifts the burden of proof, calling on the respondent states to reverse this consideration. Moreover, it holds that all individuals who prove that they are "actually and personally affected" by a disappearance shall be deemed victims as well. Accordingly, the IACtHR finds that:

> It can presume injury to the psychological and moral integrity of the families of the victims of certain human rights violations applying a *iuris tantum* presumption regarding mothers and fathers, sons and daughters, spouses, and permanent life partners (hereinafter "direct relatives"), provided that this responds to the specific circumstances of the case. As to those direct relatives, it is up to the State to disprove the presumption. In all other cases, the Court must consider whether the evidence in the case shows that the personal integrity of the alleged victim has been affected, regardless of whether he or she is a relative of another victim in the case or not. Regarding those persons to whom the Court does not presume injury to personal integrity because they are not direct family, the Court must assess, for example, whether there is a particularly close relationship between them and the victims in a case that would enable the Court to establish an effect on their personal integrity and, therefore, a violation of Article 5 of the Convention. The Court may also assess whether the alleged victims have been involved in seeking justice in the specific case, or whether they have suffered as a result of the facts of the case or of subsequent acts or omissions on the part of the State authorities in relation to the facts.[73]

The IACtHR's findings are fully aligned with the CPED's Art. 24(1). The Inter-American Court recognizes all individuals as potential victims of enforced disappearance, depending on each case's particular circumstances, and distinguishes

---

[72] The IACtHR took after the paradigm of the HRC. *See, Quinteros et al v Uruguay*, para 14.

[73] *Ibsen Cárdenas & Ibsen Peña v Bolivia*, para 127.

between direct relatives[74] and the rest[75] only with regard to the necessary evidential threshold. Direct relatives are, by virtue of their position, victims of an enforced disappearance, and thus exempted from the evidential procedure. Their anguish is taken for granted, and in turn the disappearance harms their personal integrity (the equivalent of CIDT in the Inter-American system). Their legal position as direct relatives substantiates the violation of their personal integrity, irrespective of their actual ties with the victim. In this regard, the anguish and sorrow of the relatives of abducted and disappeared kids is not questioned even though they might not have met the disappeared victims at all.[76] Conversely, children who were not born at the time of their siblings' disappearance are also considered victims, due to "the environment of suffering and uncertainty" in which they were born.[77] That is, an enforced disappearance is a violation of the right to personal integrity of direct relatives irrespective of each case's factual background, as it affects "the family nucleus".[78]

As far as alleged victims who are not direct relatives of the disappeared are concerned, the IACtHR poses a double-test to verify their suffering: they must establish

[74] For the IACtHR, relative status is an objective situation which may even run contrary to the provisions of domestic family and inheritance law. In this respect, in the *Aloeboetoe et al v Suriname* judgment, where the IACtHR examined the extrajudicial execution of seven men, the victims were polygamic, following tribal custom. Further, the victims' descendants were not registered in the state records. Although polygamy is forbidden by Surinamese law, and the children could not be connected to the victims from a legal perspective, the Court took the view that Surinamese law was not applicable to the tribe, over which the state did not exercise "effective legal control". In the Court's wording, "[in this case] local law is not Surinamese law, for the latter is not effective in the region insofar as family law is concerned". Thereby, it respected the tribal customs, to the extent that they did not contravene the IACtHR. *Aloeboetoe et al v Suriname*, para 62.

[75] The distinction between direct relatives and other potential victims is not new. In the *"Mapiripán Massacre" v Colombia* judgment, the Inter-American Court recognized four categories of victims: the direct victims of an alleged violation (a), those closest to them (the equivalent of direct relatives) (b), the next of kin of the victims (who correspond to the remaining non-related victims) (c) and the inhabitants of the community affected by the human rights violation (d). This case involved the massive extra-judicial execution of at least thirty civilians in the city of Mapiripán in Colombia. Afterwards, the victims' bodies were thrown in the closest river, leaving their next of kin unable to bury their remains, and rendering the verification of the victims' number and identity a difficult task. The legal typification of the above facts is peculiar; the Mapiripán massacre is in principle an extra-judicial execution case and does not bear the characteristics of a disappearance incident. However, the bereavement and suffering caused by the executions were worsened because the victims' bodies were thrown away, an act that resembles the practice of disappearances. In this context, the IACthR distinguished between direct victims, direct relatives, the remaining victims and finally the civilians of the massacred city. The fourth category takes into account the collective aspect of the right to the truth, or the perpetrators' intent to force them to flee from the area in which they reside. *"Mapiripán Massacre" v Colombia*, Inter-American Court of Human Rights Series C No 122 (15 September 2005) para 279 a), b); Tinta (2008), p. 259.

[76] *Gelman v Uruguay*, Inter-American Court of Human Rights Series C No 221 (24 February 2011) para 133.

[77] *Contreras et al v El Salvador*, para 122.

[78] *Gomes Lund et al ("Guerrilha do Araguaia") v Brazil*, Inter-American Court of Human Rights Series C No 219 (24 November 2010) para 239.

their close relationship with the disappeared, and in addition demonstrate that they have actively been seeking justice; or, alternatively, must show that their suffering stems from the concealment of the victim's whereabouts.[79] In the *Ibsen Cárdenas & Ibsen Peña* judgment, the IACtHR accepted that the victim's nanny, who had raised him since the age of nine, should be categorized among the members of the family unit. Her affiliation with the victim sufficed to prove their close relationship, and consequently her suffering.[80]

This judgment demonstrates the IACtHR's adaptability to the particularities of each case. Overall, its jurisprudence meets the requirements set out by CPED Art. 24(1), while the European standards move in the opposite direction, as the ECtHR does not establish any general principle that identifies that a family member of a disappeared person is a victim as well. On the contrary, the relatives of the disappeared must prove that they have suffered from "the authorities' complacency in the face of anguish and distress", which renders them "victims of treatment" under ECHR Art. 3.[81] Thereby, the ECtHR holds that the relatives of the disappeared become victims themselves as a result of the authorities' reactions and attitudes when they are informed of the disappearance, not because of the incident alone.[82] The factors taken into consideration when characterizing a relative as a victim of treatment include

> the proximity of the family tie – in that context, a certain weight will attach to the parent-child bond, – the particular circumstances of the relationship, the extent to which the family member witnessed the events in question, the involvement of the family member in the attempts to obtain information about the disappeared person and the way in which the authorities responded to those inquiries.[83]

The ECtHR introduces three "special factors": the proximity of the family ties (a), the extent to which the family member witnessed the events in question (b) and the involvement of family members in the attempts to obtain information about the disappeared person (c).[84] The European Court casts doubt on the anguish and anxiety that relatives of the disappeared may experience if they are not connected via a parental or spousal relationship with the victim. In the *Çakici v Turkey* judgment, the ECtHR did not recognize the applicant—the brother of the disappeared—as a victim of ill-treatment under Art. 3, and differentiated this from its previous verdict,

[79] The IACtHR does not apply this double-test in massacre cases, where it uses its discretionary powers to the fullest and exhausts its flexibility and latitude. In the *Ituango Massacres* case, the Inter-American Court accepted that victims whose names had not been listed in the first stage of proceedings could be added later on, provided that this did not contravene the general principle of the procedural equality of arms, and in particular the rights of defense of the respondent state. *Ituango Massacres v Colombia*, Inter-American Court of Human Rights Series C No 148 (1 July 2006) para 106. Burgorgue-Larsen and Úbeda de Torres (2011), p. 125.

[80] *Ibsen Cárdenas & Ibsen Peña v Bolivia*, para 129.

[81] *Orhan v Turkey*, paras 357–358.

[82] *Kurt v Turkey*, paras 133–134.

[83] ibid.

[84] *Janowiec et al v Russia*, App nos 55508/07, 29520/09 (ECtHR 21 October 2013) para 169.

where the petitioner was the mother of the victim. Moreover, the European Court evaluated the petitioner's attempts to bring the case to justice, and took account of the fact that the proceedings brought before the judiciary had been initiated by the father of the disappeared victim.[85] Therefore, it seems as if the ECtHR cannot recognize the pervasive nature of anguish and anxiety, which affects the family unit as a whole and not the relatives separately; it thus keeps the interpretation of judicial standing narrow, reserving it for members of the victim's next of kin. The European Court has gradually departed from this rigid view, although its approach remains circumstantial.[86] Thus, it has affirmed that the mother of the disappeared victim is a victim of ill-treatment, even if she has not been an eyewitness to her son's disappearance.[87]

Finally, the ECtHR's reasoning regarding the relatives of the disappeared differs if there is sufficient circumstantial evidence of the victims' death. In the *Varnava et al v Turkey* judgment, the European Court reversed its course of thinking: it accepted that applicants (the victims' next of kin) were to be considered victims according to ECHR Art. 34, and attributed to them the status of a victim of ill-treatment (contrary to ECHR Art. 3). Because of the disappeared's presumed death, the Court did not examine whether they should also be considered victims. Consequently, the relatives' characterization as victims was deemed a sufficient basis for lodging these petitions, and claims raised by relatives on behalf of the disappeared were not examined.[88]

Overall, the *locus standi* of relatives in disappearance cases has been enhanced. The ECtHR is gradually addressing relatives as victims of treatment, irrespective of each case's factual background, and now follows the example of the Inter-American jurisprudence. The Court's dictum in the case of *Janowiec et al v Russia* exemplifies its current approach towards the right to the truth and the status of relatives in disappearance cases, where it states that

> the suffering of family members of a "disappeared person" who have to go through a long period of alternating hope and despair may justify finding a separate violation of Article 3

---

[85] *Çakici v Turkey*, paras 98–99.

[86] *Luluyev et al v Russia*, App no 69480/01 (ECtHR 9 November 2006) para 113; *Mikiyeva et al v Russia*, App nos 61536/08 et al (ECtHR 30 January 2014) para 114; *Z & Khatuyeva v Russia*, App nos 39436/06 & 40169/07 (ECtHR 30 January 2014) para 72; *Aslakhanova et al v Russia*, App nos 2944/06 et al (ECtHR 18 December 2012) para 133.

[87] *Imakayeva v Russia*, App no 7615/02 (ECtHR 9 November 2006) paras 38, 165; *Luluyev et al v Russia*, paras 111–112; *Khamila Isayeva v Russia*, App no 6846/02 (ECtHR 15 November 2007) paras 144–145; cf the judgment in *Saidova v Russia*, where the mother of the disappeared victim was the only witness of the abduction, and her testimony alone did not suffice to establish the truthfulness of the facts. *Saidova v Russia*, App no 51432/09 (ECtHR 1 August 2013) para 69.

[88] *Varnava et al v Turkey*, paras 146, 200; *Elberte v Latvia*, App no 61243/08 (ECtHR 13 January 2015) para 99; cf *Janowiec et al v Russia*, para 186. Cf. also the judgment *Skendžić & Krznarić v Croatia* where the ECtHR concluded that the compensation received by the relatives of the disappeared during civil procedures before domestic courts deprived them of victim status under Art. 3 of the ECtHR. *Skendžić & Krznarić v Croatia*, App no 16212/08 (ECtHR 20 January 2011) para 96.

> on account the particularly callous attitude of the domestic authorities to their quest for information.[89]

Apparently, the ECHR's Art. 3 is a substitute for the right to the truth in the European human rights system. Its "separate violation" regarding the relatives' quest for information reflects the autonomous character of the right to the truth, whereas their mental distress caused by the disappearance confers upon them the status of a victim, and therefore gives them judicial standing. In the words of judges Tulkens, Spielmann, Sicilianos and Keller, in their joint concurring opinion in the *El-Masri v FYROM* judgment, "the Court is implicitly acknowledging that the right to the truth has a place in the context of Article 3, although it does not really commit itself to such a finding"; they further pointed out that "the lack of an explicit acknowledgement of [the] right [gives] the impression of a certain over-cautiousness.[90]

Moving in this direction, the ICJ acknowledged the psychological suffering of the relatives of disappeared persons and affirmed that such suffering results in mental harm. In its judgment on the Application of the Convention on the Prevention and Punishment of the Crime of Genocide it found that insufficient information with respect to the fate of individuals who are disappeared causes severe psychological distress to their relatives.[91] The International Court moved a step further and asserted that if the disappearances occurred in the context of an alleged genocide, then the mental harm that relatives undergo due to the concealment of the victims' fate meets the requirement of "mental harm" of the *actus reus* of the crime of genocide.[92] For the ICJ, when large-scale disappearances constitute genocidal acts,[93] the mental harm of the members of the attacked group (i.e. of those who are left behind, of the relatives of the disappeared) contributes to the group's destruction.[94] Although the International Court seems to employ the current jurisprudence regarding the notion of the victim in disappearance cases, it treats disappearance as a factual situation, a reality, and rejects the existing legal terminology, probably due to its

---

[89] *Janowiec et al v Russia*, para 186.

[90] *El-Masri v FYROM*, Joint Concurring Opinion of Judges Tulkens, Spielmann, Sicilianos and Keller, paras 3, 10; Heri (2014), pp. 765–766.

[91] *Application of the Convention on the Prevention and Punishment of the Crime of Genocide (Croatia v Serbia)* [2015] ICJ Gen List No 118, para 159.

[92] Article II(b) of the Convention on the Prevention and Punishment of the Crime of Genocide stipulates that "genocide means any of the following acts committed with intent to destroy, in whole or in part, a national, ethnical, racial or religious group, as such [...] (b) causing serious bodily or mental harm to members of the group".

[93] In principle, the widespread or systematic practice of enforced disappearance when committed in a certain context is a crime against humanity per se, according to CPED Art. 5 and ICC Art. 7(1)(i). UNWGEID. (21 December 2009). General comments on enforced disappearance as a crime against humanity. UN Doc A/HRC/13/31, para 39, op clause 7. Yet, if perpetrators commit disappearances aimed at the destruction of a group, then their intent (*mens rea*) is genocidal (*dolus specialis*) and subsumes the intent to forcefully disappear the victims. In this framework, mass disappearances are not a crime against humanity, but part of the crime of genocide.

[94] *Application of the Convention on the Prevention and Punishment of the Crime of Genocide* [2015], para 160.

established jurisdiction. It does not use the term "enforced disappearance", but perceives disappearances as a physical means to achieve a group's physical destruction.[95] Thus, the ICJ predictably did not establish the involved states' obligation to investigate and disclose the truth regarding the disappeared victims, nor even that relatives had an entitlement or right to the truth. It encouraged Parties "to pursue that co-operation in good faith and to utilize all means available to them in order that the issue of the fate of missing persons can be settled as quickly as possible".[96] Nonetheless, this judgment strengthened the position of the relatives of disappeared victims, and was almost revolutionary for a Court which does not examine human rights claims but focuses on state responsibility for internationally wrongful acts,[97] since it indicates a latent interplay between Art. II(b) of the Genocide Convention and the CPED's Art. 24(1).[98]

All in all, this progress coincides with the CPED's entry into force, alongside the widespread tendency recorded in the international community to bring into being a right to the truth. For this reason, references to the CPED's Art. 24 proliferate in international jurisprudence. The international community solemnly proclaims the importance of the right to the truth, affirming that it is a "particularly compelling norm" in disappearance cases.[99]

4.2 The Right to Reparation: Correcting the Ills of Enforced Disappearance

Victims' right to reparation is equally important to their right to the truth, as it guarantees restoration of their legal protection. In the framework of enforced disappearance, the right to reparation of both direct and indirect victims brings them "inside the protection of the law". The exercise of the right to reparation presumes the violation of the prohibition against disappearance and at the very least the

[95] Cf ibid, Dissenting Opinion of Judge A.A. Cançado Trindade, para 291.

[96] ibid, para 359.

[97] The massacre at the village of Plan de Sánchez in 1982 is probably the only case involving genocidal claims brought before a human rights court. The IACtHR issued a decision regarding the deaths of over two hundred and fifty people (women and children mostly) by the government of General Ríos Montt and paramilitary groups under its control. The massacre is considered an act of genocide, as the government targeted rural areas and attempted to force indigenous populations into a massive exodus. In the case of Plan de Sánchez the village was abandoned and the Maya Achi group was destroyed. The decision on the case was momentous and unique given the large number of victims, while the IACtHR stuck to a human rights victim-centered approach. Cf. *Plan de Sánchez Massacre v Guatemala*, para 51.

[98] Further, the judgment is a progressive interpretation of Art. II(b) of the Genocide Convention, as the prevailing interpretation provided for "impairments of mental faculties" of the victims, a threshold apparently not met by the anguish and anxiety suffered by the relatives of the disappeared victims. Schabas (2009), p. 184.

[99] *El-Masri v FYROM*, para 175.

acknowledgement of the right to the truth. Because of its pragmatic character, which may force the perpetrating state into acts or omissions, it is usually a stumbling block in the negotiation procedure that impedes the conclusion of an international instrument.[100] Unlike the right to the truth, the right to reparation is detached from the prohibition on disappearance and from any particular human right, since it entails the breach of all norms that reach judicial organs. Therefore, the right to reparation bears two main features: its generality compared to the other human rights norms, and its secondary character, since it emerges after the breach of a primary substantive norm.[101]

An individual's right to reparation, or their claim to collective reparations (when there is an inter-state dispute), stems from the principal legal maxim that harms should be remedied and victims ought to return to the position they would have been in if the violations had not taken place.[102] This principle was proclaimed by the Permanent Court of International Justice (hereinafter PCIJ), which held that

> it is a principle of international law that the breach of an engagement involves an obligation to make reparation in an adequate form. Reparation therefore is an indispensable complement of a failure to apply [a rule] and there is no necessity for this to be [expressly] stated.[103]

Thereby, reparation claims, and in particular reparations for human rights violations, are—alongside punishment of perpetrators—well-founded in international law, as stipulated in the International Bill of Human Rights.[104] Apart from compensating for the violations that a victim has suffered, the right to reparation is intended to restore the legal situation before the breach occurred, or to correct it (through restorative and corrective justice respectively) in accordance with the requirements of "the international legal principles of accountability [...] and the rule of law".[105]

---

[100] UN Doc E/CN.4/2005/66, paras 15–16; UN Doc E/CN.4/2004/59, para 79.

[101] Tomuschat (2002), p. 158.

[102] Roht-Arriaza (2004), pp. 157–158.

[103] *Case Concerning the Factory at Chorzów (Germany v Poland)* (Jurisdiction) PCIJ Rep Series A No 9, 21. From a human rights perspective, a state's duty to repair the damages suffered by individuals because of its wrongful behavior was first endorsed with respect to persons subjected to the so-called "scientific experiments" in the Nazi concentration camps. ECOSOC Res 353 (XII) (19 March 1951), op clause 1.

[104] UDHR Art. 8, ICCPR Art. 2(3). *See* also, ECHR, Arts 13, 41, IACHR Arts 25(2), 63. General human rights instruments do not expressly provide for a right to reparation; rather, they incorporate reparation claims into the right to an effective remedy or a fair trial and condition reparation claims on the exhaustion of domestic local remedies. The ECHR is the exception, by providing in Art. 41 that partial reparation on behalf of a contracting state party prompts the granting of just satisfaction by the ECtHR. Although this article's function is to establish the ECtHR's subsidiary role in compensating for the victim's harm, nonetheless it is an explicit provision on reparations. Similarly, IACHR Art. 63 mentions that the breaches of rights or freedoms shall be remedied and that fair compensation shall be paid to the injured party. There is seemingly no consistency in the used terminology, and variations between the terms reparation, just satisfaction and compensation may lead to doctrinal misconceptions.

[105] UNGA. (21 March 2006). Basic principles and guidelines on the right to a remedy and reparation for victims of gross violations of international human rights law and serious violations of

4.2.1 The Right to Reparation Between Justice and Impunity

Victims' right to reparation for human rights violations is crucial for the realization of justice. It restores the victims' reputation, and halts at the same time their persistent denigration by the perpetrators when human rights violations occur systematically within a state. In this sense, when international judicial organs administer justice for human rights violations revolve around three axes, namely, the investigation and establishment of the facts (legal truth), the bringing to justice of persons responsible (punishment), and reparations for the victims (reparation).[106] On one level, justice seeks to accomplish legal truth through objectivity, and to tally facts with legal rules. On another, justice has a twofold mission: to end impunity by punishing perpetrators, and at the same time to rectify the breaches that have taken place with the view to extending the victims' suffering. Punishment (or the end to impunity)[107] and the right to reparation are paired, inseparable claims, for they do not suffice alone.

The interrelation between punishment and reparations came to the attention of the international community early: it is striking that the UN adopted principles on reparation and on impunity within a few months of each other,[108] with a slight overlap between them.[109] The victims' right to reparation is complemented by the state's duty to prosecute the perpetrators. States' impunity hinders alleviation of victims' suffering and prolongs a climate of uncertainty and fear in the community. And even if victims have obtained reparation, impunity institutionalizes criminality and rewards the wrongdoers for their illegal actions, further leaving room for the repetition of egregious violations. In this regard, it is argued that the punishment of culprits is part of reparations, and therefore the duty to prosecute is a component of the right to reparation and part of truth litigations; vice versa, punishing perpetrators for

---

international humanitarian law. UN Doc A/Res/60/147, Annex, preamble.

[106] CommHR. (2 July 1993). Study concerning the right to restitution, compensation and rehabilitation for victims of gross violations of human rights and fundamental freedoms. UN Doc E/CN.4/Sub.2/1993/8, para 128. It is suggested that the term "redress" comprises the victims' right to the truth, their right to an effective remedy and the right to reparations, and is therefore preferable. This coincides with the UN Declaration of Basic Principles of Justice for Victims of Crime and Abuse of Power, which provides that "victims […] are entitled to prompt redress […] for the harm that they have suffered. Fulton (2014), p. 771; UN Doc A/Res/40/34, Annex Art. 4.

[107] Impunity is defined as "the impossibility, de jure or de facto, of bringing perpetrators of violations to account – whether in criminal, civil, administrative or disciplinary proceedings – since they are not subject to any inquiry that might lead to their being accused, arrested, tried and, if found guilty, sentenced to appropriate penalties". UN Doc E/CN.4/2005/102/Add.1, 6.

[108] van Boven, T. (2010). The United Nations basic principles and guidelines on the right to a remedy and reparation for victims of gross violations of international human rights law and serious violations of international humanitarian law, 1. Retrieved March 20, 2023, from http://legal.un.org/avl/pdf/ha/ga_60-147/ga_60-147_e.pdf.

[109] UN Doc E/CN.4/2005/102/Add.1, principles 31–34; UN Doc A/Res/60/147, Annex, principle II(b).

the crimes they commit, either under international or domestic law, does not substitute for the victims' right to obtain reparations.[110]

The doctrinal question of the inclusion of the duty to prosecute among the wide range of means to redress the victims is of minor importance, and strays far from the victim-centered approach of reparations. Assuming that the duty to prosecute falls within the reparations spectrum, any redress for the victims of gross human rights violations would be impossible via truth commissions or through the enactment of amnesty laws. Therefore, the duty to prosecute and the victims' right to reparation do not coincide, even though they complement one another due to their differing legal origin. The duty to prosecute is a facet of the principle of state accountability, while the right to reparation is a general legal standard which exceeds the international protection of human rights, originally stemming from tort law.[111] Yet, they come together on some occasions, such as public apologies by the state, which are a form of reparation that also encapsulate state accountability.

Overall, "the general tenor [regarding the rules of anti-impunity is] to reaffirm and expand on duties to investigate, prosecute, and to be critical of amnesties that preclude any of these things".[112] Impunity creates uneasiness and widespread uncertainty in those societies where violations have been systematic or excessive; it precludes the planning of lustration and national remembrance, and also dissolves official efforts to form collective truth. However, impunity is not one of the victim's top priorities, compared to reparation measures. The end of impunity must be the state's prerogative for the realization of social reform, and the accomplishment of a long-term national policy of justice for the public. Thereat, states must distinguish between and combat two forms of impunity: the one concerning the perpetrators of human rights abuses, the other regarding the disruption of the rule of law (or the historical continuity of human rights abuses).[113] According to the above, punishment for gross human rights violations is nothing but a state's commitment to justice.

---

[110] Groome (2011), p. 195; Baeza (2000), pp. 27–28. *See* also the first reparations decision by the ICC, which acknowledged the victims' right to reparation and interpreted ICC Statute Art. 75 accordingly. Thus, it ordered the establishment of a Trust Fund to provide adequate resources for the victims' reparations. *Prosecutor v Thomas Lubanga Dyilo (Decision establishing the principles and procedures to be applied to reparations)* ICC Trial Chamber I (7 August 2012) ICC-01/04-01/06; *Prosecutor v Thomas Lubanga Dyilo (Judgement on the appeals against the "Decision Establishing the principles and procedures to be applied to reparations")* Appeals Chamber (3 March 2015) ICC-01/04-01/06 AA2A3.

[111] The philosophical traces of the notion of reparation are found in Aristotle's *Nicomachean Ethics*, where the philosopher takes the view that "the law looks only at the nature of damage, treating the parties as equal, and merely asking whether one inflicted and the other has sustained damage [and] Justice in Rectification [is] the mean between loss and gain", setting the general axiom regarding redress. Aristotle (1934), p. 1132a1.

[112] Roht-Arriaza (1996), p. 95.

[113] Baeza (2000), p. 28.

4.2.2 The UN Right to Reparation for Gross Human Rights Violations

The UN from 1988 onwards has put a strong emphasis on the right to remedy and reparation for gross human rights violations and serious violations of international humanitarian law, and this resulted in the adoption of a set of related principles by the UNGA in 2006.[114] The drafting of reparation principles (also referred to as the "van Boven/Bassiouni principles" after the names of the two Special Rapporteurs entrusted with their elaboration) came as the response of the international community to grave violations and the subsequent attempts by the perpetrating states to shield state officials who committed crimes through the enactment of amnesty laws, pardons, and limitation statutes.

The UN demonstrated its focus on gross human rights violations and made headway by referring to a "right to a remedy and reparation". Unlike the right to the truth, reparations were connected with the victim from scratch, something which averted references to a duty to repair or an entitlement to reparations. However, the mandate was narrowed to gross and serious violations of human rights and humanitarian law respectively. This limitation did not cause circumspection; soon it was clear that the scope of the references to gross and serious human rights violations was to underline the urgency to redress violations which were stipulated as international crimes, and did not exclude was with no prejudice to the general concept of obtaining reparation for human rights violations, irrespective of their magnitude.[115]

Two key ideas epitomize the philosophy on which reparation principles rely: first, they are victim-oriented, and second, they appertain to the international claim to remedy and reparations, which entails a correlative international obligation on the state. The victim-oriented approach is manifested by the reference to a right, and by the acceptance that there are both direct and indirect victims. Moreover, it is generally accepted that the importance of the law on state responsibility is downgraded in the set of principles, since states bear responsibility to give reparations to the victims; in this instance, the violation is established but the perpetrators are not, or they cannot be identified. For example, in enforced disappearance cases, where several state agents are involved in a single disappearance and where state mechanisms follow the pattern of task delegation, it is impossible to bring all perpetrators to justice. Similarly, in mass conflict situations, where the number of victims and violators rises to thousands, there is no capability of the national penitentiary system, or no reason for international courts alike, to prosecute them all.[116] In such circumstances, there is no individual responsibility attributable to the state. At this

[114] For a thorough analysis of the special rapport on reparations and its course from 1988 onwards *see* Zwanenburg (2006), pp. 641–668.

[115] van Boven (2010), p. 2.

[116] Dinah Shelton aptly observes the flaw in limiting the reparation principles to gross and systematic violations: the large number of victims and perpetrators "may overwhelm the best efforts to provide redress", and thus render the principles ineffective. This is also highly probable because

point, the conduct of unidentified state organs begets state responsibility, contrary to the ARSIWA provisions, whereas the attribution of individual criminal responsibility is possible only with regards to high-ranking officials.[117] Although this scheme seems problematic as far as PIL and ICL claims are concerned, it is extremely helpful for claims brought before human rights tribunals, where, unlike national trials, the victims' primary goal is not to name and stigmatize their perpetrators but to reach justice and obtain reparation. When victims of grave acts reach international tribunals, they fulminate against the state practice and not the perpetrators themselves. Of course, this does not entail that victims waive their claim to punish perpetrators, for this would be a triumph of impunity; but such claims must be originally demonstrated before national tribunals.[118] In the IACtHR's view

> the international protection of human rights should not be confused with criminal justice. States do not appear before the Court as defendants in a criminal action. The objective of international human rights law is not to punish those individuals who are guilty of violations, but rather to protect the victims and to provide for the reparation of damages resulting from the acts of the States responsible.[119]

Secondly, the principles institute an international legal obligation to provide remedy and reparations, something which is not surprising at first sight. The improvement, though, is that Principle I provides that "States shall [...] ensure that their domestic law is consistent with their international legal obligations by (c) making available adequate, effective, prompt and appropriate remedies, including reparations", and praises a top-down approach regarding states' respective obligations. This proclamation is considered a safe choice in the context of a soft law instrument, which met with a lukewarm reception by states, which certainly showed no willingness to make it become binding. Nevertheless, this Set of Principles is the starting point for enacting an international obligation for human rights violations which is not subject to national limitations. It may be inferred that the right to a remedy and the right to a reparation are non-derogable, a characteristic which would eventually outlaw amnesties.

Further, the reparation principles are instrumental on issues of terminology; Principle VII encloses the relationship between the rights to justice, remedy and reparations. It provides that

---

Principle VIII on collective or group reparation provides for an anemic obligation towards states. Shelton (2005), p. 151.

[117] Roht-Arriaza (2004), p. 192; Tomuschat (2002), p. 181; Shelton (2005), p. 149; cf ARSIWA Art. 4 et seq.

[118] UNWGEID. (12 January 1998). General comments on article 19 of the Declaration. UN Doc E/CN.4/1998/43, para 71.

[119] *Godínez Cruz v Honduras (Merits)*, para 140; Judge Trindade expressed the opposite view in the Inter-American legal order. In his reasoned opinion in the *Myrna Mack Chang* judgment, "reparations can perfectly well be both compensatory and punitive, with the aim of putting an end to impunity and ensuring realization of justice", further adhering to the view that punitive reparations develop a dissuasive function, since they efface the "obstructions of the duty to investigate and to punish those responsible". *Myrna Mack Chang v Guatemala*, Reasoned Opinion of Judge A.A. Cançado-Trindade, para 46.

> remedies for gross violations of international human rights law [...] include the victim's right to the following as provided for under international law: (a) Equal and effective access to justice; (b) Adequate, effective and prompt reparation for harm suffered; (c) Access to relevant information concerning violations and reparation mechanisms.

There is a genus-species relationship among the three norms. Access to justice is the general norm which guarantees people's recognition before the law, and their inclusion in a particular legal order. The right to a remedy is accordingly the legal manifestation of the right to justice, whereas the right to reparation materializes the right to an effective remedy, through mechanisms set by states. There is also the opposing view, according to which the right to reparation encompasses a broader spectrum of claims than the right to a remedy, pointing at the latter's strictly legal and procedural character.[120] Their moral and philosophical interrelation explains why they are often used interchangeably, and justifies terminological inconsistencies amongst legal documents.[121] Finally, the reparation principles (Principle IX) outline the forms reparations may take, which include restitution, compensation, rehabilitation, satisfaction, and guarantees of non-repetition. These forms cover the wider possible range of both material and non-material (moral) damages suffered by victims.

These principles are of particular importance to the prohibition against enforced disappearance and victims' right to reparation, taking into account perpetrators' "intention of evading responsibility, truth and legal remedies".[122] This explains the subtle dialogue between the final version of the reparation principles and the report of the independent expert on enforced disappearance, which were drafted during the same period. Besides, it is historically verified that the UN initiative for the drafting of reparation principles was prompted by phenomena like "impunity, disappearances, and historical injustices".[123]

4.2.3 The CPED's Right to Reparation: Successes and Shortcomings

The CPED stipulates victims' right to reparation in Art. 24(4), and Art. 24(5) illustrates the content of the right to reparation in the conventional scheme. It provides that the right to obtain reparation "covers material and moral damages and, where appropriate, other forms of reparation such as: (a) Restitution; (b) Rehabilitation; (c) Satisfaction, including restoration of dignity and reputation; (d) Guarantees of non-repetition". This provision is unique in two aspects: first, it promotes compensation as the primary form of reparation, and second, it explicates by way of

---

[120] UNWGEID, General comments on article 19 of the Declaration, para 70; UN Doc E/CN.4/2002/71, para 84.

[121] UN Doc E/CN.4/2005/66, para 16.

[122] UN Doc E/CN.4/2002/71, para 84.

[123] Shelton (2005), p. 143.

example the forms that satisfaction may take in enforced disappearance cases. In the remaining part, the provision follows the standards of the UN reparation principles.

The explicit mention of compensation in Art. 24(4), alongside the provision that other forms of reparation will be applied to cover "material and moral damages where appropriate", signals the priority of compensation over the other forms, which are eventually allocated a subsidiary role. This order of prioritization flows from the well-established connection in international law between compensation and the damages caused[124] to the victim for the harm suffered.[125] The placement of compensation in paragraph 4 denotes that the other forms of reparation are subsidiary yet complementary to it. With respect to the forms of satisfaction, reference to the restoration of the disappeared's dignity and reputation is justified by the defamation an enforced disappearance may entail for the victim. More specifically, archetypical disappearances are those "carried out primarily with the purpose of elimination of political opponents [and] victims [are] often cast as terrorists, subversives, or undesirables by their prosecutors".[126] By spreading rumors about the disappeared, the perpetrating governments managed to sow doubts among the population about the victims' dissenting behavior. As a result, the majority would mumble the motto "por algo será" (where there is smoke, there is fire) in order to disassociate themselves from the alleged subversives, and avoid potentially disappearing themselves.[127] In this context, restoration of the victims' dignity and reputation is equally important when they are presumed dead, for it terminates the social marginalization suffered by their next of kin. To restore their dignity, victims most often request that international tribunals publicly apportion responsibility for the facts established so as to nullify national court judgments which contaminate the reputation of the disappeared (particularly judgments which convict them of acts of terrorism) and to expunge the relevant state archives, with the view to facilitate the re-assimilation of the disappeared (if alive) and their relatives into society.[128]

The CPED's provision on the right to reparation and its content is fairly deemed a success compared to Art. 19 of the 1992 Declaration, which provides that

> the victims of acts of enforced disappearance and their family shall obtain redress and shall have the right to adequate compensation, including the means for as complete a rehabilitation as possible. In the event of the death of the victim as a result of an act of enforced disappearance, their dependants shall also be entitled to compensation.

First and foremost, from the 1992 Declaration up to the CPED the position of the relatives of the disappeared has certainly improved. The CPED systematically

[124] *Gabčikovo-Nagymaros Project (Hungary/Slovakia)* [1997] ICJ Rep 7, 81, para 152.

[125] *Velásquez Rodríguez v Honduras (Compensatory Damages)*, Inter-American Court of Human Rights Series C No 7 (21 July 1989) para 39.

[126] Fulton (2014), p. 774.

[127] Roht-Arriaza (2004), p. 160.

[128] *Cantoral-Benavides v Peru (Reparations)*, Inter-American Court of Human Rights Series C No 88 (3 December 2001) para 64; *19 Merchants v Colombia*, para 72(g); *Bámaca-Velásquez v Guatemala (Reparations and Costs)*, Inter-American Court of Human Rights Series C No 91 (22 February 2002) paras 70(d), 84.

places the definition of the persons considered victims before the stipulation of the right to the truth and to reparation and clarifies from the outset the position of the next of kin of the disappeared. Secondly, Art. 19 is confusing as far as the relatives' right to compensation is concerned. While the first period affords that the relatives, alongside the disappeared victim, are entitled to adequate compensation, the second period makes unclear who the beneficiaries of compensation are. The UNWGEID's General Comments on Art. 19 resolves this uncertainty through a historical interpretation of the provision. The relatives of the disappeared victim are entitled to compensation irrespective of the victim's reappearance, presumption of death, or unacknowledged fate. Accordingly, the Working Group advocates that "the right of compensation in relation to an act of enforced disappearance shall not be made conditional on the death of the victim" and draws a clear line between extrajudicial executions and enforced disappearances resulting in the victim's death.[129] In this context, the second period of Art. 19 emphasizes states' obligation to compensate the relatives of the disappeared; this addition was historically an imperative, bearing in mind the simultaneous evolution of the prohibition of disappearance and the phenomenon of extrajudicial executions. Moreover, the absence of a prohibition on enforced disappearance alongside a limited understanding of the phenomenon resulted in equating enforced disappearance with state-sponsored murder in domestic legal orders. In effect, many states did not award compensation unless the victim's death could safely be presumed or proven.[130] Thirdly, Art. 19 employs "rehabilitation" as an umbrella term, which comprises satisfaction and guarantees of non-repetition,[131] even though at the time of the Declaration's adoption, international jurisprudence had already elaborated on these facets of reparation, rendering this omission unjustifiable.[132] The distinction between the two provisions affirms the positive assessment of CPED Art. 24, which clearly sets out the forms a reparation shall take.

4.2.3.1 The Right to Obtain Compensation: CPED Art. 24(4)

Compensation is the most typical remedy awarded by international bodies for human rights violations, a reality which usually leads to the wrong assumption, or oversimplification, that the right to obtain reparation is limited to the awarding of

---

[129] UNWGEID, General comments on article 19 of the Declaration, para 74.

[130] UN Doc E/CN.4/1998/43, paras 26–46; Citroni (2014), pp. 790–791.

[131] ibid, para 75.

[132] The HRC, in its first communication regarding enforced disappearance, requested that the impugned state compensate the victim and his/her family for the injury suffered, as well as ensure that similar violations do not occur in the future. *Eduardo Bleier v Uruguay*, para 15; *Joaquín David Herrera Rubio et al v Colombia*, HRC (1990) UN Doc CCPR/C/OP/2/161/1983, para 12; *Godínez Cruz v Honduras (Reparations and Costs)*, Inter-American Court of Human Rights Series C No 8 (21 July 1989) paras 24–25; *Velásquez Rodríguez v Honduras (Compensatory Damages)*, paras 25–27.

compensation. This is a general proposition that exceeds the prohibition on enforced disappearance, usually expressed as a form of criticism of the practice of international tribunals.[133] The rule of "prompt, fair and adequate compensation" is a common legal principle, originally framed in the context of private-wealth state deprivations (namely expropriation and nationalization). The features of promptness, adequateness and fairness indicate the point when compensation shall be awarded so as to be satisfactory, will correspond to the harm caused, and will be equal to the value of the harm respectively.[134]

With respect to enforced disappearance, the principle of proportionality applies, and thus compensation should be proportionate to the harm suffered by the victim,[135] not be designed either to enrich or to impoverish them.[136] Despite theoretical considerations about the outdated value of awarding compensation alone, compensation remains vital for the victims of enforced disappearance. The UNWGEID reached this conclusion when it sought information about the legal, procedural and financial aspects of compensation by those countries where at least twenty complaints of enforced disappearances had been reported at that time.[137] The IACtHR's jurisprudence has been a catalyst at this point. In the first three cases of enforced disappearance that it undertook (which also happened to be its first three judgments), not only did the Court depict the pattern and delimit the practice of enforced disappearance but it also set the scope and content of compensation. In the *Velásquez-Rodríguez* judgment, the Court held that "'fair compensation' [...] to the 'injured party' is compensatory and not punitive [and] includes reparation to the family of the victim of the material and moral damages they suffered because of the involuntary disappearance of Manfredo Velásquez"; while, with regards to emotional harm, the IACtHR stated that "indemnity may be awarded under international law and, in particular, in the case of human rights violations. Indemnification must be based upon the principles of equity".[138] There are two main inferences to be drawn from the above excerpts: first, compensation covers both material and moral damages (also referred to as pecuniary and non-pecuniary, or patrimonial and non-patrimonial damages), and second, emotional harm, which is the main symptom of moral damages, is the consequence of breaching an international legal rule. Consequently, compensation for emotional harm is not subject to domestic law standards.

Based on these two major principles, the IACtHR built its doctrine on the calculation of compensation. Material damages are the actual damages suffered because of the victim's disappearance. For Inter-American jurisprudence, material damages

---

[133] Fulton (2014), pp. 776–782; Antkowiak (2008), pp. 357–359; Cassel (2006), p. 92; van Boven (2003), p. 654.

[134] Dawson and Weston (1962), pp. 737–738.

[135] UN Doc E/CN.4/2002/71, para 84.

[136] *Tibi v Ecuador*, para 225; *Caracazo v Venezuela*, Inter-American Court of Human Rights Series C No 95 (29 August 2002) para 78.

[137] UN Doc E/CN.4/1998/43, paras 23, 65.

[138] *Velásquez Rodríguez v Honduras (Compensatory Damages)*, paras 38–39, 27. *See* also, *Godínez Cruz v Honduras (Reparations and Costs)*, paras 36–37, 25.

are synonymous with the victim's loss of earnings. To calculate them, the Court applies a complex formula consisting of three criteria, readjusted according to each case's particularities: the victim's salary at the time of their disappearance, their life expectancy, and the number of their direct dependants.[139] The formula is an example of the way the IACtHR perceives equity, as it combines international and national standards to calculate the amount of lost earnings. Although the state is complicit in an internationally wrongful act, compensation is calculated pursuant to national rates regarding the salaries received and the person's life span. Of course, it is accurately observed that it is quite difficult for the IACtHR to calculate the amount of money that the disappeared victims would have earned if they had disappeared while pursuing their studies or during their early livelihood.[140]

The IACtHR has gradually begun to fix its jurisprudence regarding the content of pecuniary damages, "which presumes the loss of or harm to the income of the victims, the expenditure incurred as a result of the facts, and the pecuniary consequences that have a causal link to the facts of the case *sub judice*".[141] In other words, pecuniary damages includes the victim's loss of earnings, the expenses incurred in the search for the victim, and most often the medical expenses for the victim's next of kin (or other consequential damages).[142]

With respect to moral damages and indemnity for emotional harm, in the *Velásquez-Rodríguez* and *Godínez Cruz* judgments the Inter-American Court exhausted its discretion in the calculation of moral damages, since it provided no indication on how it decided the exact amount of money owed by the impugned state to the victims. It appears that in its subsequent judgments the IACtHR determined that a fixed amount of money was owed for moral damages suffered, and that this was significantly less than the moral damages it awarded in its first judgments. However, a set amount of money is not compatible with the principles of equity and proportionality for the pain suffered by the indirect victims of disappearance, although it ensures legal certainty. The only factor the Court reckoned in the calculation of the fixed amount of moral damages was whether the respondent state had acknowledged international responsibility for the disappearances, something which is still supposed to extenuate the moral suffering of the victim's family.[143] The Court soon abandoned this reasoning and settled on a more flexible scheme, acknowledging that "it is not possible to allocate a precise monetary equivalent to non-pecuniary damage". Based on this proposition the IACtHR currently holds that

---

[139] Pasqualucci (1996), pp. 26–29.

[140] Pasqualucci (2013), p. 231.

[141] *Serrano-Cruz Sisters v El Salvador*, para 150; *Gómez-Paquiyauri Brothers v Peru*, para 205; *19 Merchants v Colombia*, para 236.

[142] *Trujillo-Oroza v Bolivia*, para 75.

[143] Pasqualucci (1996), pp. 35–36.

> non-pecuniary damage can include the suffering and hardship caused to the direct victims and to their next of kin, the harm of objects of value that are very significant to the individual, and also changes, of a non-pecuniary nature, in the living conditions of the victims.[144]

By affirming the inability to allocate a precise monetary equivalent to moral damages, it demonstrates its unwillingness to treat all cases evenly and to relinquish the established case by case approach.[145] Thereat, the IACtHR attempts to strike a balance between a consolidated jurisprudence which will guarantee the victims' right to obtain reparation while simultaneously paying attention to the particular circumstances that surround a case, reserving its authority to differentiate between its judgments accordingly. It admits that while case law may establish a precedent, it "cannot be invoked as an absolute criterion".[146]

Moreover, it follows from the IACtHR's later judgments that it may award compensation for non-pecuniary damages to the relatives of the disappeared person, as well as to the direct victims of enforced disappearance themselves ("suffering and hardship caused to the direct victims and to their next of kin"). This is anticipated in rare cases where the disappeared victim reappears and brings proceedings before the Court. However, the IACtHR has granted compensation to the direct victims for the moral damage it assumes they have suffered while under the command of their captors. Of course, this compensation does not substitute for the indemnity awarded to the relatives due to their moral suffering and distress. The IACtHR gradually reached the conclusion that

> the non-pecuniary damages inflicted on [the direct victim] are evident, and it is human nature that each person submitted to forced disappearance experiences profound suffering, anguish, terror, impotence, and insecurity, for which this harm does not require evidence.[147]

For the Court, enforced disappearance is a state practice designed to exterminate or inflict pain on the victim. This is an objective observation that is beyond doubt, hence evidence of the moral pain suffered by the disappeared is unnecessary so long as the IACtHR finds an established state pattern of enforced disappearance. Even the Court or the petitioners are in most cases unable to discover information regarding the exact circumstances of each disappearance incident. In this context, the IACtHR sets a high evidentiary threshold in order to establish that a systematic practice of enforced disappearance exists in the impugned state, and consequently absolves victims and their next of kin from any proof requirement.[148]

---

144 *Serrano-Cruz Sisters v El Salvador*, para 156; *19 Merchants v Colombia*, para 244.

145 Donoso (2009), pp. 43–44.

146 *Neira-Alegría et al v Peru (Reparations and Costs)*, Inter-American Court of Human Rights Series C No 29 (19 September 1996) para 55.

147 *Chitay Nech et al v Guatemala*, paras 274, 276. *See* also, *Radilla-Pacheco v Mexico*, para 375.

148 In this context, it is striking that the IACtHR has awarded compensation for non-pecuniary damages to victims whose death was certified long before adjudication, and the victims were not technically disappeared. The Court has granted compensation to victims of extrajudicial execution for the moral distress they suffered from the time they were taken in custody until their execution. This is not the regular approach adopted by the IACtHR; rather, it is a deliberate choice of the Court, either when it has evidence of excessive brutality by state agents or when it aims at underlining a

Furthermore, the IACtHR upheld this position in cases where the disappeared victims are "presumed alive", cases which typically involve the forced disappearance of children. The *Contreras et al v El Salvador* judgment related to the disappearance of six children, five of whom were not found by state authorities. The Court adjudicated that "the physical and moral integrity of the then children who were victims of forced disappearance in this case were affected, resulting in feelings of loss, abandonment, intense fear, uncertainty, anguish and pain".[149] The decision is definitive particularly with regards to the payment of compensation awarded to the non-found disappeared victims. The IACtHR ordered the impugned state to create bank accounts in the name of the disappeared victims, with the prospect that within ten years the victims would be identified and would claim compensation. The IACtHR provided that, if the victims were not found after ten years then their next of kin would be able to collect the compensation. This scheme presupposed that state authorities will be actively engaging in investigations to locate the disappeared during this period of time.[150]

The Inter-American Court is pioneering, proving its deep understanding of the phenomenon of enforced disappearance. By granting compensation to the direct victims of enforced disappearance who are "presumed alive", it recognizes the mental distress and anguish suffered by the disappeared themselves. This view has shifted the general approach to archetypical enforced disappearance to where the principal legal concern regarding direct victims is their helplessness and their placement outside the protection of the law, while mental distress is a term usually employed to explain the position of indirect victims. The IACtHR also breaks definitively the latent jurisprudential dichotomy by which the relatives of victims who remain disappeared are entitled to compensation for pecuniary damages in their name, whereas non-pecuniary damages are directly awarded to the relatives themselves. In this judgment, the Court neither calculated the lost earnings of the disappeared victims, nor awarded pecuniary damages in their name, for this would imply

state's aggravated responsibility towards a vulnerable group of people. In the first instance, the IACtHR granted compensation for non-pecuniary damage to the victims of the *Aloeboetoe* case, taking into account that the victims were forced to dig their own graves. The Court adopted a similar reasoning to this regarding enforced disappearance and held that "the victims suffered moral damages, for it is characteristic of human nature that anybody subjected to the aggression and abuse described above will experience moral suffering". *Aloeboetoe et al v Suriname*, para 52. In the second case, the IACtHR awarded non-pecuniary damages to abducted and executed minors in Colombia. This incident did not form part of a state pattern; it was a totally unprovoked expression of the state agents' barbarism. In the second event, although the IACtHR had no information regarding the minors' execution, it took for granted that the fear of death is a feeling which undoubtedly causes severe mental distress to children. Moreover, the Inter-American Court took pains to stress that the impugned state not only failed to protect its citizens but also was unable to protect children, whose defenselessness and vulnerability is given. In this case, the IACtHR could not rely either on a set state practice or on evidence for this particular event. The only factor it took into consideration was that the victims were children. *"Street Children" (Villagrán-Morales et al) v Guatemala*, Inter-American Court of Human Rights Series C No 77 (26 May 2001) paras 90–91.

[149] *Contreras et al v El Salvador*, para 228.

[150] ibid, para 243.

a presumption of their death. Instead, the IACtHR granted pecuniary damages only to the relatives of the disappeared, to compensate them for the expenses they incurred in their attempts to locate the victims.[151]

From a doctrinal perspective, the Court's "presumption of the victims' non-death" creates a series of questions. First of all, in the event that disappeared victims do not reappear within a set time, their relatives will receive compensation for non-pecuniary damages twice. From a moral perspective there is nothing wrong in this; instead, the remedial power of compensation is by definition sufficient to heal the victim's family for the pain the disappearance has caused. From a legal standpoint, though, the twofold collection of compensation for non-pecuniary damages contravenes the general principle that compensation shall not render the victim either richer or poorer. Otherwise, if the disappeared victims reappear and claim compensation, this alone will not suffice as a measure of redress, and victims will have to institute proceedings anew if they are to pursue legal restitution. With regards to the legal basis for the awarding of compensation to disappeared children, the IACtHR relies on a violation of IACHR Art. 5(1), according to which "every person has the right to have his physical, mental, and moral integrity respected". For the Court, a child's involuntary separation from its family environment is an outright violation of their personal integrity, irrespective of the conditions in which the child was raised after the abduction.[152] Regarding the evidence provided to the IACtHR on the state conduct of child disappearances, the state pattern covers only the performing and purpose of abduction, while the fate of these children afterwards varies: some are officially adopted by families, others are raised by the families of the members of the military who capture them, and finally there are reports of child trafficking.[153] In this regard, the IACtHR cannot presume the ill-treatment of the abducted children, and this is why compensation is given to cover the separation from their families alone. Of course, in the present case the testimony of the found victim is dominant in the judgment with respect to the abominable treatment she received from the family that raised her, leaving little room to consider that the disappeared children may have grown up properly.

Although the ECtHR has not confronted a set state pattern of forcible children abductions, even it had done so hypothetically it would still not be able to apply a reasoning close to the one promoted by the IACtHR, due to lack of a legal basis. The ECtHR traditionally adjudicates enforced disappearance cases based on ECHR Arts 2 and 3. In the present case, given that the victims are presumed to be alive, there can be no violation of Art. 2, which would give rise to reparations, while there can be no presumption of ill-treatment under Art. 3 either. In this respect, the closest provision to IACHR Art. 5 is ECHR's Art. 8 on the right to respecting private and

---

[151] ibid, para 225.

[152] Even if there is no suggestion that the child has been ill-treated during the disappearance, the Court holds the view that "the State is responsible for the suppression and substitution of the identity [....] which took place since [...] birth, until [the child's] true identity [is] determined and expressed as a form of enforced disappearance". *Gelman v Uruguay*, para 312(3).

[153] *Contreras et al v El Salvador*, para 54.

family life. Yet, a violation of Art. 8 would not justify the award of compensation for non-pecuniary damages to a person who has not appeared before the ECtHR, and for whom there is no information. In other words, the reasoning of the IACtHR is not aligned with the high evidentiary threshold set by the ECtHR regarding compensation. Moreover, the ECtHR is not familiar with the concept of enforced disappearances as part of systematic state conduct, which would then allow it to consider disappearance as a situation which involves by definition insurmountable suffering for the disappeared victim and to then award them compensation for non-pecuniary damages.

The European jurisprudence is certainly more comprehensive regarding compensation due to its extensive range of examined cases, whilst it remains embryonic concerning compensation to disappearance victims and reveals the ECtHR's lack of familiarity with the phenomenon. The European Court is constantly neglecting "judicial and doctrinal developments on the issue of reparation for [...] enforced disappearance, notwithstanding the demands of the applicants, no forms of reparation different from pecuniary compensation have ever been taken into account".[154] The "flaws in the remedial framework of the ECtHR" are commonly acknowledged,[155] putting the European Court at a disadvantage compared to the IACtHR. In terms of compensation awarded for the violation of the prohibition on disappearance, the European jurisprudence is primitive, since it remained until recently at the level of the *Velásquez-Rodríguez* standards. In its first disappearance judgment, the Court awarded an amount of money to the victim's next of kin without specifying the grounds of compensation,[156] while there have been judgments where it awarded compensation for non-pecuniary damages to the victim's relatives but not in favor of the disappeared victim, since it was unable to clarify the conditions of and reasons behind his vanishing.[157] In its subsequent jurisprudence, the ECtHR granted compensation for pecuniary damages to the direct victim of enforced disappearance, and non-pecuniary damages to the victim's next of kin, who petitioned before the Court as a CIDT victim because of the state's unwillingness to investigate the conditions of the victim's loss. Yet, the ECtHR did not examine the petitioner's request to receive compensation as a victim of "a practice of "disappearances" in south-east Turkey".[158]

The ECtHR has recognized a systematic practice of enforced disappearance in the regions of Turkey and Russia. In its *Aslakhanova et al v Russia* judgment it held *ex post facto* that it had confronted a state "'pattern of enforced disappearances' occurring principally between 1992 and 1996 in South Eastern Turkey"; moreover, it accepted that there is "a systemic practice, [...] an accumulation of identical breaches which are sufficiently numerous and inter-connected to amount not merely

[154] Scovazzi and Citroni (2007), p. 372.

[155] Antkowiak (2008), p. 354.

[156] *Aksoy v Turkey*, para 113.

[157] *Kaya v Turkey*, App no 158/1996/777/978 (ECtHR 19 February 1998) para 122.

[158] *Kurt v Turkey*, paras 171, 174–175; *Timurtaş v Turkey*, paras 116, 127–128.

to isolated incidents or exceptions but to a pattern or system" of enforced disappearance in the region of the northern Caucasus.[159] By affirming the existence of a pattern of disappearances, the ECtHR, although it typically maintained the same standard of proof "beyond reasonable doubt", accepted that "such proof may follow from the coexistence of sufficiently strong, clear and concordant inferences or of similar, unrebutted presumptions of fact".[160] Accordingly, the European Court has come to the conclusion that it is "sufficient for the applicants to make a *prima facie* case of abduction by servicemen, thus falling within the control of the authorities", and it is then for the Government "to discharge their burden of proof".[161] The gradual evolution of the ECtHR's jurisprudence regarding the established patterns of enforced disappearance performed by particular states is extremely helpful in supporting the victims' attempts to find vindication, and is a considerable improvement on previous ways to confront the phenomenon. It is generally noted that the Court, in its recent jurisprudence, awards without exception both pecuniary and non-pecuniary damages to the disappeared and their relatives respectively.

The latest development in the European jurisprudence concerning its remedial authority was accomplished in the *Cyprus v Turkey* judgment on just satisfaction under Art. 41 ECHR.[162] In this judgment, the ECtHR broke the deadlock resulting from the *Varnava* judgment and the subsequent jurisprudence. In *Varnava*, the European Court actually transmuted the question of "missing persons" to an issue of "dead people". In that judgment, presuming the missing people to be dead rendered inadmissible claims under Art. 3 on their behalf, because the certainty of their death was deemed to end the ambiguity surrounding the victims' status, which a disappearance necessarily involves.[163] This approach rendered inadmissible the ensuing claims raised by the missing people's relatives because they were not considered disappeared (their death was a given),[164] while claims made under Art. 2 stumbled because of their corpses' non-identification. Aware of this jurisprudence, Cyprus initiated proceedings before the ECtHR and submitted satisfaction claims

---

[159] *Aslakhanova et al v Russia*, paras 66, 219.

[160] *Bazorkina v Russia*, para 130.

[161] *Aslakhanova et al v Russia*, para 98.

[162] In the European legal order the term "just satisfaction" refers to monetary measures, additional to compensation, ruled by the ECtHR. Because of the pecuniary character attributed to the term, the judgment's analysis falls under compensation, something which may cause terminological confusion. Yet, this categorization is doctrinally imperative, considering that satisfaction includes everything except from monetary measures.

[163] *Varnava et al v Turkey*. *See* also, *Palić v Bosnia & Herzegovina*, App no 4704/04 (ECtHR 15 February 2011) paras 74–75. The IACtHR adopts the opposite reasoning: even when the death of the disappeared victim is certain, their families' anguish and suffering persist when there is no specific information regarding the conditions of their disappearance. Thereat, the Court holds that clarifying the whereabouts or fate of the victim "is of utmost importance for the relatives of the disappeared victim [...] since by doing so, the relatives would be relieved from the anguish and suffering". *Ticona Estrada et al v Bolivia*, para 155.

[164] Citroni (2014), p. 791.

only on behalf of those missing after the Turkish invasion.[165] Thus, the applicant state exercised a *sui generis* diplomatic protection on behalf of the injured parties, seeking satisfaction for a finite number of victims (the applicant state excluded from its pleas those victims whose bodies had already been exhumed and identified, and those covered by the *Varnava* judgment). That is, "the Cypriot Government's claim for just satisfaction is not a claim for pecuniary damages directly caused to Cyprus as a State, but rather a claim for the awarding of just satisfaction to the individual injured parties, its nationals".[166] This judgment is unique in European jurisprudence in two aspects: it was the first time the ECtHR restored its jurisdiction over a dispute the merits of which it had already issued a judgment, and the first time it had applied Art. 41 to an inter-state dispute. On the first point, the ECtHR had delivered its "principal judgment" evaluating the human rights violations stemming from the Turkish military operations in northern Cyprus in 2001, and the ECtHR at that time "had expressly instructed the applicant Government not to submit any claim for just satisfaction [because] the issue of the possible application of Article 41 of the Convention was not ready for decision",[167] though without limiting its jurisdiction. This choice involved a certain political reading, even though the European Court attempted to diminish potential negative legal repercussions, which it managed to do eventually by asserting its jurisdiction. Further, the application of Art. 41 in an inter-state dispute was a "judicial amalgam" of public international and human rights law. By ordering just satisfaction, the European Court closed the cases of missing persons from the 1974 military operations. That is, the victims' relatives could only lodge a petition for subsequent procedural violations of the state's duty to prompt an investigation on the victims' conditions of death, insofar as investigations were still a national duty and not conducted by an international body. The judgment received a warm welcome by the Cypriot legal community, proving the significance of compensation for victims of gross human rights violations. Yet, it cast doubt on the effectiveness of the legal remedies provided by the European legal order, or, more precisely, on the interpretation of ECHR provisions by the Court, bearing in mind the procedural obstacles confronted by the relatives of the missing.

Overall, the divergence between the two regional courts concerning the award of compensation is apparent. The IACtHR perceives compensation like an arrow in its quiver, while the ECtHR has exhausted its remedial power to compensate, considering it the quiver in its entirety. The European approach is timid, influenced by the principle of subsidiarity; even when the ECtHR diagnosed the systematic performance of enforced disappearance by a member-state, it underlined that "it is not in a position to order the exact general and individual measures to be implemented by [the state] in order to comply with the judgment. Nor does it find it necessary to set

[165] Cyprus submitted just satisfaction claims on behalf of the enclaved Greek Cypriot residents of Karpas peninsula as well; this claim is not examined in the present analysis for the sake of consistency.

[166] *Cyprus v Turkey (Just satisfaction)*, App no 25781/94 (ECtHR 12 May 2014) para 35.

[167] ibid, para 25.

a time-limit for the implementation of any such measures".[168] In this regard, its jurisprudence continues to be strictly limited to claims raised by petitioners, although it has taken steps towards a more victim-centered approach. Therefore, even when the ECtHR acknowledges the existence of a state pattern of enforced disappearance, it does not consider claimants to be victims of the practice. On the contrary, their victim status lies within the context of the established facts, isolated from the general conduct of the impugned state. As a result, the acknowledgement of a state practice does not influence the award of compensation.

4.2.3.2 The Right to Restitution: CPED Art. 24(5)(a)

Victims' right to restitution for human rights violations they have suffered is the core of all reparation schemes. Restitution enjoys priority over the other forms of reparations, precisely because it incorporates the attempts of every legal order to erase the occurrence of human rights violations. It relies on the general legal proposition that "every violation of an international obligation which results in harm creates a duty to make adequate reparation [which] consists in full restitution (*restitutio in integrum*)",[169] which means the restoration of the situation existing prior to the violation (restoration of the status *quo ante*).[170] Yet, it is correctly pointed out that restitution claims are based on the paradox that they are "intended to return the victim to the position he or she would have been in had the violations not occurred"—something that it is impossible to do practically.[171]

From a theoretical standpoint, violations of the "irreducible core of human rights" cannot be restored, as they cause irreparable harm to one's dignity. According to the dignitarian discourse of human rights, breaches pertaining to the principle of human inviolability cannot be restored by any means. In this respect, in the rare cases in which disappeared victims survive and reappear there cannot be full restoration that can heal their suffering while they are under their captors' full control. Even if the victim has not been subjected to torture or CIDT, the fear they experience due to their deracination from their family, their segregation from societal structures, and their placement outside the legal order, cannot be repaired. In general terms, full restitution for direct victims of enforced disappearance is not possible, while restitution requires in principle the victim's reappearance. Full restitution is thus a misused term in the context of enforced disappearance, and only partial restitution applies; this means that restitution for disappearance victims is synonymous with rehabilitation.[172]

---

[168] *Aslakhanova et al v Russia*, para 220.

[169] CommHR, Study concerning the right to restitution, compensation and rehabilitation for victims of gross violations of human rights and fundamental freedoms, para 90.

[170] This principle is incorporated in ECHR Art. 46 as well.

[171] Roht-Arriaza (2004), p. 158.

[172] The IACtHR acknowledged this systemic deficiency and concluded that "redressing the damage caused by the breach of an international duty requires, as far as possible, *restitutio in integrum*,

Judicial bodies seldom come across cases where the disappeared are not executed by state authorities and can therefore submit claims against those authorities. The IACtHR made recent judgments in *García Lucero et al v Chile* and *J v Peru*, where the victims were subjected to enforced disappearance within the framework of widespread repression policies by the impugned governments for their alleged anti-governmental actions. Yet, unlike the majority of disappearance cases, they were forcibly expelled and exonerated respectively.[173] In both cases, the victims were held in military camps configured to accommodate terrorist suspects, and their captors intended to disorient them to ensure that they were unaware of the place of their captivity. It goes without saying that the victims were also severely tortured. These cases are excellent examples of how the IACtHR can explore in depth ways to give restitution to victims of enforced disappearance, and in general the cases offer an excellent opportunity to disassociate disappearance from extrajudicial executions. All the same, the Inter-American Court treated these cases as incidents of arbitrary detention accompanied by torture, despite the established state patterns against alleged terrorists under the auspices of the military and the perpetrators' proven aim to disconnect the victims from the outside world.[174] Besides, the NGO that submitted the petition on behalf of Mr. García considered it a disappearance case.[175]

Unfortunately, the IACtHR considers disappearance in terms of result, as the detainees were not permanently disappeared, and breaks down the crime into its constituent elements—that is, arbitrary detention and ill-treatment—and this would seem to be a definite gap preventing Inter-American jurisprudence from resembling European reasoning. According to this course of thinking, only those whose fate is still undetermined qualify as victims of enforced disappearance. Were that true, then enforced disappearance should not be characterized a continuous crime, nor should the international community care about the disappeared victims' traces. After all, the legal stipulation of enforced disappearance is not exhausted by the administration of justice for past disappearance events or by the prevention of future disappearances, but also aims at the location and rescue of the victims of ongoing disappearances. Consequently, the status of a "victim of disappearance" is not affected by the victim's potential reappearance, but depends on the pattern employed

---

which means restoring the situation to that prior to the violation. Should this be impossible, it is for the international court to establish a series of measures aimed not only at ensuring respect for the violated rights, but also at redressing the consequences of the breach and ordering the payment of compensation for the damage suffered. It is also necessary to add the positive measures a State must undertake to guarantee that injurious acts like the ones of the instant case do not occur again". *Almonacid-Arellano et al v Chile*, para 136. *See* also, Laplante (2004), p. 352.

[173] *García Lucero et al v Chile*, Inter-American Court of Human Rights Series C No 267 (28 August 2013) para 57; *J v Peru*, Inter-American Court of Human Rights Series C No 275 (27 November 2013) para 1.

[174] *García Lucero et al v Chile*, para 174; *J v Peru*, paras 59, 325; *see* also, *Cantoral-Benavides v Peru (Merits)*, para 43.

[175] Redress, Leopoldo García Lucero. Retrieved March 22, 2023, from http://www.redress.org/case-docket/leopoldo-garcia-lucero-v-chile.

by the state and on the actual conditions of isolation suffered by the victim. Moreover, the IACtHR's rationale eliminates disappearance claims, as it leaves modern state patterns outside the prohibition's protective scope. Should reappearance automatically render the injured party a "victim of torture or arbitrary detention", then extraordinary renditions, or unacknowledged administrative detentions, cannot be considered forms of enforced disappearance. In this framework, the *García Lucero* and *J* cases are not formally recorded as enforced disappearances, and there is no reference to the victims' restitution. The Court adjudicates a set of measures in favor of the victims in order to satisfy their right to "integral reparation", and eventually to accomplish their legal restoration and social recovery.[176] Similarly, the ECtHR rejected all claims for long-term restorative measures in the *El-Masri* judgment. Although the European Court attributed to the petitioner the status of "disappearance victim", it did not deviate from its standard reparatory tactic, but limited itself to compensation. The reappearance of El-Masri was not an element assessed by the ECtHR in the reparation part of its decision.[177] The jurisprudence of both regional courts contradicted the genuine interpretation of CPED Art. 24(5)(a), according to which restitution "means that the disappeared person, if still alive, must be immediately released".[178]

In general, restitution for direct victims of enforced disappearance includes the provision of medical and psychological care for torture after-effects,[179] or recovery of their original name and the correction of the respective state records when identity substitution has taken place.[180] It may also include reinstatement to positions of employment, and thus restitution of salaries, pensions, dividends, corporate earnings or other tangible items,[181] if the victims are in a position of returning to their ordinary lives.[182] In this context, restorative measures comprise the expunction of the victim's criminal record, or of official records that label or stigmatize them as state enemies.[183] What is more, it includes the return of the victim and their family to their residence.[184] Furthermore, if the death of the disappeared victim is certified then restitution includes the location of the corpses by the state and their return to the victims' next of kin, if they so wish.[185] Although this measure does not correspond *prima facie* to the notion of restitution, care of the dead body is prompted by cultural beliefs, whereas all religions provide for burial rituals; hence it is crucial for

---

[176] *García Lucero et al v Chile*, para 185; *J v Peru*, para 393.

[177] *El-Masri v FYROM*, para 177.

[178] UN Doc E/CN.4/2002/71, para 86.

[179] Pasqualucci (2013), p. 192.

[180] *Contreras et al v El Salvador*, paras 193–196.

[181] Roht-Arriaza (2004), p. 168.

[182] Cassel (2006), pp. 91, 93.

[183] *Cantoral-Benavides v Peru*.

[184] *Vélez Restrepo & Family v Colombia*, Inter-American Court of Human Rights Series C No 248 (3 September 2012) para 264.

[185] *Moiwana Community v Suriname*, Inter-American Court of Human Rights Series C No 145 (15 June 2005) para 208.

the relatives of the victims to seek their corpses or remains in order to honor their memory. Finally, the restitution of disappeared children entails the "annulment of any adoption which originated in enforced disappearance"[186] and reunification with their family.

Clearly, the aforementioned restorative judicial actions are attached to legal restitution, and mostly appertain to the notions of rehabilitation and just satisfaction. On the one hand, the material aspect of restitution is naturally diminished for the disappeared victims, while on the other there is an interrelation between the various forms of reparation. Hence, measures of legal restitution are often categorized theoretically as measures of rehabilitation or satisfaction. Although determining doctrinal classification is difficult, because it is obscured, the nexus where these concepts are situated conforms with the broad range of measures that restitution includes compared to rehabilitation and satisfaction, since it seeks the full recovery of the victim's prior status. Besides, when restoration of the status *quo ante* is impossible, rehabilitation and just satisfaction "must take a great role in human rights law".[187]

4.2.3.3 The Right to Rehabilitation: CPED Art. 24(5)(b)

Rehabilitation is the formal embodiment of a society's "recognition, remorse and atonement for harms inflicted"[188] to the victims of enforced disappearance. It comprises all necessary measures to guarantee the victims' return to their habitual rhythms. Apart from state-paid medical and psychological treatment, which may be considered a restorative obligation, rehabilitation exceeds the strict legal framework and requires the restructuring of social processes and mechanisms so as to allow the victim's full re-integration. It is associated with the political aspects of enforced disappearance, i.e. the victim's alienation from the political community (*polis*). In this respect, rehabilitation is dependent first of all on a change in those political motives which initiated the state pattern of enforced disappearance. When enforced disappearances are a policy of totalitarian regimes, then rehabilitation would ideally require the regime's overthrow, whereas if disappearances occur as part of discriminatory practices (racial, religious or gendered), then rehabilitation demands their abolishment. In practical terms, victims' rehabilitation comprises political initiatives that would ensure a stable and safe political environment for them.

Thereby, rehabilitation at the Southern Cone was attained after the fall of totalitarian regimes and the commitment of the succeeding governments to wipe out the remnants of disappearance policies, while in countries where civil conflicts persist, rehabilitation cannot be fully accomplished, mainly because the fear of disappearances remains. In light of the traditional paradigm of enforced disappearance, rehabilitation expresses the individual's inseparable connection with a *topos*, be it

[186] UN Doc E/CN.4/2002/71, para 93.

[187] Antkowiak (2008), p. 361.

[188] Roht-Arriaza (2004), p. 157.

individuals' inner connection with the land, their place of birth, residence, or neighborhood, or, from a broader perspective, their ability to regain their political standing in the society to which they belong. In this respect, successful rehabilitation for a disappeared trade unionist or political leader would entail the continuance of their activities, as well as enjoyment of their right to freedom of speech for them and their family members. Similarly, rehabilitation for the victims of a discriminatory religious policy would correspond to the exercise of their right to freedom of religion. Of course, these examples are still theoretical, firstly because enforced disappearances usually result in the victim's death, and secondly because actual rehabilitation requires a developed legal system coupled with mature social structures, the establishment of which is a long-term challenge for countries that have experienced such conflicts.[189]

Two key conclusions arise from this analysis: rehabilitation reveals that the *polis* is locus-dependent, and also that it outstrips strict juridical standards. The interdependence of *polis* and *topos* was introduced in Aristotle's *Politics*, where it is pointed out that "a single city [*polis*] occupies a single site [*topos*], and the single city belongs to its citizens in common".[190] Analyzing this extract, a *topos* is the main prerequisite for the existence of a *polis*, yet a "*topos* is not simply a *topos*. The idiosyncrasies of a particular location will always affect a polis in ways that are not simply traceable to its law or its regime".[191] For the victim's right to rehabilitation, this means that *topos* individualizes the means through which rehabilitation is accomplished, according to the cultural and legal particularities of each political community.[192] Further, the influence of *topos* on *polis* surpasses the field of spatial peculiarities; it is the determining factor of political equilibria in each society. In turn, this means that rehabilitation relies on a stable political environment, the constituents of which are unique to each country. In other words, rehabilitation means the victim's return to the political *topos* from which they have been ousted. After all, the embracing of the outlawed remains the primary goal of all political societies, either when their exclusion forms part of punishment under the law (regarding people sentenced for their illegal acts), or when it is the result of a state practice, which infringes their human rights (like an enforced disappearance).

As far as the juridical aspects of rehabilitation are concerned, national tribunals are vested with the power to monitor the rehabilitation of those convicted, and the respective international human rights tribunals ought to control member-states' actions to repair the harm suffered because of their wrongdoing. However, the

[189] The UNWGEID pays special attention to the process of rehabilitation, with particular reference to children. When children are the direct victims of enforced disappearance it is crucial that "states [...] ensure children's physical and psychological recovery and social integration", because the well-being of a child "is best promoted through family and community-based solutions designed to rebuild a child's self-esteem and improve his or her relationships with adults". UNWGEID. General comment on children and enforced disappearances, para 34.

[190] Aristotle, *Politics*, Book B, 1260b.

[191] Davis (1996), p. 41.

[192] *Aloeboetoe et al v Suriname*, (n 280).

second is not possible because of the low integration levels of the international human rights legal order. Put simply, human rights courts are not in a position to monitor to what extent member-states take positive measures to facilitate and realize victims' rehabilitation. Despite the absence of a vertical international system, human rights tribunals confine themselves to providing a set range of rehabilitation measures, including offering medical and psychological assistance to the victims and their relatives and the deletion of all national documents (criminal records, judicial decisions etc.) that affect negatively the victims' status[193]—measures akin to those previously examined under legal restitution. In this sense, rehabilitation is attainable only via moderate judicial activism; that is, a teleological and broad interpretation of the authority of international tribunals.

As a result, the IACtHR has shown in a number of cases that it perceives itself as a *quasi* constitutional court. In the *Gómez-Palomino* judgment, the Inter-American Court examined in depth the notion of rehabilitation,[194] and ordered the respondent state to launch special educational programs for the disappeared victim's next of kin. It observed that the disappearance had a detrimental effect on the life plans of the victim's relatives, ceasing their education. Taking into account the relatives' ages, the IACtHR ruled that if they did not wish to pursue educational programs, they might assign such benefits to their descendants.[195] By expanding the circle of beneficiaries, the Court put emphasis on the actual rehabilitation of the victim's family, instead of sticking to measures which would probably turn into a dead letter. Moreover, the IACtHR ordered the respondent state to provide a fellowship for advanced university studies to the direct victim, who was abducted while a university student.[196] Despite this progress, the IACtHR is not fully equipped to monitor states' compliance with its decisions. In the *Cantoral-Benavides v Peru* case, although Peru paid the victim and his family the compensation awarded by the Court, it invoked national legislation and closed the ongoing investigation regarding the victim's ill-treatment, contrary to the judgment.[197]

In conclusion, any rehabilitation analysis is deficient since it stumbles at the lack of jurisprudential examples. Apart from a few examples in Inter-American jurisprudence, the European Court does not engage in rehabilitation issues; hence rehabilitation is the most neglected form of reparation. A final point arising from the political-topical aspects of reparation is what measures rehabilitation for victims of extraordinary renditions would include; or, in other words, is rehabilitation possible for those subjected to non-topical disappearances? The novelty of extraordinary renditions is that they deprive the disappeared victim of a "place of reference". Although they still have very strong political underpinnings (covered by an

---

[193] Citroni (2012), p. 55.

[194] Scovazzi and Citroni (2007), p. 372. The authors aptly classify these remedial measures as rehabilitation measures, although the IACtHR refers to them as satisfaction.

[195] *Gómez-Palomino v Peru*, Inter-American Court of Human Rights Series C No 136 (22 November 2005) paras 143–145.

[196] *Cantoral-Benavides v Peru (Reparations)*, para 80.

[197] Laplante (2004), pp. 363–364.

anti-terrorist veil), extraordinary renditions are designed on a trans-border basis—a characteristic that hampers the victim's return to a "political *topos*". From a legal standpoint, judicial bodies do not possess the means to guarantee rehabilitation for these people. Taking the *El-Masri* case as an example, the ECtHR could not have done much for the victim's rehabilitation, given that it could not order the erasure of his records by the US (lack of jurisdiction *ratione loci*), or require FYROM to ensure his orderly return, since the victim had no connection with this "political community". Evidently, the IACtHR's dictum that a "judgment is in itself a type of reparation [...] the victims" is sometimes true.[198] The declaratory value of an international judgment is the only applicable remedial tool for extraordinary renditions.

4.2.3.4 The Right to Satisfaction (Restoration of Dignity and Reputation): CPED Art. 24(5)(c)

Satisfaction covers the widest range of remedial non-monetary measures, and it now has a special role in enforced disappearance cases.[199] The CPED's explicit reference to the restoration of dignity and reputation highlights the severe social consequences a disappearance entails. During the CPED's drafting, the term "dignity" was preferred over "honor" as a term more relevant to the good protected by the disappearance prohibition.[200] Measures of satisfaction are classified into five categories:

> acknowledgement of responsibility and public admission of the facts; search for and return of the remains of victims of human rights violations; official declarations and court rulings to restore the victim's honor and reputation; enforcement of judicial and administrative sanctions against those responsible for the violations; and measures designed to keep the victims' memory and/or legacy alive by building monuments, memorials, and the like.[201]

Satisfaction measures address victims, their families, the perpetrating state, and the community as a whole; they are measures mostly "of a public scope or repercussion"[202] meant "to send a message".[203] Hence, they are a holistic remedial approach. So far, satisfaction measures are applied exclusively by the IACtHR, which has proved resourceful. At the other extreme, the ECtHR consciously refuses to offer any kind of satisfaction, adhering to a compensation-centered remedial policy.

A brief account of the IACtHR's satisfaction ambit includes first of all the publication of the judgment by the impugned state. Informing the public of the judgment is a means to restore the victim's dignity and reputation, and to "disseminate the

[198] *Velásquez Rodríguez v Honduras (Compensatory Damages)*, para 36.

[199] UN Doc E/CN.4/2002/71, para 88.

[200] UN Doc E/CN.4/2003/71, para 86; UN Doc E/CN.4/2004/59, para 135.

[201] IACommHR. (2013). Impact of the friendly settlement procedure. OEA/SerL/V/II Doc 45/13, para 107.

[202] *Servellón-García et al v Honduras*, Inter-American Court of Human Rights Series C No 152 (21 September 2006) para 186.

[203] Pasqualucci (2013), p. 204.

historical truth of the facts".[204] States are instructed to publish those extracts which establish the facts, as well as the Court's ruling. What is more, the IACtHR orders states to use the most popular media, so as to guarantee the maximum possible publicity,[205] or to publish the judgment in a foreign state, if the victim resides there.[206] Apart from the judgment's publication, the IACtHR requires states to assume responsibility for the unlawful acts they commit, and afterwards to apologize publicly to the injured party. Undoubtedly, this measure is of paramount importance for the victim's relatives, while it has far-reaching legal consequences too. Apology is a common form of satisfaction in interstate disputes, provided by ARSIWA Art. 37(2), which states that "requests for, or offer of an apology are a quite frequent feature of diplomatic practice [...] which may be given verbally or in writing by an appropriate official".[207] Apology by a state for the injury caused to another state, or to its individuals if the state has exercised diplomatic protection, is common in international law, a remedial form compatible with the principle of state sovereignty and the rules of state responsibility. In the field of human rights, though, a state's apology to its citizens somehow disrupts the traditional hierarchy between the subjects and actors of international law. As a result, the IACtHR is innovative by ordering the impugned states to apologize to the victims' families, although this practice is common within public international law. It is accurately pointed out that the scheme whereby states directly apologize to individuals is a "step in humanizing reparations in international human rights law".[208]

Besides the declaratory relief an apology entails, the measure's importance relies on the fact that it presupposes the state's responsibility for a wrongful act. In the Inter-American regime in particular, this means that an act must be wrongful under the IACHR. Further, since the Court's well-founded jurisprudence subsumes incidents of disappearance under an established state pattern of enforce disappearance, a state's apology is tantamount to a formal denunciation of the practice of enforced disappearances. Therefore, an apology extends beyond the victim's family, reaching all members of a society. As such, it expresses the state's commitment to refrain from this practice in the future, and serves as a measure of non-recidivism, too. This reading of formal apologies in the Inter-American legal order justifies the criticism in the IACtHR's recent jurisprudence which distinguishes patterns of short-term disappearance from the traditional disappearance practices that end in a victim's execution. Ergo, the IACtHR misses the opportunity to secure formal denunciations of the practice of unacknowledged administrative or secret arbitrary detention (similarly with the missed chance to develop the law of restitution). Apparently, the declaratory strength of a state apology renders it the most efficient measure of

[204] *Osorio Rivera & Family Members v Peru*, para 257.

[205] *Radilla-Pacheco v Mexico*, para 350; *González Medina & Family v Dominican Republic*, para 295.

[206] *Tibi v Ecuador*, para 261.

[207] Crawford (2002), pp. 233–234.

[208] Pasqualucci (2013), p. 205.

satisfaction, because it allows the international human rights regime to challenge a state's internationally wrongful acts.[209] Official apologies also serve as guarantees of non-repetition because they are thought to prevent the recurrence of enforced disappearances in the future.[210] Moreover, the IACtHR concluded that the element of publicity is indispensable in apologies. Consequently, a state's apology to a victim's family during a hearing before the Court does not suffice as a measure of satisfaction. Accordingly, it held that for a "statement to attain full effect as reparation for the victims and to serve as a guarantee of non-recidivism, the Court deems that the State must carry out a public act of acknowledgment of its responsibility regarding the facts in this case".[211] The IACtHR has gradually developed its jurisprudence over states' duty to make an official apology, requiring the attendance of high-ranking officials alongside the victim's family and the preparation of a ceremony for the restoration of their dignity and reputation.

The next category of satisfaction measures includes the creation of public memorials. Inter-American jurisprudence considers that public monuments are powerful means of satisfaction, functioning simultaneously as guarantees of non-repetition. More specifically, when museums, streets, parks, squares, hospitals, or schools are named after the victims,[212] there is a permanent tribute to the disappeared. Compared to public ceremonies, sites are a perpetual reminder of the atrocities of the past; they materialize the restorative social process, while contributing to historical consciousness.[213] In addition, the IACtHR deploys a multi-faceted remembrance strategy,

[209] As with state apologies, declaratory relief is accomplished through declaratory judgments. In international law, it is often requested that an appropriate tribunal should declare the wrongfulness of a state's act as a means of giving satisfaction to the injured party. The only disappearance case where the injured party sought a declaratory judgment is in *Cyprus v Turkey*. The Cypriot government requested that the ECtHR declare that "Turkey is required to abide by the judgment [...] by abstaining from [...] the unlawful sale and exploitation of Greek Cypriot homes and property in the northern part of Cyprus". The ECtHR rejected the claim on the premise that Turkey is "formally bound by the relevant terms of the main judgment". *Cyprus v Turkey (Just satisfaction)*, para 61(i), 63. The ECtHR seems to equate a declaratory judgment with the obligatory character of its decisions. By rejecting the claim for declaratory relief, the ECtHR disregards the ongoing character of human rights violations in northern Cyprus—a definite shortcoming of this decision. In his concurring opinion, Judge Pinto de Albuquerque emphasized the importance of a declaratory judgment as a measure of satisfaction, on the grounds that "[t]he power to declare the cessation of an ongoing human rights violation is implied logically in the power to establish the existence of the human rights violation itself. [...] The provision of compensation as a remedy [...] is not to be confused with the duty of States not to commit and to put to end to violations of the Convention. Were it otherwise, the European human rights protection system would be flawed, because States could commit violations with impunity so long as they provided compensation to the victims of the violations". Judge Albuquerque espoused the Inter-American conduct, which values compensationless measures, in favor of satisfaction measures. *Cyprus v Turkey (Just satisfaction)*, Concurring Opinion of Judge Pinto de Albuquerque Joined by Judge Vučinić, para 21.

[210] *Cantoral-Benavides v Peru (Reparations)*, para 81.

[211] *Molina-Theissen v Guatemala*, para 87.

[212] Citroni (2012), p. 56.

[213] The importance of public sites for the preservation of collective memory in Latin America extends as well to the use and reformation of those places which were used as torture units or secret

ordering states to designate a national day and to create audiovisual documentaries to honor the victims, or to establish internet databases and inquiry committees[214] so as to facilitate the process of victim identification and family reunification.[215] Undoubtedly, these measures exceed the limits of the Court's judicial competence, since they do not focus on the relief of the injured party; rather, they aim at the alleviation of the suffering of all victims of enforced disappearance, whose numbers are undetermined. These measures are not victim-centered; to the contrary, their focal point is the remedial policies of the respondent state. The IACtHR, having recognized state patterns of widespread enforced disappearance, provides for judicial "corrective patterns" and interferes with the structure of national remedial mechanisms.

Finally, the IACtHR obligates the impugned state to conduct investigations to locate victims, or their remains, and to punish the perpetrators and masterminds of the disappearances under examination.[216] The adjudication of these measures is a concession by the IACtHR of the imperfection of the international legal order. In other words, the Court cannot fully administer justice, as it is not in a position to control public authorities or to guarantee the perpetrators' punishment or the promotion of human rights in general. Consequently, these measures are only a sort of admonition or reminder to states to make use of all their resources to accomplish justice. At this point, there is a vicious circle: these cases reach the IACtHR precisely because of the state's failure to conduct a thorough and effective investigation for a disappeared victim. After all, it is the state's inefficiency that prolongs the relatives' anguish and constitutes ill-treatment. In this respect, the IACtHR clarifies that international tribunal judgments cannot substitute for states' obligations towards

---

detention centers. The memorialization of disappearance is an issue currently involving public agencies and NGOs. Proposals vary and express two trends; either to turn these places into sites for the promotion of human rights, or to reform them but preserve their character as places of former ill-treatment. Although the first trend is reasonable, it is considered insufficient, as it restricts "the memory of the disappeared to a particular moment", while it is argued that the second allows "a nation to engage with disappearance" in a temporary manner. Bishop (2014), p. 559.

[214] The launch of national commissions for searches for the disappeared is classified by the IACtHR in other cases as a guarantee of non-repetition, proving the interrelation of remedial measures depending on the particularities of each case. *García & Family Members v Guatemala*, Inter-American Court of Human Rights Series C No 258 (29 November 2012) para 221.

[215] *Serrano-Cruz Sisters v El Salvador*, paras 183–191; *Contreras et al v El Salvador*, paras 208–210.

[216] The ECtHR is moving timidly in this direction. Unlike the Turkish and Cypriot cases, it recognizes that a contemporary state practice of enforced disappearance exists in the northern Caucasus, and has conceded the ongoing character of the right to the truth, which persists even after international adjudication. This view deviates from the European precedent, creating an *ad hoc* evaluation of enforced disappearance incidents in Russia. In *Aslakhanova et al v Russia*, although the ECtHR did not stray from its standard practice regarding the right to obtain reparation, it acknowledged that "[i]nvestigation into a disappearance does not serve the sole purpose of establishing the circumstances of the killing, and finding and punishing the perpetrator. The crucial difference [is that] the authorities also aim to find the missing person or find out what happened to him or her. [...] Crucial evidence may not come to light until later". *Aslakhanova et al v Russia*, para 214.

their citizens; securing full reparation is not feasible unless the state recognizes the rightfulness of the victims' claims and cooperates to the fullest extent. Consequently, these measures underline that a state's duty to seek the truth does not end with the payment of compensation, or with international adjudication in general. This view coincides with the restorative character of the right to the truth; for revealing the truth is by itself a form of satisfaction for the injured party.

4.2.3.5 Guarantees of Non-repetition: CPED Art. 24(5)(d)

Guarantees of non-repetition come last in the listing of reparation measures; yet, they, too, are not victim-centered. In the strict context of enforced disappearance, guarantees of non-repetition "start with the cessation of continuing violations"; that is, the human rights violation "only stops when the fate and whereabouts of the disappeared person are considered clarified beyond reasonable doubt".[217] As far as indirect victims are concerned, non-repetition is equal to establishing effective state mechanisms for the investigation of the disappeared. From this angle, guarantees of non-repetition fulfill a pedagogic mission[218] aimed at combating the phenomenon of disappearance, thus surpassing both strict legal terms and the structure of international claims for human rights violations.

To the Inter-American Court, guarantees of non-repetition require the reform of the executive branch to prevent the occurrence of disappearances in the future, as well as legislative adaptation in support of the executive's structural changes. Accordingly, the IACtHR, under the title "human rights training", reached the conclusion that to adequately secure the prohibition of disappearance:

> the State must adopt the necessary measures to train and educate the members of intelligence services, the Armed Forces and the National Police on legality issues and restrictions related to the use of force in general situations, armed conflict and terrorism, the due obedience concept and the role of said institutions in situations such as the events in the instant case. In doing so, the State must implement, on a permanent basis and within a reasonable time, human rights-oriented programs for all-rank members of the above-mentioned institutions. The State must also adopt the necessary measures to train and educate prosecutors and judges, including officers of military criminal courts, on international standards related to the judicial protection of human rights. [...] Said programs shall specially focus on the instant Judgment and the international instruments on human rights.[219]

The Court is striving to intensify the effect of human rights training programs by broadening the list of addressees; to wit, it is extending its ambit to include judges and attorneys as well. In the *Gelman v Uruguay* judgment, it ordered the state to

> implement, at the Center for Judicial Studies of Uruguay [...] permanent human rights programs, offered to district attorneys and judges of the Judicial Branch of Uruguay, that

---

[217] UN Doc E/CN.4/2002/71, para 89.

[218] *Miguel Castro Castro Prison v Peru*, paras 451–452; *Ituango Massacres v Colombia*, para 409.

[219] *La Cantuta v Peru*, paras 240–242. *See*, also *Goiburú et al v Paraguay*, para 178; *Servellón-García et al v Honduras*, para 200.

> entail courses or training programs on the diligent investigation and judgment of acts which constitute enforced disappearance of persons and abductions of minors. [220]

This is an elementary form of vertical harmonization of national judicial systems with the Inter-American legal order implemented by the Court, with the view to tackling judicial deficiencies in addressing disappearances. The IACtHR is endeavoring to strengthen the right to a judicial remedy of the victims' relatives and to render it efficient in the domestic system so that recourse to a regional tribunal is needless.

The second set of guarantees of non-repetition pertains to the necessary legislative amendments for the comprehension and punishment of the prohibition against disappearance. In this context, the judgment of *Trujillo-Oroza v Bolivia* was a landmark, because the IACtHR tried to weigh up the different *de jure* obstacles regarding the punishment of enforced disappearance. The Court adopted the view that the absence of a definition of enforced disappearance as an offence was one of the factors that impeded the investigation of the victim's fate. The IACtHR took into account the fact that the respondent state was a member of the IACFDP and had failed to define forced disappearance as an offense in its penal code, contrary to Arts 1(1) and 2 of the said Convention. To reach this decision, the IACtHR reversed the reasoning adopted by Bolivia's constitutional court. The Bolivian Supreme Court argued that the ratification of the IACFDP was too recent to create legal obligations for the state; hence Bolivia did not fail to abide by its international obligations.[221]

The IACtHR then referred explicitly to the obligation of IACFDP member-states to incorporate the definition of disappearance into their national legal order and to stipulate the commission of disappearance as a crime, turning to the case of *Heliodoro Portugal v Panama*. It observed that Panama's "failure to define forced disappearance of persons as an autonomous offense has prevented the development of effective criminal proceedings [...] and this allows impunity to be perpetuated".[222] The IACtHR moved a step further, and, although it welcomed the belated incorporation of the crime of enforced disappearance into Panama's penal code, it examined thoroughly whether the national provision was in compliance with the IACFDP. The Court concluded that Panama had "failed to comply with its obligation to define forced disappearance as an offense" pursuant to IACFDP and ordered the state's legislative reform.[223] In other cases, it called upon respondent states to set aside national limitations or amnesty provisions and to comply with the international peremptory norm that provides that statutes of limitations are not applicable to crimes against humanity.[224]

[220] *Gelman v Uruguay*, para 278.

[221] *Trujillo-Oroza v Bolivia*, paras 103, 105, 116. *See* also, *Gomes Lund et al ("Guerrilha do Araguaia") v Brazil*, para 287.

[222] *Heliodoro Portugal v Panama*, para 183.

[223] ibid, paras 209, 259.

[224] *Almonacid-Arellano et al v Chile*, para 153.

Overall, guarantees of non-repetition are intended to minimize international human rights law violations by states. The IACtHR reminds states of their duty to enact legislation in conformity with their international legal obligations.[225] So far, it is proven that states are more receptive to such reparation measures when they are already in the process of amending their national legislation,[226] for this lessens the Court's interference with their domestic legal order. Guarantees of non-repetition have triggered criticisms of the Inter-American Court, because the Court is considered to interfere excessively in member-states' domestic affairs. However, Pasqualucci aptly observes that

> if the Court did not have the authority to order a State to repeal offending domestic laws, every subsequent victim of the law would be required to exhaust domestic-remedies before resorting to the Inter-American human rights system to remedy the violation. That would be expensive and time-consuming for the victims and result in a flood of similar cases before the Court and other international human rights bodies.[227]

4.2.4 Enforced Disappearance and the Right to Obtain Reparation: Issues of Implementation

The right to obtain reparation signifies the failure to prevent the occurrence of enforced disappearance, meaning that there is a breach of the prohibition. The right to obtain reparation depends on the particularities of each national legal system and the available resources. International standards are by definition imperfect and of a subsidiary character, taking into account the loose and decentralized structure of the international system. This means that the right to obtain reparation is inherently doomed: with regards to national protection, reparation is a state's formal attempt to fix its wrongdoings, yet disappearance is not receptive to *restitutio in integrum*. On the international plane, the right to reparation collapses because of the lack of enforceability. Therefore, analyses on individuals' reparations are mostly of a theoretical value, focusing on the legal options provided to the injured party and not on their implementation. In this light, Art. 24(5) of the CPED is still in uncharted territory: neither has the CED elaborated on it in the context of individual complaint procedure, nor is there proof of the potential influence of Art. 24(5) in the domestic legal orders of the CPED's member-states. Accordingly, Art. 24(5) is evaluated by virtue of its conformity with the standards set in the UN Principles on the Right to

[225] In the European human rights system, member-states proceed to legislative reforms, or amendments, in order to avoid future convictions by the ECtHR. Although the European Court does not adjudicate guarantees of non-repetition, it has succeeded indirectly in the harmonization of national legal orders. The probability a state modifying its national legislation increases when the ECtHR identifies continual violations of the ECHR under a state pattern in contravention of the Convention. Σισιλιάνος (2010), pp. 93–94.

[226] Pasqualucci (2013), p. 216.

[227] ibid, p. 217.

a Remedy and Reparations and in the relevant articles on state responsibility, as well as with jurisprudential standards. Art. 24(5) of the CPED is fairly considered a comprehensive provision, as it incorporates all measures of reparation, with special care paid to the victim's reputation and dignity; no other judgment may be as well-founded, despite its shortcomings.

In this frame of reference, only a jurisprudential analysis is possible, which leads necessarily to a comparison between the two regional courts. The evaluation of their jurisprudence varies according to one's perception of their role; and as a result its activism has been well-received. Yet at the same time, the IACtHR's decisions are considered incremental; from a positivist perspective, the Inter-American Court exceeds its jurisdictional powers. Its approach is perilous, as it interferes with its member-states' legal orders. In this regard, it is the ECtHR that has gradually evolved the jurisprudence on enforced disappearance reparations. The European Court is taking cautious steps towards building a complete reparation scheme without jeopardizing "the subsidiary nature of its role [while it avoids] the role of a first-instance tribunal of fact".[228] European developments can be summarized by the expansion of the definition of victim status, the recognition of ongoing patterns of enforced disappearance in the European continent, and the fixed jurisprudence regarding compensation. In strict positivist terms, the provided reparations suffice for victims, while the Court does not compromise its distinct role vis-à-vis national courts. Consequently, part of the theory disavows the Inter-American approach because the approach becomes entangled even with the legislative and judicial branches of its member-states, assuming powers it is not vested with.

The Inter-American perspective towards reparations, though, is momentous for two reasons. From the victims' standpoint, the Inter-American system offers the widest possible range of reparation measures, tailored to the particularities of each case. This evaluation is self-evident; besides, applicants before the ECtHR employ the dicta of the IACtHR in their allegations. Secondly, in legal terms the Inter-American jurisprudence contributes to the establishment of the customary prohibition of enforced disappearance. This happens in two steps: first, the IACtHR tends to recognize state patterns of disappearance, and does not consider them single incidents. Second, if it finds the respondent state responsible for the victim's disappearance, it orders the state to give a formal apology to their family, and denounces the relevant state's pattern of behavior. Both these official statements are part of the Court's satisfaction measures. By ordering states to proceed with explicit statements against the practice of enforced disappearance, the IACtHR contributes to the formulation of their *opinio juris*. States' official repudiation of enforced disappearance signifies their commitment to the prohibition, irrespective of whether they abide by it or not. At least at a regional level, the Court strengthens the customary prohibition of disappearance, as it shapes states' *opinio juris*. What is more, the Court controls the content of these statements, since it requires states to publish part of its decisions; hence, it also influences the content of the customary prohibition.

---

[228] *Hassan v the United Kingdom*, App no 29750/09 (ECtHR 16 September 2014) para 47.

In this way, the Inter-American Court sets high standards for the prohibition on disappearance. Its jurisprudence not only cements the customary prohibition on a regional level, but also specifies its content, so as not to be vague or to stray far from the conventional standards. The IACtHR's remedial power becomes a material source of customary prohibition. The Court's jurisprudence is a source of "healing" for the injured parties, as well as reparation for the norm which has been violated, since it verifies its existence and content. Moreover, it emboldens national judges to deal with the atrocities of the past, and it has inspired revolutionary decisions in the field of disappearances.[229]

A final remark concluding the examination of the right to obtain reparations for the violation of enforced disappearance will be made on how the HRC copes with reparations. This observation ultimately comes in the form of a comment, because the HRC lacks remedial power; that is, it was intentionally omitted from the previous analysis. If the HRC finds a violation of the Covenant, it requires the impugned state-party to provide the author of the communication with an effective remedy. In its later communications regarding disappearances, it specified what an effective remedy is. The Committee follows the footsteps of the IACtHR, as it

> urges the State party a) to conduct a thorough and effective investigation into the disappearance and death of the [direct victim]; to provide adequate information resulting from its investigation; c) to return to the family the mortal remains [...] d) to prosecute, try and punish those held responsible for the violations; and e) to provide adequate compensation for [the victim and his family. The State party is also under an obligation to take measures to prevent similar violations in the future [Finally] the State party is also requested to publish the Committee's Views.[230]

Although the Committee's decisions are not enforceable, the HRC provides for the entire range of reparations. Repeated references to such reparation measures consolidate the HRC's case law and create a sort of precedent for victims of enforced disappearance who submit individual communications. Even if this set of reparation measures is of symbolic value only, it nevertheless enhances the naming and shaming policy directed against those countries practicing disappearances, which is a powerful tool in the human rights field.

[229] Iovane (2012), p. 619.

[230] *Salem Saad Ali Bashasha v the Libyan Arab Jamahiriya*, paras 9–10. *See* also by way of example *Yubraj Giri v Nepal*, paras 9–10; *Mohamed el Awani Ibrahim v the Libyan Arab Jamahiriya*, paras 9–10; *El Hassy v the Libyan Arab Jamahiriya*, paras 8–9; *Khaled Il Khwildy v Libya*, paras 9–10; *El Abani v the Libyan Araba Jamahiriya*, paras 9–10; *Mufteh Younis Muftah Al-Rabassi v Libya*, paras 9–10; *Hisham Abushaala v Libya*, paras 8–9; *Abdelahim Ali Mussa Benali v Libya*, paras 8–9; *Selimovic et al v Bosnia and Herzegovina*, paras 14–15; *Duric v Bosnia and Herzegovina*, paras 11–12.

4.3 The CPED's System of Human Rights: An Appraisal

The rights to the truth and to reparations are indispensable for the realization of the right not to be subjected to enforced disappearance, even in legal orders where the latter right is not stipulated. In judicial proceedings before international human rights tribunals, truth and reparation serve as guarantees of the victims' vindication. On the one hand, truth triggers states' positive obligation to investigate the alleged violation, as well as victims' demands to reveal the exact conditions in which a disappearance occurred, while on the other hand, reparations give substance to justice, making up for the ills of a disappearance. Both in the CPED's framework and also in judicial terms, these rights have a secondary character vis-à-vis the disappearance prohibition; to wit, they are not autonomous. Contrary to the UNWGEID's comments, where the right to the truth is deemed autonomous in an attempt to stress its significance, these rights are prohibition-dependent. Precisely because truth and reparation are context-based, the preceding analysis referred exclusively to their function relating to enforced disappearance.

For this reason, there has been no separate analysis concerning their character—whether absolute or not—or the potential existence of customary rules on truth and reparation. Given that truth and reparation draw their origin from the prohibition on disappearance, it therefore follows that they bear the characteristics of it; namely, they are non-derogable, absolute rights, having attained a customary character. This view is reasonably radical, albeit consistent on the basis of victim protection. In the same way that peace disruptions are not an excuse for practicing disappearances, truth and reparations during administrative or judicial proceedings cannot be suspended (non-derogability). Moreover, once prohibition of disappearance is inflicted, it is a *sine qua non* condition that the state responsible bears the duty to investigate the violation and provide reparations to the victim, a proposition non-susceptible to restrictions and limitations (absoluteness). Last, in the framework of disappearance, truth and reparations are customary norms. Bearing in mind the value of customary law for human rights, including the expansion of *opinio juris* to include negative rules, truth and reparation are crucial aspects of the customary norm, for the perpetrating states have always refused to fully cooperate with the victims' families in order to trace the victims' whereabouts, as well as to give due diligence during the investigatory process. All in all, truth and reparation create a protective system which aims at preventing or deterring the occurrence of disappearance, and at the same time at rectifying the errors made by giving reparation to the victims and castigating the perpetrators.

Jurisprudence

PCIJ

Case Concerning the Factory at Chorzów (Germany v Poland) (Jurisdiction) PCIJ Rep Series A No 9.

ICJ

Application of the Convention on the Prevention and Punishment of the Crime of Genocide (Croatia v Serbia) [2015] ICJ Gen List No 118.
Gabčikovo-Nagymaros Project (Hungary/Slovakia) [1997] ICJ Rep 7.

ICC

Prosecutor v Thomas Lubanga Dyilo (Judgement on the appeals against the "Decision Establishing the principles and procedures to be applied to reparations") Appeals Chamber (3 March 2015) ICC-01/04-01/06 AA2A3.
Prosecutor v Thomas Lubanga Dyilo (Decision establishing the principles and procedures to be applied to reparations) ICC Trial Chamber I (7 August 2012) ICC-01/04-01/06.

IACtHR

Bámaca-Velásquez v Guatemala (Reparations and Costs), Inter-American Court of Human Rights Series C No 91 (22 February 2002).
Caesar v Trinidad & Tobago, Inter-American Court of Human Rights Series C No 123 (11 March 2005).
Cantoral-Benavides v Peru (Reparations), Inter-American Court of Human Rights Series C No 88 (3 December 2001).
Caracazo v Venezuela, Inter-American Court of Human Rights Series C No 95 (29 August 2002).
García & Family Members v Guatemala, Inter-American Court of Human Rights Series C No 258 (29 November 2012).
García Lucero et al v Chile, Inter-American Court of Human Rights Series C No 267 (28 August 2013).
Godínez Cruz v Honduras (Reparations and Costs), Inter-American Court of Human Rights Series C No 8 (21 July 1989).

Gómez-Palomino v Peru, Inter-American Court of Human Rights Series C No 136 (22 November 2005).
Ituango Massacres v Colombia, Inter-American Court of Human Rights Series C No 148 (1 July 2006).
J v Peru, Inter-American Court of Human Rights Series C No 275 (27 November 2013).
Lori Berenson-Mejía v Peru, Inter-American Court of Human Rights Series C No 119 (25 November 2004).
"Mapiripán Massacre" v Colombia, Inter-American Court of Human Rights Series C No 122 (15 September 2005).
Moiwana Community v Suriname, Inter-American Court of Human Rights Series C No 145 (15 June 2005).
Neira-Alegría et al v Peru (Reparations and Costs), Inter-American Court of Human Rights Series C No 29 (19 September 1996).
Servellón-García et al v Honduras, Inter-American Court of Human Rights Series C No 152 (21 September 2006).
"Street Children" (Villagrán-Morales et al) v Guatemala, Inter-American Court of Human Rights Series C No 77 (26 May 2001).
Velásquez Rodríguez v Honduras (Compensatory Damages), Inter-American Court of Human Rights Series C No 7 (21 July 1989).
Vélez Restrepo & Family v Colombia, Inter-American Court of Human Rights Series C No 248 (3 September 2012).

ECtHR

Aslakhanova et al v Russia, App nos 2944/06 et al (ECtHR 18 December 2012).
Charalambous et al v Turkey, App no 46744/07 (ECtHR).
Chauvy et al v France, App no 64915/01 (ECtHR 29 June 2004).
Cyprus v Turkey (Just satisfaction), App no 25781/94 (ECtHR 12 May 2014).
Cyprus v Turkey, App no 25781/94 (ECtHR 10 May 2001).
Elberte v Latvia, App no 61243/08 (ECtHR 13 January 2015).
Emin (Mustafa) et al v Cyprus, App no 59623/08 (ECtHR).
Gelman *v Uruguay*, Inter-American Court of Human Rights Series C No 221 (24 February 2011).
Giniewski v France, App no 64016/00 (ECtHR 31 January 2006).
Gomes Lund et al ("Guerrilha do Araguaia") v Brazil, Inter-American Court of Human Rights Series C No 219 (24 November 2010).
Hassan v the United Kingdom, App no 29750/09 (ECtHR 16 September 2014).
Imakayeva v Russia, App no 7615/02 (ECtHR 9 November 2006).
Ireland v the United Kingdom, App no 5310/71 (ECtHR 18 January 1978).
Janowiec et al v Russia, App nos 55508/07, 29520/09 (ECtHR 21 October 2013).
Kaya v Turkey, App no 158/1996/777/978 (ECtHR 19 February 1998).
Khamila Isayeva v Russia, App no 6846/02 (ECtHR 15 November 2007).

Lawless v Ireland (n 3), App no 332/57 (ECtHR 1 July 1961).
Lehideux & Isorni v France, App no 55/1997/839/1045 (ECtHR 23 September 1998).
Lingens v Austria, App no 9815/82 (ECtHR 8 July 1986).
Luluyev et al v Russia, App no 69480/01 (ECtHR 9 November 2006).
Mikiyeva et al v Russia, App nos 61536/08 et al (ECtHR 30 January 2014).
Öcalan v Turkey, App no 46221/99 (ECtHR 12 May 2005).
Palić v Bosnia & Herzegovina, App no 4704/04 (ECtHR 15 February 2011).
Saidova v Russia, App no 51432/09 (ECtHR 1 August 2013).
Skendžić & Krznarić v Croatia, App no 16212/08 (ECtHR 20 January 2011).
Varnava et al v Turkey, App nos 16064/90 et al (ECtHR 18 September 2009).
Z & Khatuyeva v Russia, App nos 39436/06 & 40169/07 (ECtHR 30 January 2014).

Human Rights Chamber for Bosnia & Herzegovina

Dordo Unković v the Federation of Bosnia & Herzegovina Human Rights Chamber for Bosnia and Herzegovina CH/99/2150 (9 November 2001).

UN Documentation

UNGA

UNGA. (21 February 2014). The safety of journalists and the issue of impunity. UN Doc A/Res/68/163.
HRCouncil (22 March 2010). Progress report of the Human Rights Council Advisory Committee on Best Practices on the issue of missing persons. UN Doc A/HRC/14/42.
HRCouncil. (12 October 2009). 12/12. Right to the truth. UN Doc A/HRC/12/12.
UNGA. (29 November 1985). Declaration of Basic Principles of Justice for Victims of Crime and Abuse of Power. UN Doc A/Res/40/34.
UNGA Res 3220 (XXIX) (6 November 1974).
UN Doc A/Res/60/147.
UN Doc A/Res/40/34.
UN Doc A/Res/35/193.

ECOSOC

UN Doc E/CN.4/2006/57.
CommHR (20 April 2005). Right to the truth. UN Doc E/CN.4/Res/2005/66.

CommHR (8 February 2005). Updated set of principles for the protection and promotion of human rights through action to combat impunity. UN Doc E/CN.4/2005/102/Add.1.
UN Doc E/CN.4/2004/59
UNWGEID. (12 January 1998). General comments on article 19 of the Declaration. UN Doc E/CN.4/1998/43
CommHR. (2 October 1997). Question of the impunity of perpetrators of human rights violations. UN Doc E/CN.4/Sub.2/1997/20/Rev.1.
CommHR. (2 July 1993). Study concerning the right to restitution, compensation and rehabilitation for victims of gross violations of human rights and fundamental freedoms. UN Doc E/CN.4/Sub.2/1993/8.
UN Doc E/CN.4/2005/102/Add.1.
UN Doc E/CN.4/2003/71.
UN Doc E/CN.4/2002/71.
ECOSOC Res 353 (XII) (19 March 1951).
UNWGEID. (12 January 1998). General comments on article 19 of the Declaration. UN Doc E/CN.4/1998/43

HRC

Joaquín David Herrera Rubio et al v Colombia, HRC (1990) UN Doc CCPR/C/OP/2/161/1983.
María del Carmen Almeida de Quinteros et al v Uruguay, HRC (1990) UN Doc CCPR/C/OP/2/1981.

Miscellaneous

UNWGEID. (21 December 2009). General comments on enforced disappearance as a crime against humanity, UN Doc A/HRC/13/31.
Secretariat. (6 August 1999). Observance by United Nations forces of international humanitarian law. UN Doc ST/SGB/1999/13.
Fact Sheet No.6/Rev/3.

CoE Documentation

PACE (3 October 2005). Enforced disappearances. Res 1719 (2005).
PACE. (3 October 2005). Enforced disappearances. Res 1463 (2005).

OAS Documentation

IACommHR. (2013). Impact of the friendly settlement procedure. OEA/SerL/V/II Doc 45/13.

OAS Permanent Council. (23 May 2005). Persons who have disappeared and assistance to members of their families. OEA/Ser.G, CP/CAJP.2278/05/rev.4.

Online Material

UNWGEID. General comment on the right to the truth in relation to enforced disappearance. Retrieved March 22, 2023, from http://www.ohchr.org/Documents/Issues/Disappearances/GC-right_to_the_truth.pdf.

Nuremberg Trial Proceedings, (4 December 1945), 3. Retrieved March 22, 2023, from http://avalon.law.yale.edu/imt/12-04-45.asp.

Redress, Leopoldo García Lucero. Retrieved March 22, 2023, from http://www.redress.org/case-docket/leopoldo-garcia-lucero-v-chile.

van Boven, T. (2010). The United Nations basic principles and guidelines on the right to a remedy and reparation for victims of gross violations of international human rights law and serious violations of international humanitarian law, 1. Retrieved March 20, 2023, from http://legal.un.org/avl/pdf/ha/ga_60-147/ga_60-147_e.pdf.

References

Books

Arendt H (1973) The origins of totalitarianism: new editions with added prefaces. Hancourt

Aristotle (1934) Nicomachean ethics (trans: Rackham H). Harvard University Press

Aristotle, Metaphysics

Aristotle, Politics, Book A

Aristotle, Politics, Book B

Burgorgue-Larsen L, Úbeda de Torres A (2011) The Inter-American Court of Human Rights, case law and commentary. Oxford University Press

Crawford J (2002) Articles on state responsibility, introduction, text and commentaries. CUP

Davis M (1996) The politics of philosophy, a commentary on Aristotle's politics. Rowman & Littlefield

Pasqualucci JM (2013) The practice and procedure of the Inter-American Court of Human Rights, 2nd edn. Cambridge University Press

Raz J (1986) The morality of freedom. Clarendon Press

Schabas WA (2009) Genocide in international law, the crime of crimes, 2nd edn. Cambridge University Press

Scovazzi T, Citroni G (2007) The struggle against enforced disappearance and the 2007 United Nations Convention. Martinus Nijhoff Publishers and VSP

Shelton D (2005) Remedies in international human rights law, 2nd edn. Oxford University Press
Tinta MF (2008) The landmark rulings of the Inter-American Court of Human Rights on the rights of the child, protecting the most vulnerable at the edge. Martinus Nijhoff
Σισιλιάνος Λ-Α (2010) Η Ανθρώπινη Διάσταση του Διεθνούς Δικαίου, Αλληλεπιδράσεις Γενικού Διεθνούς Δικαίου και Δικαιωμάτων του Ανθρώπου, Νομική Βιβλιοθήκη

Articles

Antkowiak TM (2008) Remedial approaches to human rights violations: the Inter-American Court of Human Rights and beyond. Columbia J Transnatl Law 46(2):351–419
Baeza PR (2000) Impunity: an impossible reparation. Nordic J Int Law 69(1):27–34
Bishop KE (2014) The architectural history of disappearance: rebuilding memory sites in the Southern Cone. J Soc Archit Hist 73(4):556–578
Citroni G (2012) Measures of reparation for victims of gross human rights violations: developments and challenges in the jurisprudence of two regional human rights courts. Inter-Am Eur Hum Rights J 5(1–2):49–71
Citroni G (2014) The pitfalls of regulating the legal status of disappeared persons through declaration of death. J Int Crim Justice 12(4):787–804
Dawson FG, Weston BH (1962) "Prompt, adequate and effective": a universal standard of compensation? Fordham Law Rev 30(4):727–758
Donoso G (2009) Inter-American Court of Human Rights' reparation judgments. Strengths and challenges for a comprehensive approach. Revista Instituto Interamericano de Derechos Humanos 49:29–68
Dworkin R (2006) Objectivity and truth: you'd better believe it. 25(2) PPA 87
Ferejohn MT (1981) Aristotle on necessary truth and logical priority. Am Philos Q 18(4):285–293
Finucane B (2010) Enforced disappearance as a crime under international law: a neglected origin in the laws of war. YaleJInt'lL 35(1):171
Fulton S (2014) Redress for enforced disappearance, why financial compensation is not enough. J Int Crim Justice 12(4):769–786
Gaynor F (2012) Uneasy partners – evidence, truth and history in international trials. J Int Crim Justice 10(5):1257–1276
Groome D (2011) The right to truth in the fight against impunity. Berkeley J Int Law 29(1):175–199
Heri C (2014) Enforced disappearance and the European Court of Human Rights' *Ratione Temporis* jurisdiction. J Int Crim Justice 12(4):751–768
Laplante LJ (2004) Bringing effective remedies home: the Inter-American human rights system, reparations, and the duty of prevention. Neth Q Hum Rights 22(3):347–388
Naqvi Y (2006) The right to the truth in international law: fact or fiction? Int Rev Red Cross 88(862):245–274
Pasqualucci JM (1996) Victim reparations in the Inter-American human rights system: a critical assessment of current practice and procedure. Mich J Int Law 18(1):1–58
Roht-Arriaza N (1996) Combating impunity: some thoughts on the way forward. Law Contemp Problems 59(4):93–102
Roht-Arriaza N (2004) Reparations decisions and dilemmas. Hastings Int Comp Law Rev 27(2):157–220
Rombouts H, Vandeginste S (2000–2003) Reparation for victims of gross and systematic human rights violations: the notion of victim. Third World Leg Stud, pp 89–114
Tomuschat C (2002) Reparation for victims of grave human rights violations. Tulane J Int Comp Law 10:157–184
Waldron J (2008) The concept and the rule of law. Georgia Law Rev 43(1):1–62
Zwanenburg M (2006) The van Boven/Bassiouni principles: an appraisal. Neth Q Hum Rights 24(4):641–668

Book Chapters

Cassel D (2006) The expanding scope and impact of reparations awarded by the Inter-American Court of Human Rights. In: De Fayter K et al (eds) Out of the ashes: reparations for gross violations of human rights, Intersentia, pp 191–217

Iovane M (2012) Domestic courts should embrace sound interpretative strategies in the development of human rights-oriented international law. In: Cassese A (ed) Realizing utopia, the future of international law. Oxford University Press

Sarigiannidis M (2014) On a right and a duty to the truth, and its relevance to international peace and justice. In: Skouteris T, Vagias M (eds) International organizations and the protection of human rights, essays in honor of Prof. Paroula Naskou-Perraki. Themis, pp 31–46

van Boven T (2003) Reparations; a requirement of justice. In: Memoria del Seminario, El Sistema interamericano de protección de los derechos humanos en el umbral del siglo XXI, T1, 2nd edn. IACtHR

Chapter 5
Conclusions

5.1 The Right Against Enforced Disappearance: CPED's Contribution

Reaching the final point, this study is still searching for its key argument, which ought to run through it and function as a central link connecting the previous chapters. From beginning to end, the most attractive legal aspect when entering the field of enforced disappearance has been the pronouncement of the right not to be subjected to enforced disappearance set out in Art. 1(1) of the 2007 Convention. The inclusion of a new right in the international human rights regime is by itself a development which requires examination, albeit not a positive development by definition. From this viewpoint, the doctrinal analysis of the prohibition against enforced disappearances has been the central tenet of this research. Yet, the mere analysis of a provision is analytical and may lack argumentation.

At this point, three considerations are necessary. First, the right against disappearances as such has so far not received a thorough theoretical analysis. Most scholars place emphasis on the definition and constitutive elements of enforced disappearances, equating them to the right's content. However, the two are not identical, since the definition of enforced disappearance forms just part of the right.

Second, the right's decryption essentially requires prior analysis of the phenomenon: the practice, patterns, and offence of enforced disappearance. As such, a scholar cannot escape delving into the historical and definitional features of enforced disappearances. This is due to the practice's complex nature, which cannot be understood without exploring the particular patterns of it, or by exemplifying some of the important events which have taken place. For this reason, the thesis distinguishes between archetypical and modern forms of enforced disappearances. After all, the inherent conceptual difficulty surrounding enforced disappearances has been proclaimed as the main reason for the belated conclusion of international, legally binding instrument. This observation serves both to excuse the international

I. Pervou, *The Right not to Be Subjected to Enforced Disappearance*,
https://doi.org/10.1007/978-3-031-36731-1_5

community for its lax responses and also to justify the perpetual legal difficulty in addressing disappearances. It is true, though, that an enforced disappearance causes an abstract image of fear and uncertainty, something comparable to torture, which consists either of a physical or a mental action directed by the captor towards the victim: tangible, and thus understandable.

In other words, there cannot but be a descriptive-based analysis of enforced disappearances. In this regard, the first two chapters attempted to bring forth to the greatest extent possible the elements of enforced disappearances. That is, to describe the phenomenon through a holistic, historical approach and then to break it down into its constituent parts in order to establish links between the paradigms of the past and the challenges of the present. In this regard, there is a double connecting link between Chaps. 1 and 2. On the one hand, they juxtapose typical with atypical disappearance patterns, while on the other hand they point to the phenomenon's transformation and progression in perpetration methods. This second link is practically an unfolding interpretation of enforced disappearance that relies on the first connecting link, and vice-versa. Put simply, a teleological—or at least elastic—interpretation of the definition of enforced disappearance allows theory to subsume modern practices under the notion of disappearance, while conversely this teleological course of thinking is attainable simply because we can accept the evolution of the phenomenon of enforced disappearance. This empirical position is radical, to say the least, given that it focuses on the evolution of the perpetrator's perversity in order to apply a teleological interpretation to the definition of disappearances. In this way, Chap. 2 expands the definition of enforced disappearances to apply it to methods like extraordinary rendition, not because it finds the definition suitable for this purpose, but primarily because it perceives extraordinary renditions as the evolution of the Latin American paradigm of disappearances.

Finally, the third consideration relates to the pronouncement of the prohibition against disappearances as stipulated in the 2007 Convention. The factual nature of a right's pronouncement is prima facie undoubted; to wit, the provision of a right by an international instrument either happens or it does not. Therefore, there seems to be no argument behind the provision that "no one shall be subjected to enforced disappearance". This view, though, is misleading: it enmeshes the factual façade of such a provision with the ontological argument, embedded in the creation of such a norm. More specifically, although the pronouncement of a right is a sine qua non as far as the technocratic part of a special legal document is concerned, the creation of a prohibition is disputable as such; the drafters of the 2007 Convention unwittingly made a doctrinal statement through Art. 1(1). The prohibition against enforced disappearances is constitutive for the 2007 Convention, and in the meantime it bears an irrefutable declaratory power as far as the international human rights regime is concerned. CPED Art. 1 is the international community's thesis vis-à-vis the perpetrators of enforced disappearances, and it is therefore the most significant measure taken to combat the phenomenon. This line of argument is supported by the fact that the prohibition on disappearances is a norm which is not stipulated in any other international legal document. It is an addition to the other international Bill of Human Rights. This proposition is at the heart of the study's central argument.

Right after one accepts that the norm against disappearances presupposes a stance towards the international system of human rights, a series of questions arise. Is the norm against disappearances bound by the conventional boundaries of the CPED, which stipulates it? Are the two interdependent? How is the CPED assessed in terms of the right's pronouncement? And finally, how does this right contribute to the protection against enforced disappearances? Answers to the above questions have formed the final argument of this thesis: the prohibition of enforced disappearance under Art. 1(1) of the CPED is thrust into a position of legal isolation. The norm's constitutive power does not exceed the CPED's confines. The right against disappearances stands amidst international instruments which do not provide for equivalent measures, simply because their drafters could not have foreseen the evolution of human perversity in the second half of the twentieth century. The right's "non-recognition" by the body of other legal documents also sharply reduces the norm's declaratory power. Clearly there has been an attempt to draw parallel between the constitutive and declaratory theories of state recognition and the constitutive and declaratory power of a "human right's legal recognition".

5.2 The Right Against Enforced Disappearance: Its Legal Isolation

The legal stipulation of a human right cannot in any event guarantee an improvement in the protection of human rights. The opposite would contravene the cardinal legal axiom according to which a law cannot be assessed by the number of its breaches. The starting point in examining the contribution of Art. 1 to the protection against enforced disappearances is the protection offered by the CPED. The CPED provides for its own monitoring mechanism, the CED. The latter is responsible for reporting the Convention's implementation by its member-states. So far, the CED is the Convention's Achilles heel, its deadly weakness. The CED's limited powers ratione temporis have rendered it inactive. It is highly improbable that the Committee receives individual complaints for alleged enforced disappearances, something which renders the CPED redundant. In addition, the CED's reluctance, or even recalcitrance, to proceed with general interpretative comments on the Convention's provisions reduce it to an inadequate monitoring mechanism. This view is reinforced by the fact that the UNWGEID continues to operate actively after the CPED's entry into force, a novelty in the UN system. Then again, assessing the right against disappearances within the conventional framework would automatically confine it to the number of the CPED's member-states. In turn, this would overly circumscribe any assessment attempt, given that most of the CPED's member-states are countries that do not apply the practice of enforced disappearance, a common problem regarding human rights instruments. This means that an intra-conventional assessment of the right's impact on the protection against disappearances is by definition deficient.

The greatest challenge is to evaluate the norm's influence beyond the Convention's orbit. This analysis is twofold. First, it involves the customary prohibition against disappearances, with a second phase involving the judicial treatment of enforced disappearance. By shedding light on the customary value of the prohibition on disappearances, there is an attempt to associate this norm with the International Bill of Human Rights. The connection between a disappearance norm and the general principle of human dignity is only possible through the lens of customary enforced disappearance. The second positive element is that reference to a customary prohibition against disappearances broadens its field of application. It immediately acquires a global reach, as it extends its ratione materiae to all states. Yet, recourse to a customary enforced disappearance is not a panacea. The inherent conceptual difficulty the phenomenon entails is magnified when talking of a customary norm, given that the norm's delimitation definitely becomes more difficult.

Moving on to the second strand of this analysis, the judicial treatment of enforced disappearance practices is examined throughout the study. A basic remark is that there is a critical divergence between the approaches of the three key judicial bodies addressing enforced disappearance cases. On the one hand, the IACtHR clearly adopts a victim-friendly stance. Given that its jurisprudence has been built on enforced disappearance incidents, the Inter-American Court has a sense of victim empathy. The IACtHR recognized the norm against enforced disappearance, although the provisions of the IACHR are the basis of its adjudication.

On the other hand, the ECtHR has been until recently troubled when addressing enforced disappearances. The European Court has been trying to fit the practice under the provisions of the ECHR and to assimilate it with practices it had already in place, to the victims' and the norm's detriment. Further, the ECtHR's long legal tradition prevented the European Court from sufficiently conceptualizing enforced disappearance. The ECtHR vacillates between the right to life and the prohibition of torture and freedom from liberty deprivation, depending on each case's factual background. It may be argued that the range of enforced disappearance patterns that the European Court confronts cause such a vacillation, which would require more of an adjustment. However, the reported fluctuations of the European jurisprudence are not restricted exclusively to the broad case law; rather, they stem from the ECtHR's positivist criteria and strict thresholds. In effect, the ECtHR is not a victim-friendly forum with regards to enforced disappearances.

The HRC stands somewhere in the middle of the two regional tribunals. It is quite difficult to discern a particular attitude, not only towards disappearance communications but also in general. The HRC's lack of enforcement capacity affects the Committee's reasoning, which is not outlined in detail in its communications. Overall, it is a safe conclusion that the HRC is selective in following a few of the progressive steps made by the IACtHR and promotes a more conciliatory approach between victims and the impugned states. It may be suggested that the divergence in these approaches is reasonable, tailored to the idiosyncrasies of each case and to the respective forums: a well-founded proposition. Yet, these inconsistencies persist, they are systemic and they hinder the establishment of international legal standards for victim protection. This persisting problem can be attributed to the absence of the right not to be subjected to enforced disappearance from the general human rights treaties. Their judicial organs refer sometimes to the right of the 2007 Convention (primarily the IACtHR), but they are bound ratione materiae to adjudicate these cases by the cumulative application of other norms.

As a result, the right against disappearances is now experiencing a state of quasi-legal isolation. Except from the 2007 Convention itself, it is only the Argentinean Constitution which stipulates such a norm.[1] Thus, the final question is whether a norm may improve individual protection in its absence from legally binding instruments.

I would expect that the proposal of this study would be added to the norm in the general human rights treaties' catalogues. Protocols added to the ECHE and the ICCPR would be a solution, while an expansion of the IACtHR's jurisdiction over the IACFDP would suffice. Hence, this proposal is completely mismatched with the preceding analysis on the natural perception of human rights, the renunciation of positivism, and the value of customary human rights rules. After all, the natural-empirical reading of human rights does not need Additional Protocols of constitutional affirmations to function. Indeed, this is the utopian concept of the international human rights regime. The protection of a right, though, is highly dependent on the right's positive affirmations ("declaratory recognitions" according to the previous metaphor). The international community—that is, its subjects and the system they create—is still a highly positivist one. This is neither positive nor negative; it is just a factual observation. Thus, from a human rights perspective, where the victim-centered approach is the key axiom permeating this legal order, it is the individuals' actual protection which is at stake. Consequently, there is a need to strengthen the norm against enforced disappearance to enhance victim protection. In a positivist-constructed system, this strengthening shall take an appropriate form. It is too early for the establishment of a natural human rights regime, or, according to its critics, for a utopian system. The right not to be subjected to enforced disappearances has long been the lost child of the international human rights regime, and is still the lost child of the positivist human rights protection system.

[1] Article 43 of Argentina's Constitution provides for protection from unjustified restraint, which mentions: "When the harmed, restricted, altered, or threatened right is that of physical liberty, or in case of illegal worsening in the manner or conditions of detention, or in case of the forced disappearance of persons, the writ of habeas corpus may be filed by the affected person or by anyone else on his behalf and the judge shall immediately resolve it, even while a state of siege is in effect". Retrieved March 22, 2023, from https://www.constituteproject.org/constitution/Argentina_1994.pdf?lang=en.

5.3 What Future for the Protection of Enforced Disappearances

Although the 2007 Convention is the most important step taken so far by the international community for the protection against enforced disappearances, so far individual protection is not satisfying. Enforced disappearances is a persisting phenomenon worldwide. In addition, disappearances take nowadays multiple forms, rendering their protection a difficult riddle to solve. In this context, the future for the protection of enforced disappearance seems to be ominous. There are three considerations respectively: if there is normative agreement between the right's conceptualization and the stipulation of enforced disappearance offences in international criminal law and the national penal codes (a), if the particular forms disappearances take are well understood (b), and finally if there is sufficient information, so that the international community is well aware of states' practicing disappearances (c). Only the first consideration is of legal interest and brings forth the general issue regarding the discrepancy between human rights norms and their stipulation as criminal offences. Enforced disappearance did not make an exception to the rule; as such, the prevailing interpretation of the crime in international criminal law, does not offer full protection to victims and places emphasis on the perpetrators' treatment. This is inevitable, given the legal domains' different scopes. However, it is not beneficial for the phenomenon's conceptualization. The second consideration relates to states' countless ways to commit disappearances. The phenomenon takes multiple forms and the archetypical or historical approach are of no value anymore. In this regard, it is imperative that the normative understanding of disappearances prevails over a descriptive one. This is a difficult path the international community shall follow; it is only through jurisprudence and legislative initiatives that the gradual consolidation of the legal norm can take place. Finally, the issue which seems insurmountable currently is information about disappearances. Perpetrating states are not revealing information about their practice, nor do they concede they commit disappearances. The international community is unaware of the systematic practice of enforced disappearance on many occasions; and even if reports suggest that enforced disappearances are an established party by a particular state, then again there is not much more to be done. During the last years, there are numerous examples that verify this proposition. During the 2011 civil war which torn Libya, the UNSC expressly mentioned in its resolutions that enforced disappearances were reportedly a systematic practice by both parties to the conflict.[2] Nevertheless, apart from acknowledging that disappearances took place, there was no other evidence that could be used either legally, or politically to the victims' protection. The same observation comes for North Korea too. Although there is international awareness of the non-democratic governance of

[2] UN Doc S/Res/1973 (2011) (17 March 2011) preamble.

the state and the systemic violation of human rights, there is no further evidence that could prompt international concern.[3] In addition, this proposition is affirmed by far during conflicts. The example of the Russian war in Ukraine is laminating.[4] There are so far reports on the systematic practice of enforced disappearances, which takes two forms. There are either mass disappearances of people who are presumed to be the victims of extra-judicial executions, or the disappearance of juveniles and children from their birthland to Russia's inland, without any information for their whereabouts. On both occasions, the prerequisites for an enforced disappearance exist. Yet again, there are no means of assistance to the victims.

Overall, information on the commission of disappearances is probably the most serious handicap the international community needs to overcome. Enforced disappearances are meant to remain secret and the perpetrating states are never expected to admit committing such a crime. Thus, enforced disappearances are addressed *ex post facto*, when they form part of a state's historical course.

References: UN Documentation

UN Security Council

UN Doc S/Res/1973 (2011) (17 March 2011).

UN Human Rights Office of the High Commissioner

UN Human Rights Office of the High Commissioner. (28 March 2023) These Wounds Do Not Heal, Enforced Disappearance and Abductions by the Democratic People's Republic of Korea. Retrieved 28, March 2023, from https://www.ohchr.org/sites/default/files/documents/countries/korea-dpr/2023-03-28-Enforced-disappearance-DPRK-en.pdf

UN Human Rights Office of the High Commissioner. (24 March 2023). Report on the Human Rights Situation in Ukraine, 1 August 2022 – 31 January 2023.

[3] UN Human Rights Office of the High Commissioner. (28 March 2023) These Wounds Do Not Heal, Enforced Disappearance and Abductions by the Democratic People's Republic of Korea. Retrieved 28, March 2023, from https://www.ohchr.org/sites/default/files/documents/countries/korea-dpr/2023-03-28-Enforced-disappearance-DPRK-en.pdf.

[4] UN Human Rights Office of the High Commissioner. (24 March 2023). Report on the Human Rights Situation in Ukraine, 1 August 2022–31 January 2023. Retriever 28, March 2023, from https://www.ohchr.org/sites/default/files/documents/countries/ukraine/2023/23-03-24-Ukraine-35th-periodic-report-ENG.pdf.

Retriever 28, March 2023, from https://www.ohchr.org/sites/default/files/documents/countries/ukraine/2023/23-03-24-Ukraine-35th-periodic-report-ENG.pdf.

Online Material

https://www.constituteproject.org/constitution/Argentina_1994.pdf?lang=en

The manufacturer's authorised representative in the EU is Springer Nature Customer Service Centre GmbH, Europaplatz 3, 69115 Heidelberg, Germany. If you have any concerns regarding our products, please contact ProductSafety@springernature.com

Printed and bound by CPI Group (UK) Ltd, Croydon, CR0 4YY

01/10/2026

02225865-0005